CREATED BY **ROBERT KIRKMAN**
AND **CHRIS SAMNEE**

ROBERT KIRKMAN
Creator, Writer

CHRIS SAMNE
Creator, Artist

FIRE POWER VOLUME 3: FLAME WAR
JULY 2021 FIRST PRINTING
ISBN: 978-1-5343-1908-0

Published by Image Comics, Inc. Office of publication: PO BOX 14457, Portland, OR 97293. Copyright © 2021 Robert Kirkman, LLC and Chris Samnee. Originally published in single magazine format as FIRE POWER™ #7-12. FIRE POWER™ (including all prominent characters featured herein), its logo and all character likenesses are trademarks of Robert Kirkman, LLC and Chris Samnee, unless otherwise noted. Image Comics® and its logos are registered trademarks and copyrights of Image Comics, Inc. All rights reserved. No part of this publication may be reproduced or transmitted in any form or by any means (except for short excerpts for review purposes) without the express written permission of Image Comics, Inc. All names, characters, events and locales in this publication are entirely fictional. Any resemblance to actual persons (living or dead), events or places, without satiric intent, is coincidental. Printed in the U.S.A.

FOR IMAGE COMICS, INC.

FOR SKYBOUND ENTERTAINMENT

SKYBOUND.COM

IMAGECOMICS.COM

MATT WILSON
olorist

RUS WOOTON
etterer

SEAN MACKIEWICZ
Editor

ANDRES JUAREZ
Logo, Collection Design

CARINA TAYLOR
Production

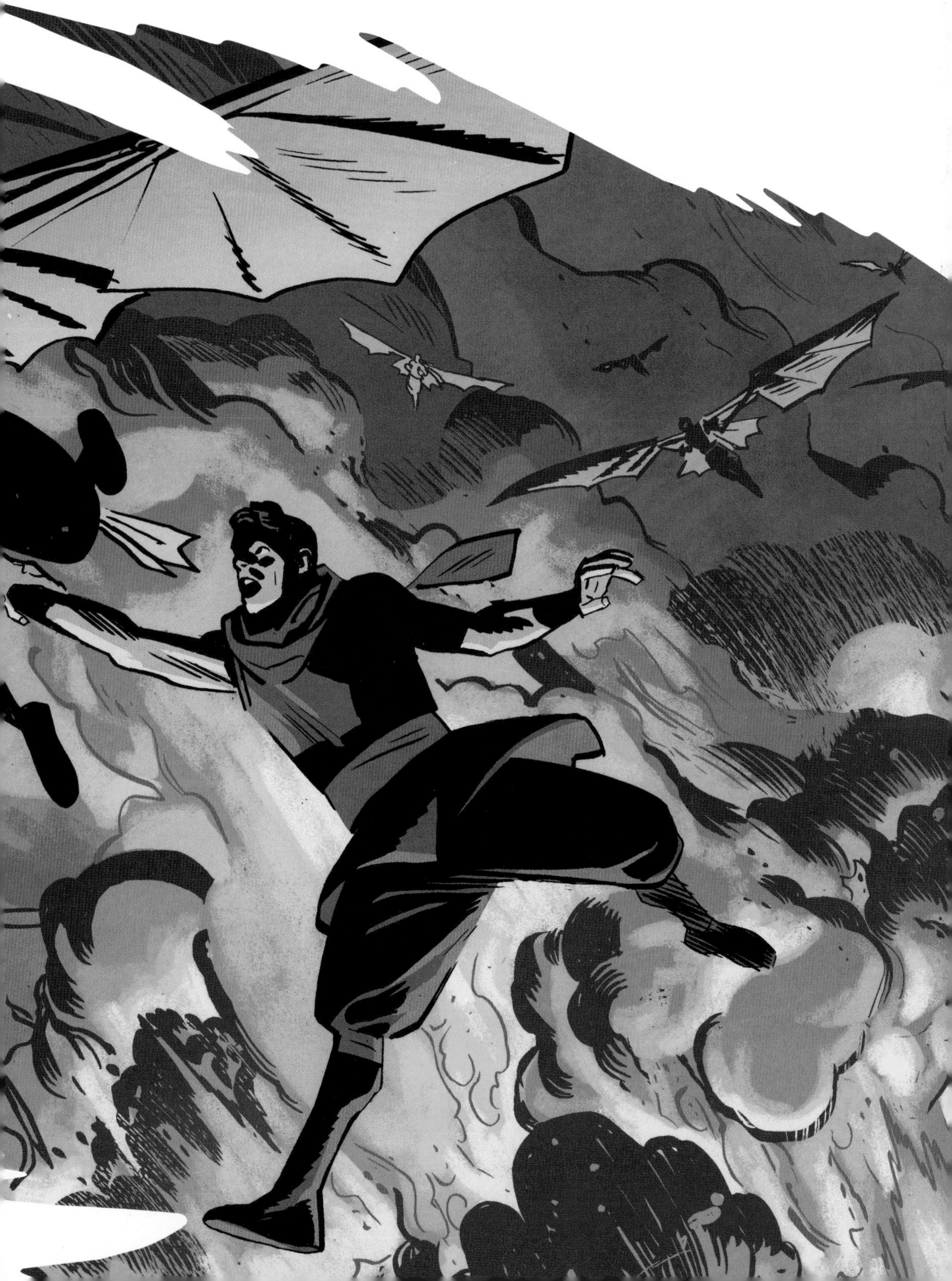

CHAPTER
THREE

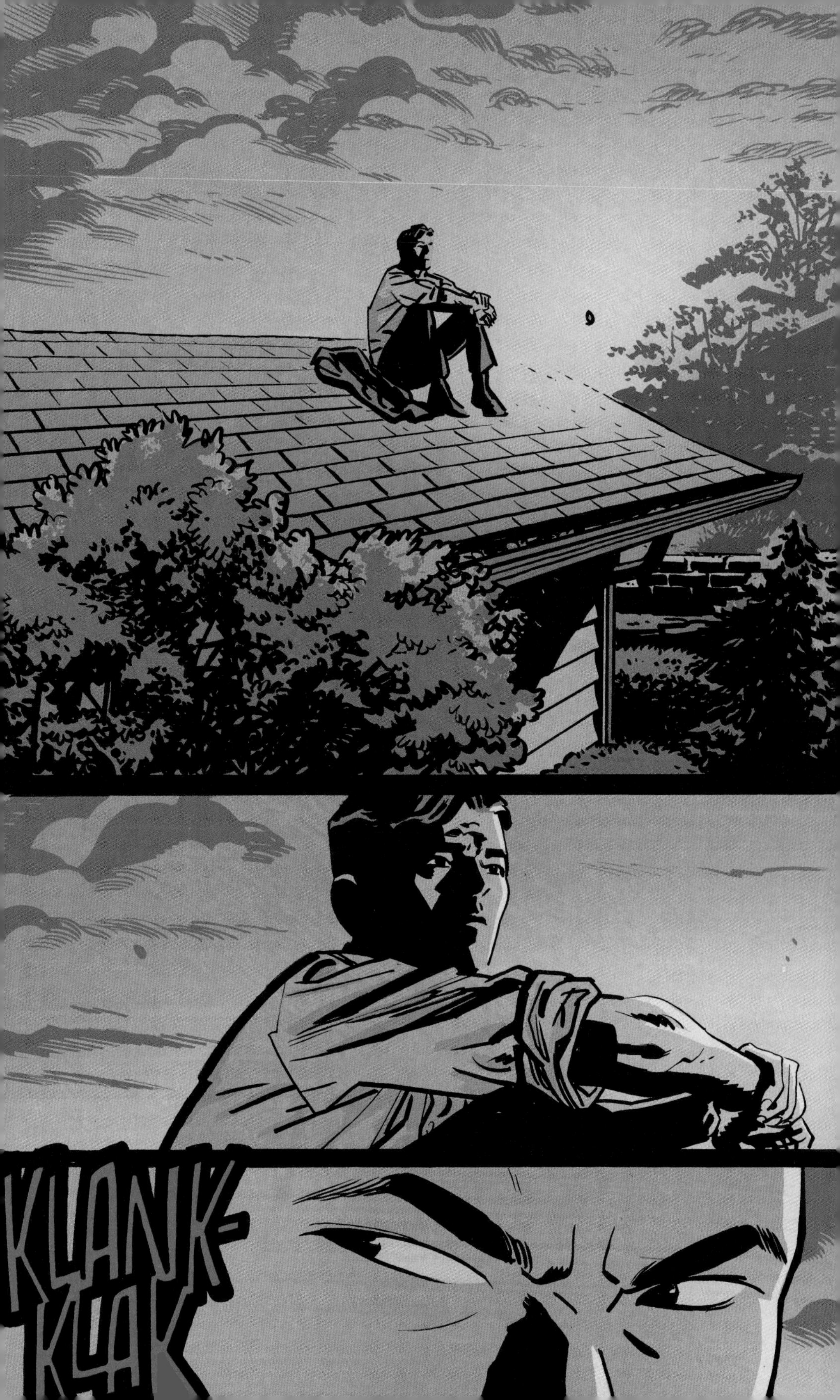
KLANK-
KLAK

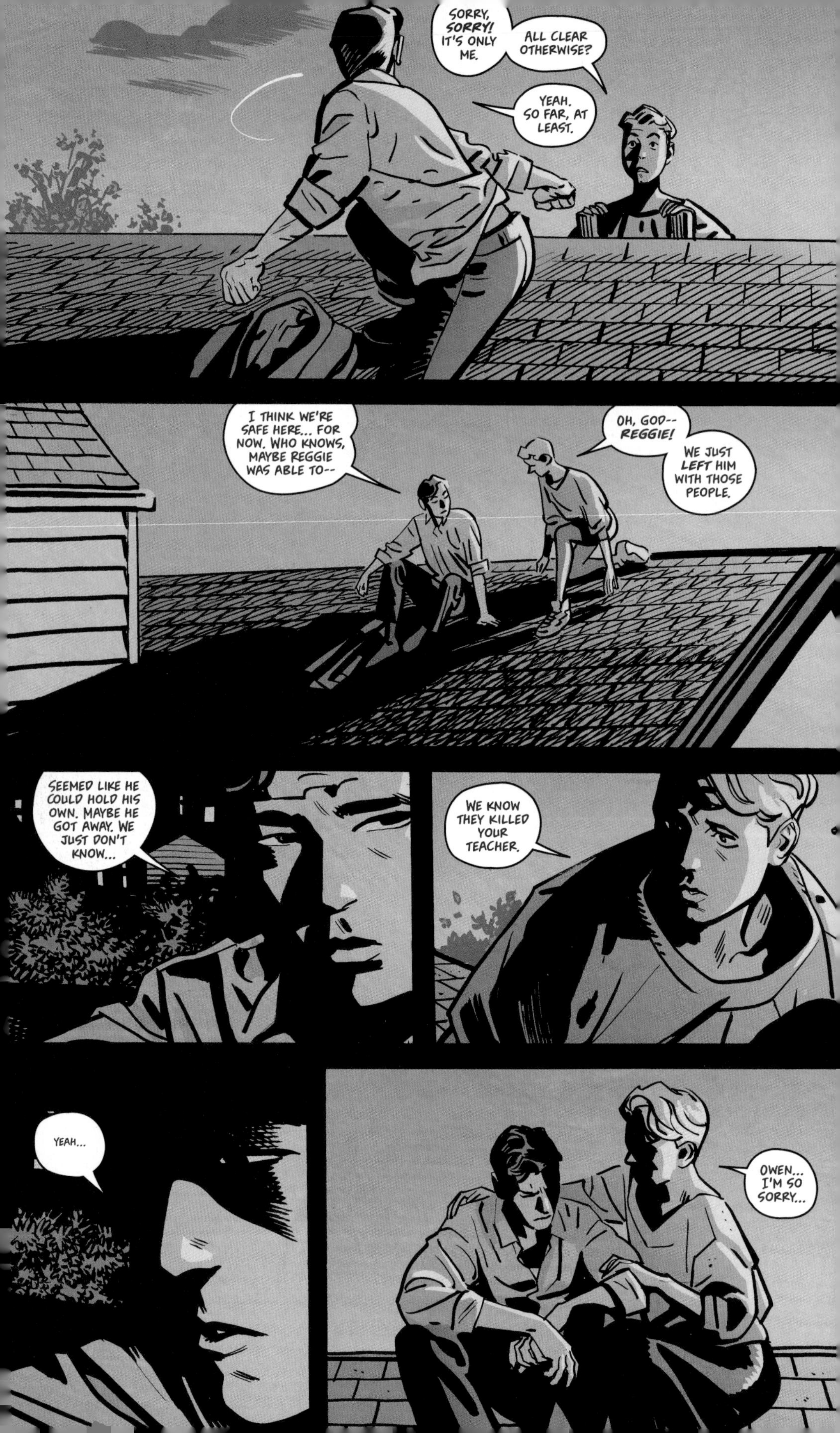
SORRY, SORRY! IT'S ONLY ME.
ALL CLEAR OTHERWISE?
YEAH. SO FAR, AT LEAST.
I THINK WE'RE SAFE HERE... FOR NOW. WHO KNOWS, MAYBE REGGIE WAS ABLE TO--
OH, GOD-- REGGIE!
WE JUST LEFT HIM WITH THOSE PEOPLE.
SEEMED LIKE HE COULD HOLD HIS OWN. MAYBE HE GOT AWAY. WE JUST DON'T KNOW...
WE KNOW THEY KILLED YOUR TEACHER.
YEAH...
OWEN... I'M SO SORRY...

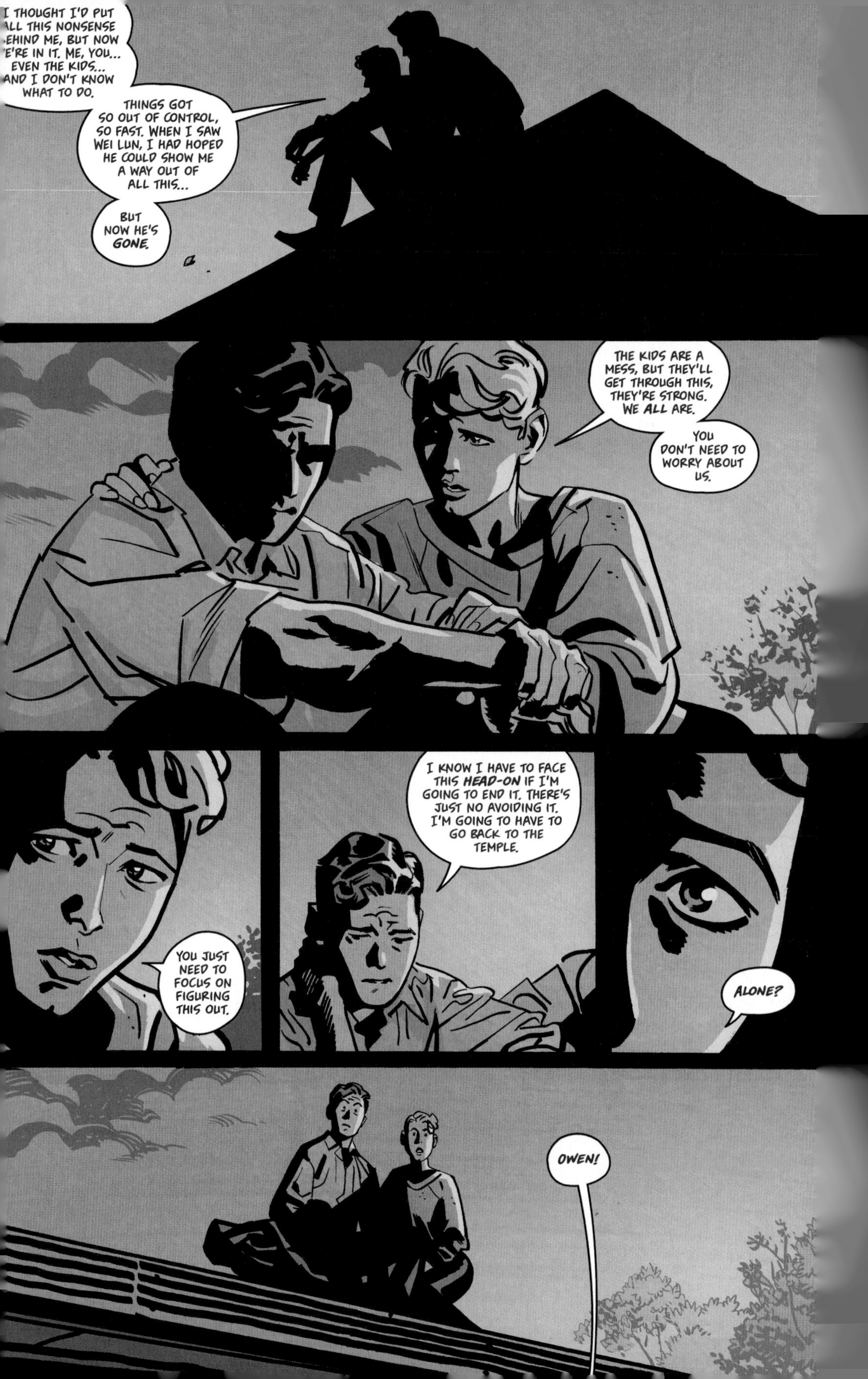
I THOUGHT I'D PUT ALL THIS NONSENSE BEHIND ME, BUT NOW WE'RE IN IT. ME, YOU... EVEN THE KIDS... AND I DON'T KNOW WHAT TO DO.
THINGS GOT SO OUT OF CONTROL, SO FAST. WHEN I SAW WEI LUN, I HAD HOPED HE COULD SHOW ME A WAY OUT OF ALL THIS...
BUT NOW HE'S GONE.
THE KIDS ARE A MESS, BUT THEY'LL GET THROUGH THIS, THEY'RE STRONG. WE ALL ARE.
YOU DON'T NEED TO WORRY ABOUT US.
YOU JUST NEED TO FOCUS ON FIGURING THIS OUT.
I KNOW I HAVE TO FACE THIS HEAD-ON IF I'M GOING TO END IT. THERE'S JUST NO AVOIDING IT. I'M GOING TO HAVE TO GO BACK TO THE TEMPLE.
ALONE?
OWEN!

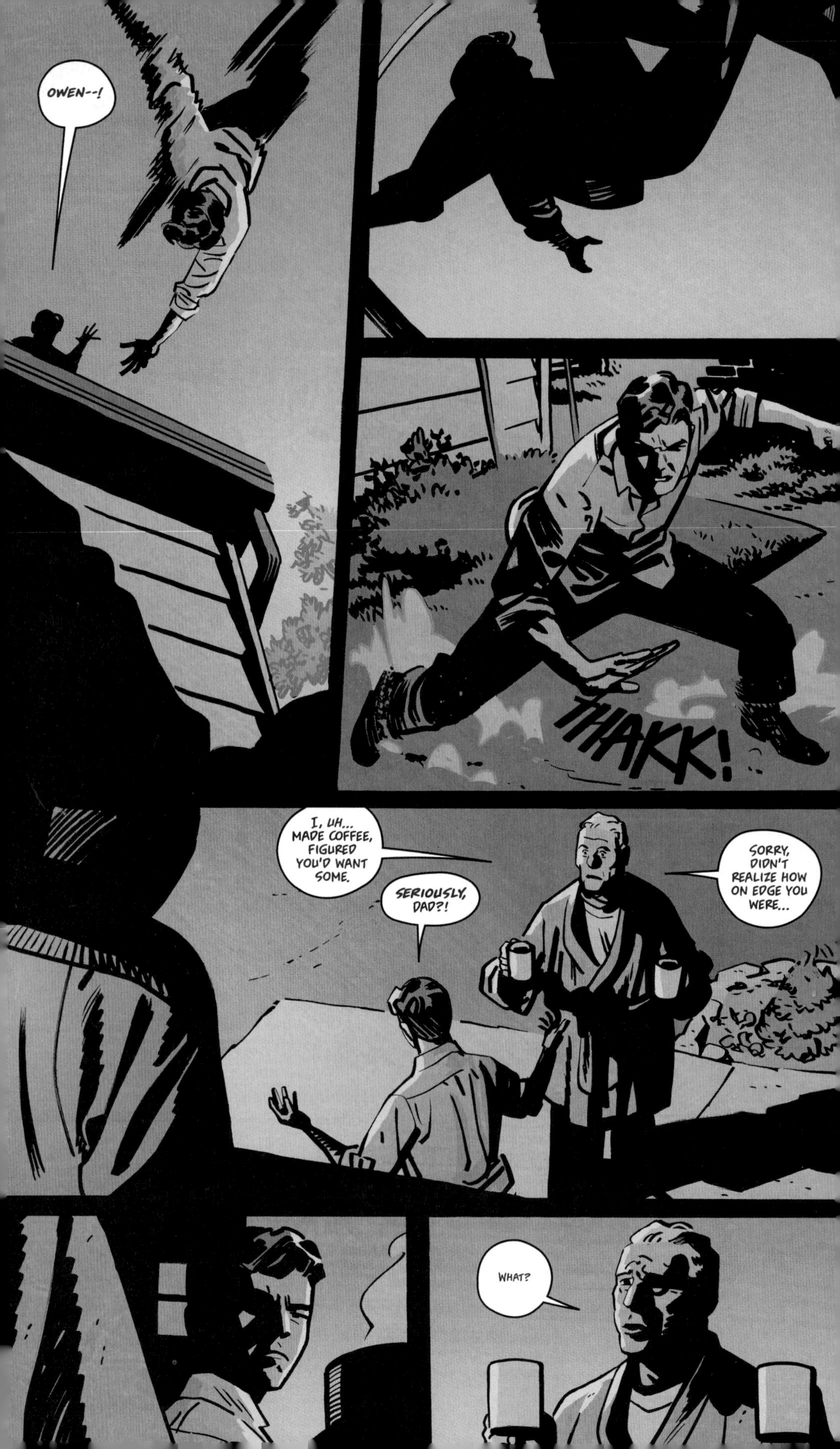
OWEN--!
THAKK!
I, UH... MADE COFFEE, FIGURED YOU'D WANT SOME.
SERIOUSLY, DAD?!
SORRY, DIDN'T REALIZE HOW ON EDGE YOU WERE...
WHAT?

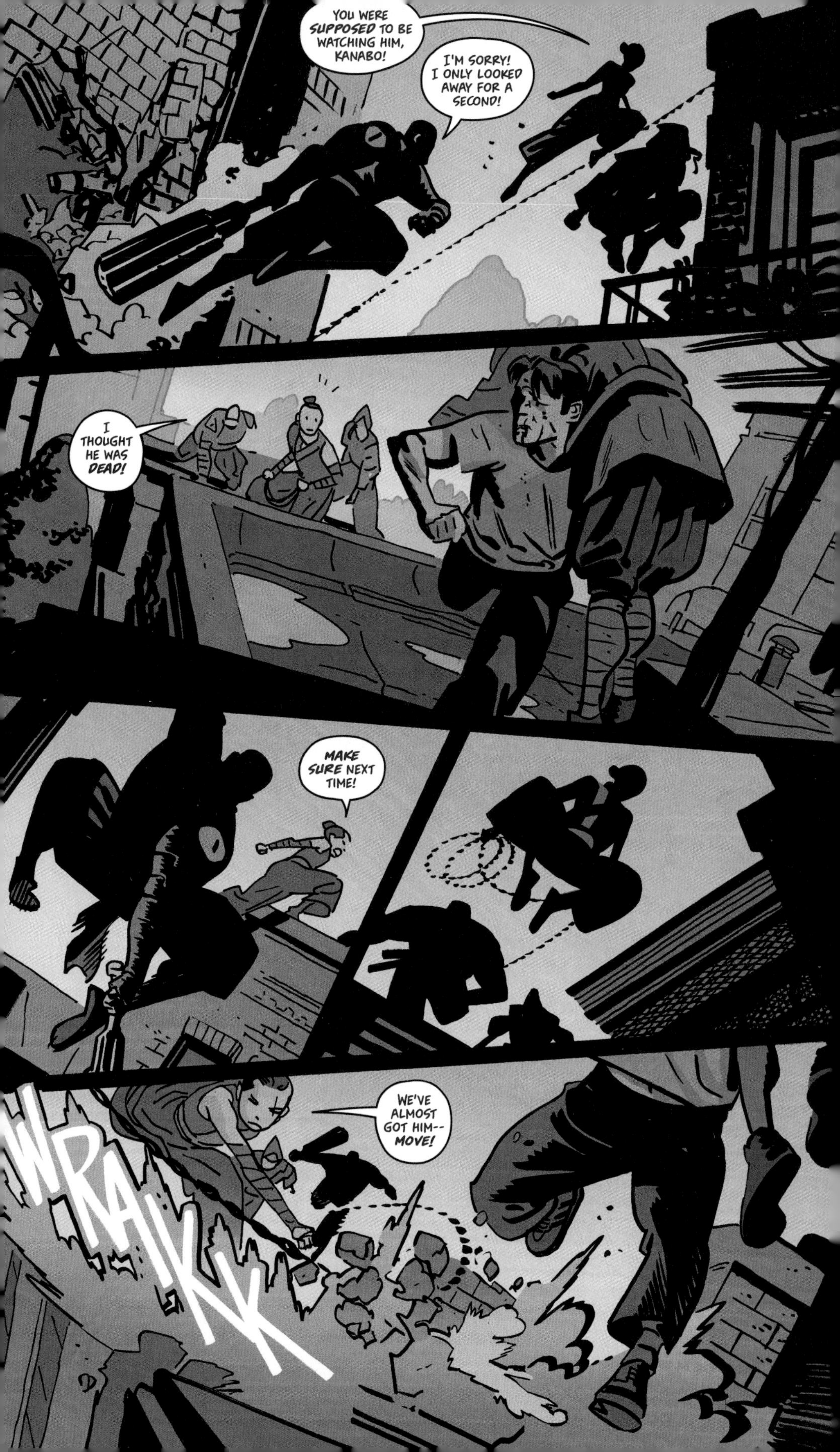
YOU WERE SUPPOSED TO BE WATCHING HIM, KANABO!
I'M SORRY! I ONLY LOOKED AWAY FOR A SECOND!
I THOUGHT HE WAS DEAD!
MAKE SURE NEXT TIME!
WE'VE ALMOST GOT HIM-- MOVE!
WRAAKK

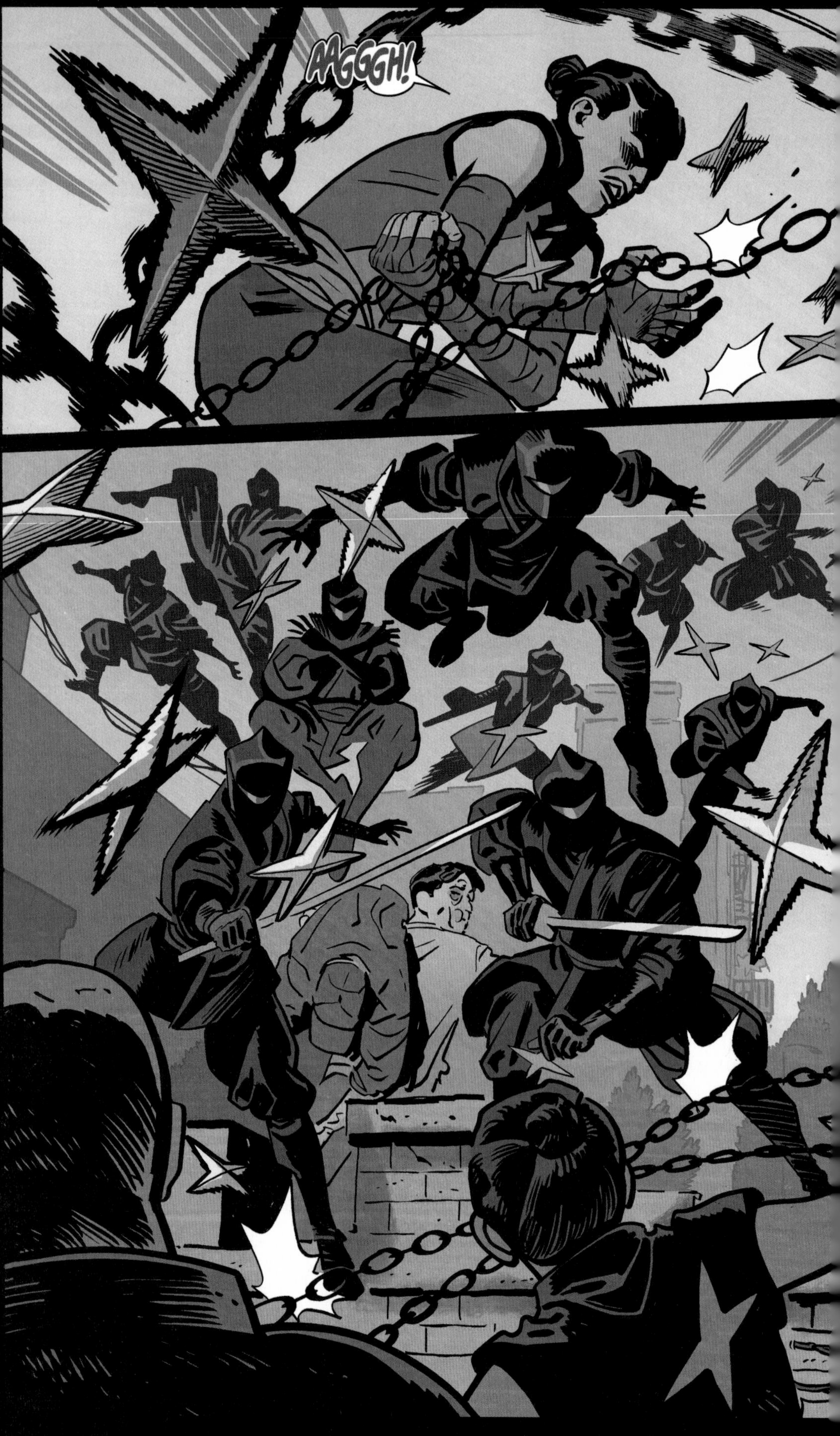
AAGGGH!

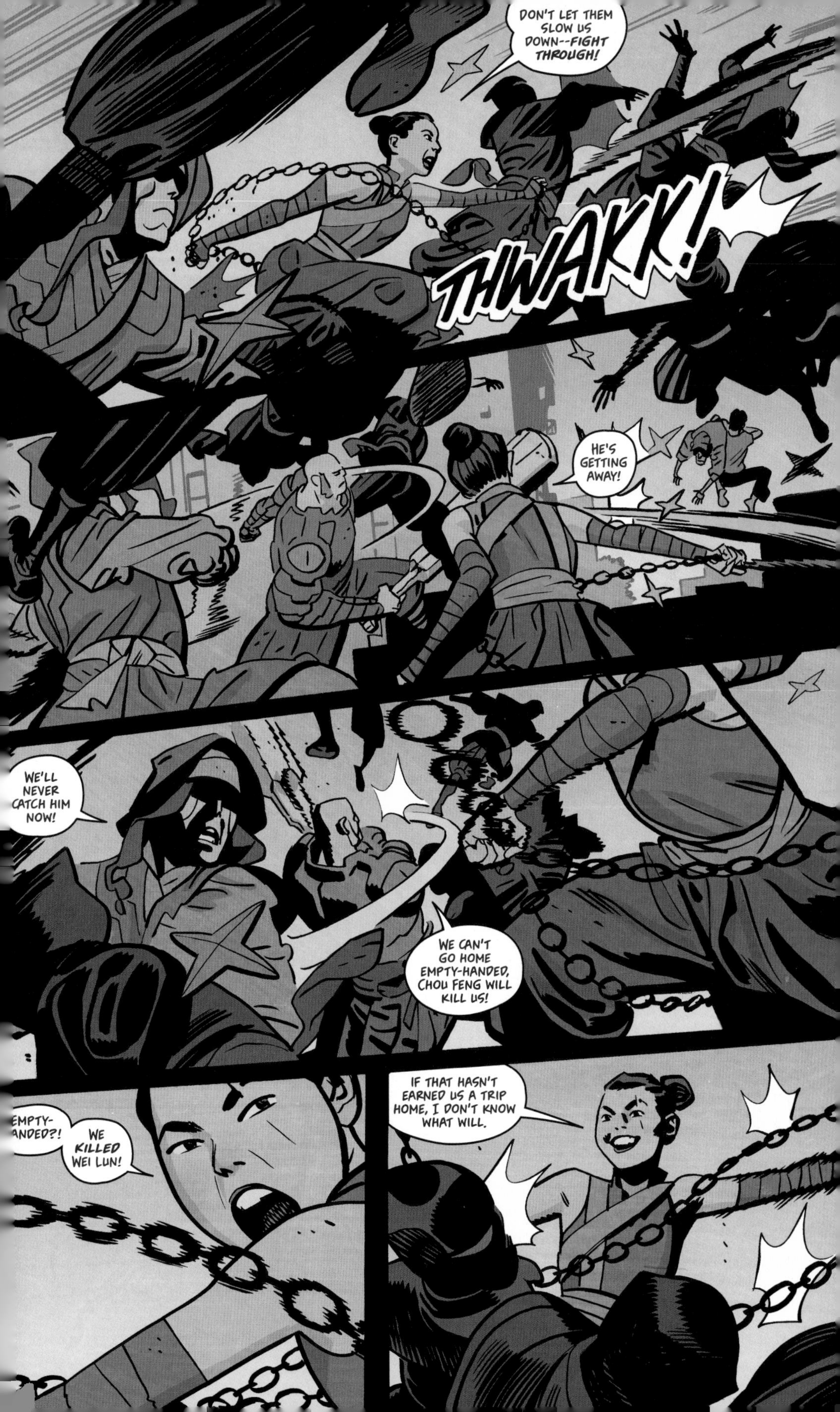

DON'T LET THEM SLOW US DOWN--FIGHT THROUGH!
THWAKK!
HE'S GETTING AWAY!
WE'LL NEVER CATCH HIM NOW!
WE CAN'T GO HOME EMPTY-HANDED, CHOU FENG WILL KILL US!
EMPTY-HANDED?!
WE KILLED WEI LUN!
IF THAT HASN'T EARNED US A TRIP HOME, I DON'T KNOW WHAT WILL.

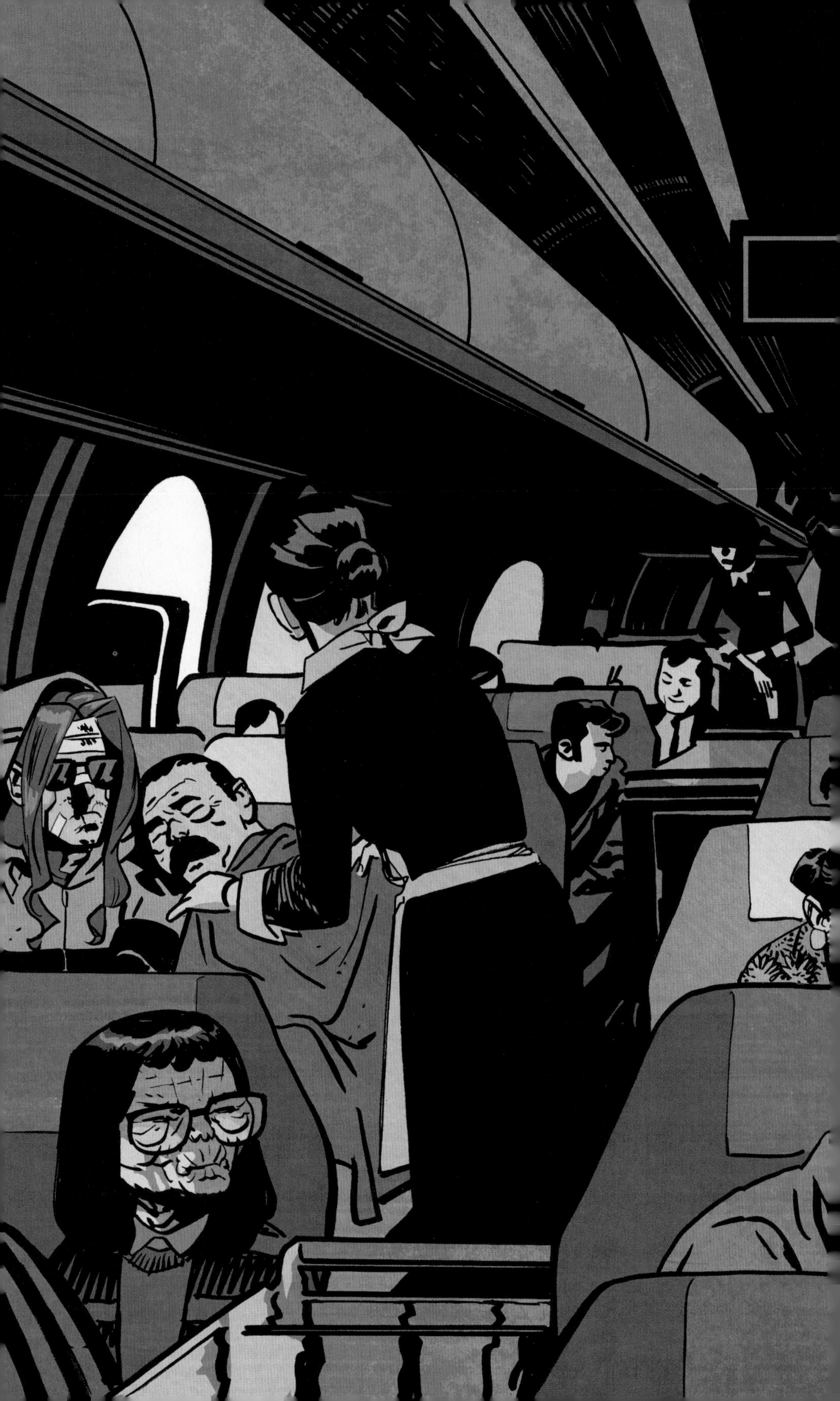

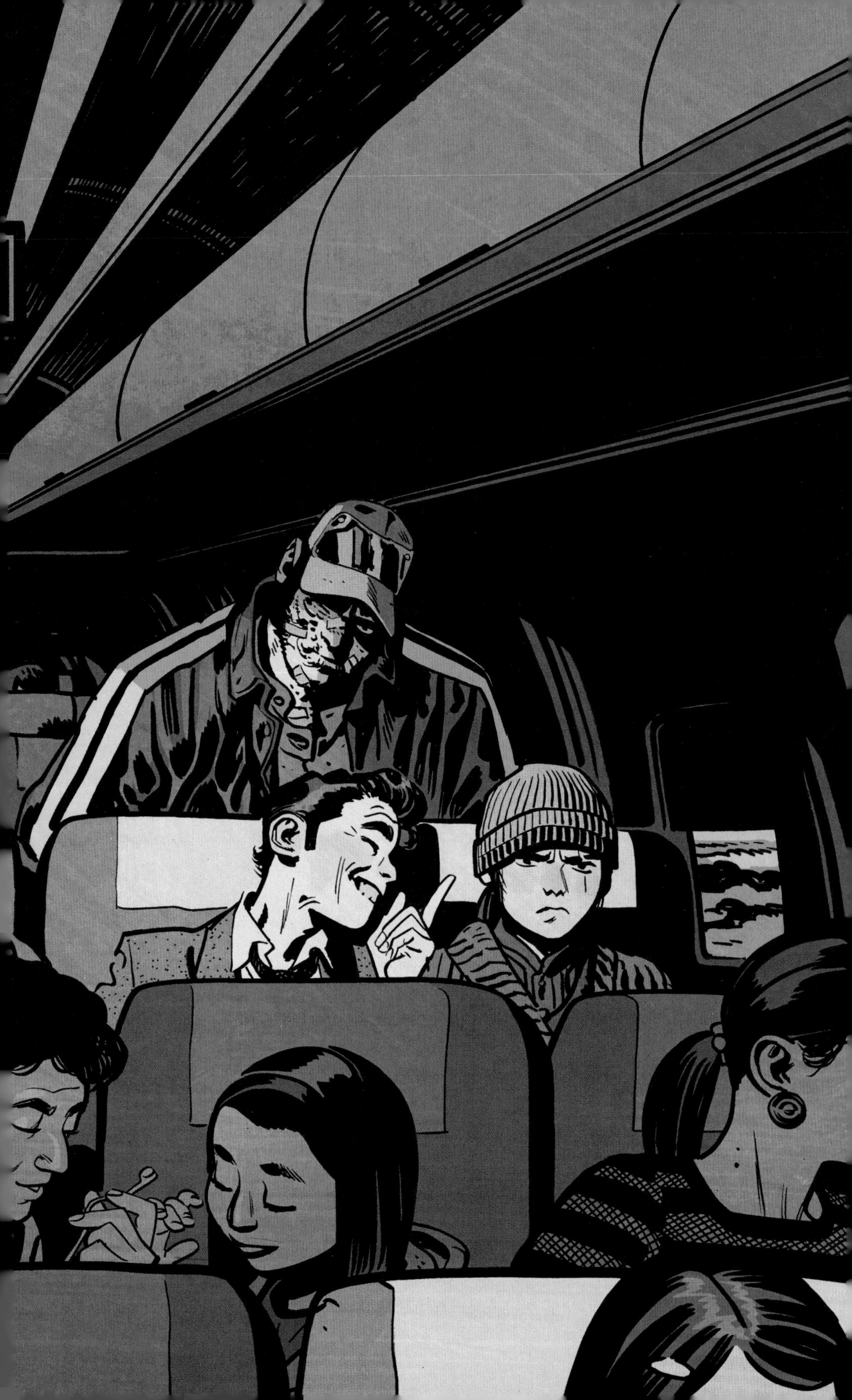

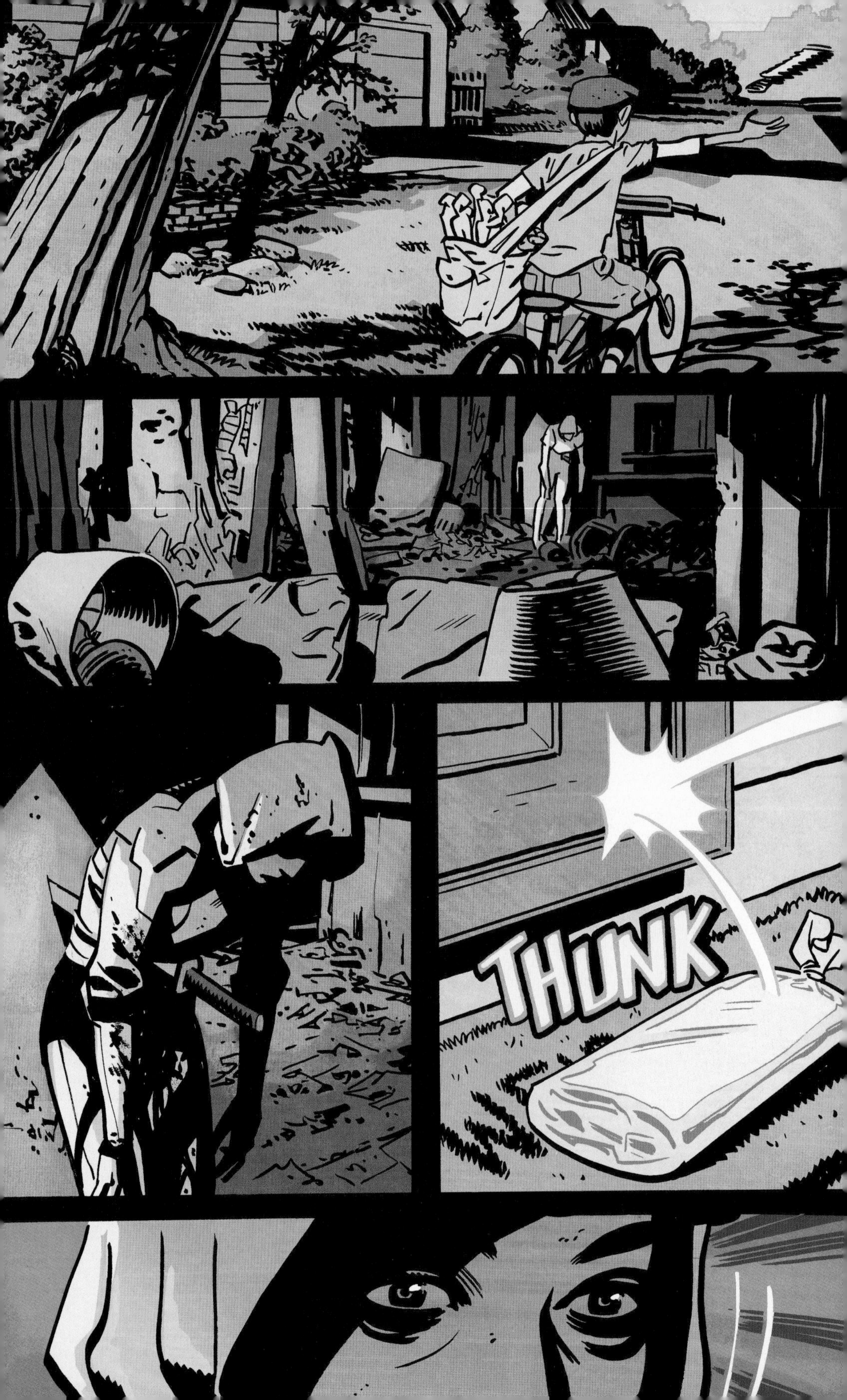
THUNK

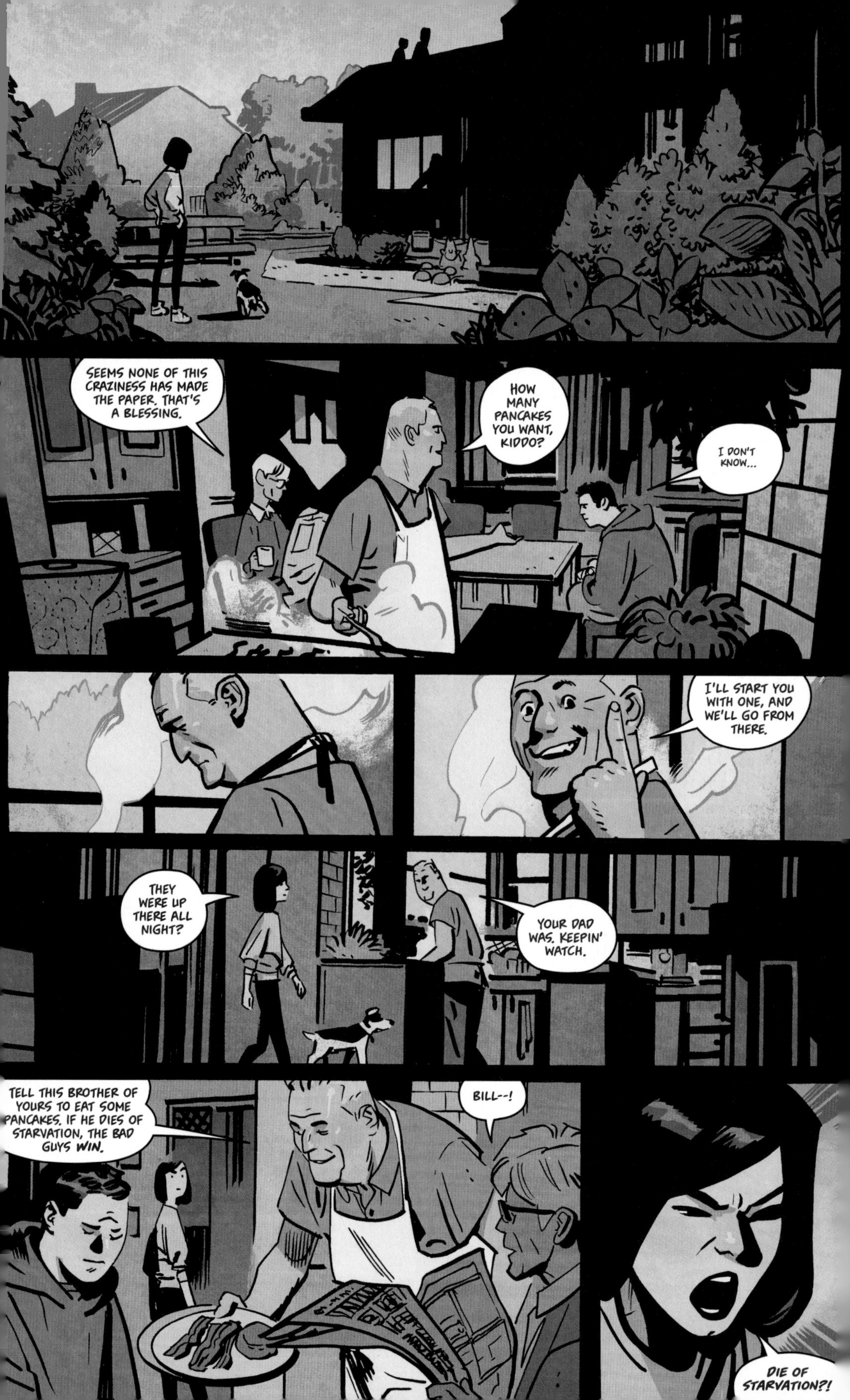
SEEMS NONE OF THIS CRAZINESS HAS MADE THE PAPER. THAT'S A BLESSING.
HOW MANY PANCAKES YOU WANT, KIDDO?
I DON'T KNOW...
I'LL START YOU WITH ONE, AND WE'LL GO FROM THERE.
THEY WERE UP THERE ALL NIGHT?
YOUR DAD WAS. KEEPIN' WATCH.
TELL THIS BROTHER OF YOURS TO EAT SOME PANCAKES. IF HE DIES OF STARVATION, THE BAD GUYS WIN.
BILL--!
DIE OF STARVATION?!

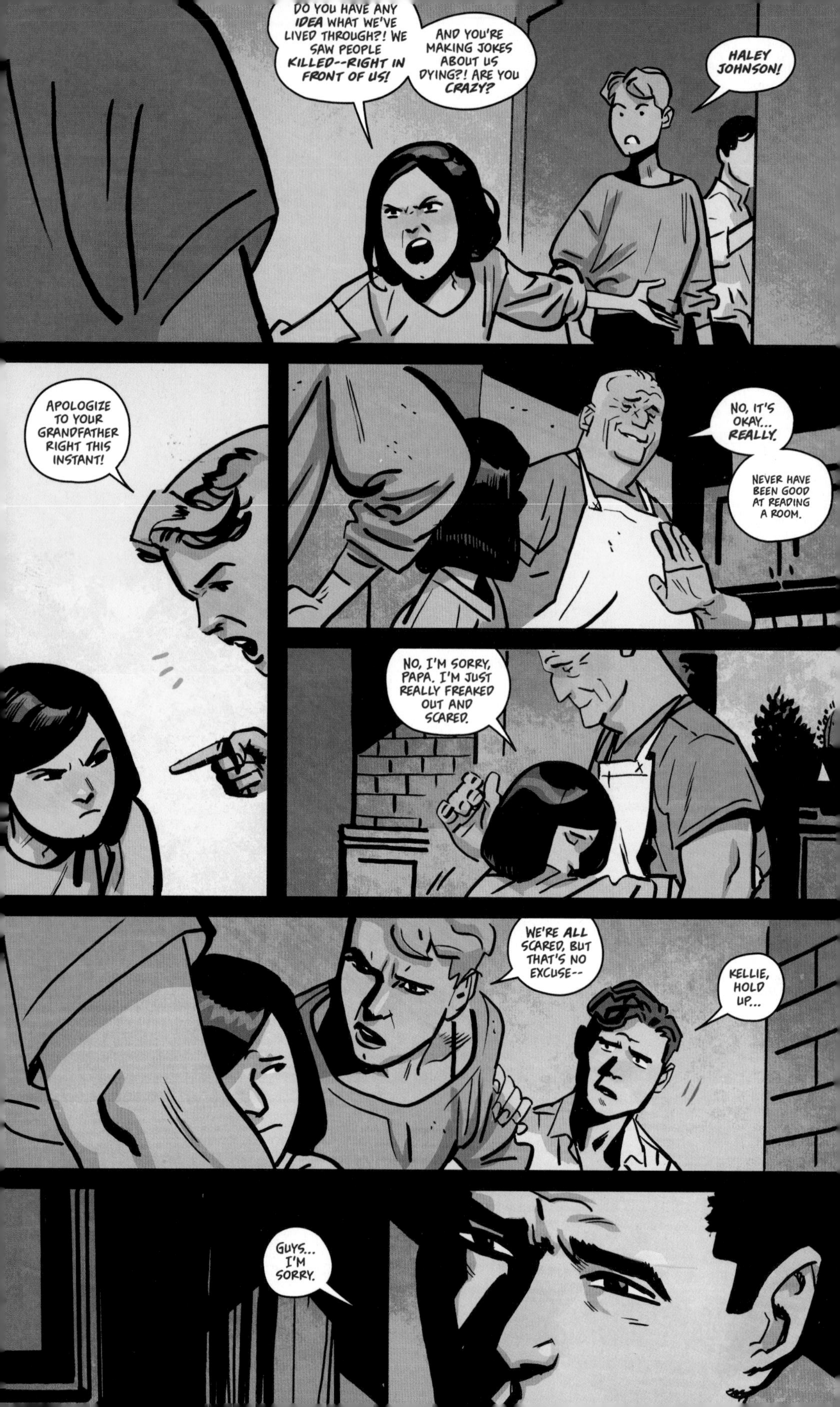
DO YOU HAVE ANY IDEA WHAT WE'VE LIVED THROUGH?! WE SAW PEOPLE KILLED--RIGHT IN FRONT OF US!
AND YOU'RE MAKING JOKES ABOUT US DYING?! ARE YOU CRAZY?
HALEY JOHNSON!
APOLOGIZE TO YOUR GRANDFATHER RIGHT THIS INSTANT!
NO, IT'S OKAY... REALLY.
NEVER HAVE BEEN GOOD AT READING A ROOM.
NO, I'M SORRY, PAPA. I'M JUST REALLY FREAKED OUT AND SCARED.
WE'RE ALL SCARED, BUT THAT'S NO EXCUSE--
KELLIE, HOLD UP...
GUYS... I'M SORRY.

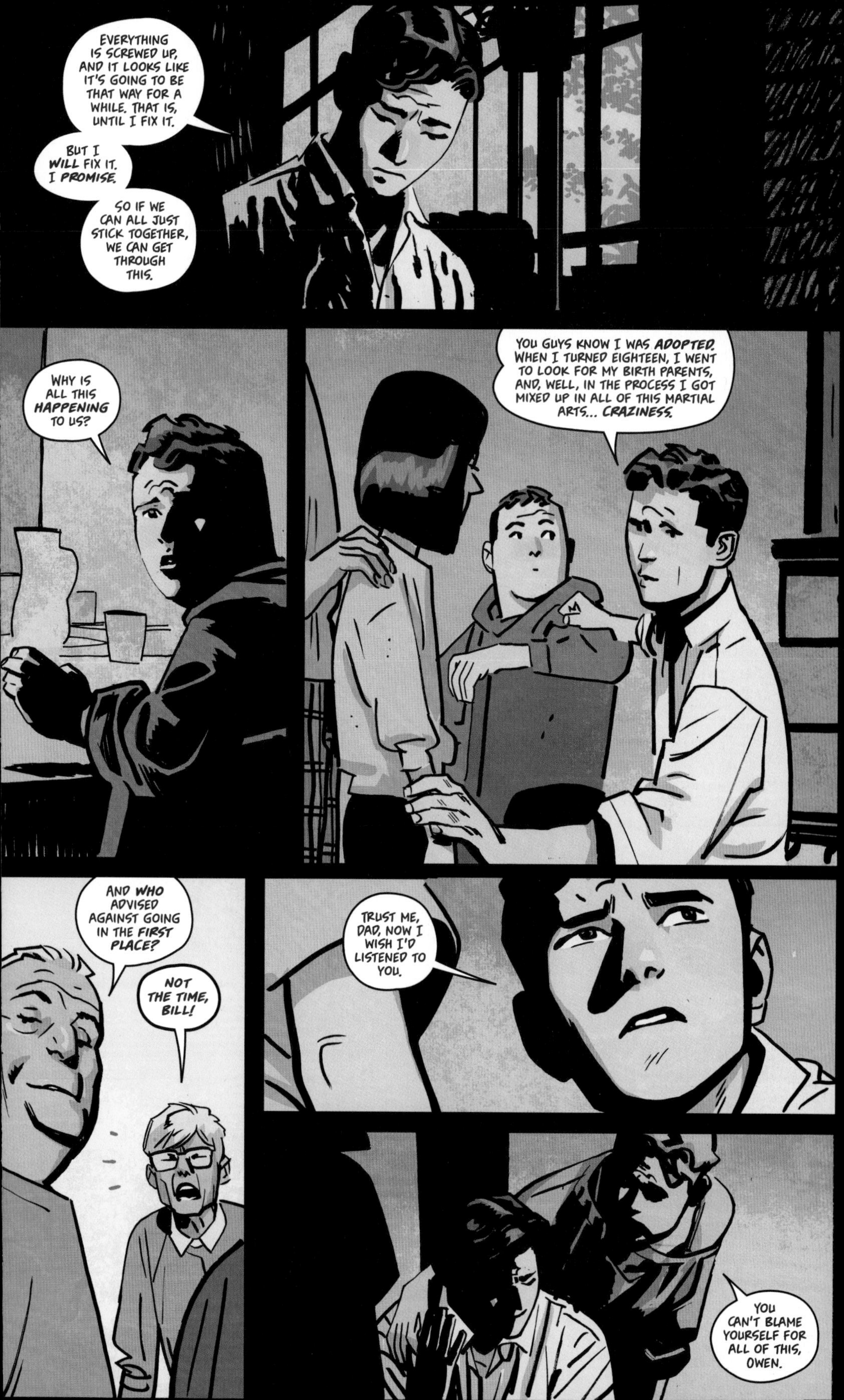

EVERYTHING IS SCREWED UP, AND IT LOOKS LIKE IT'S GOING TO BE THAT WAY FOR A WHILE. THAT IS, UNTIL I FIX IT.
BUT I **WILL** FIX IT. I ***PROMISE.***
SO IF WE CAN ALL JUST STICK TOGETHER, WE CAN GET THROUGH THIS.
WHY IS ALL THIS ***HAPPENING*** TO US?
YOU GUYS KNOW I WAS ***ADOPTED.*** WHEN I TURNED EIGHTEEN, I WENT TO LOOK FOR MY BIRTH PARENTS, AND, WELL, IN THE PROCESS I GOT MIXED UP IN ALL OF THIS MARTIAL ARTS... ***CRAZINESS.***
AND ***WHO*** ADVISED AGAINST GOING IN THE ***FIRST PLACE?***
NOT THE TIME, BILL!
TRUST ME, DAD, NOW I WISH I'D LISTENED TO YOU.
YOU CAN'T BLAME YOURSELF FOR ALL OF THIS, OWEN.

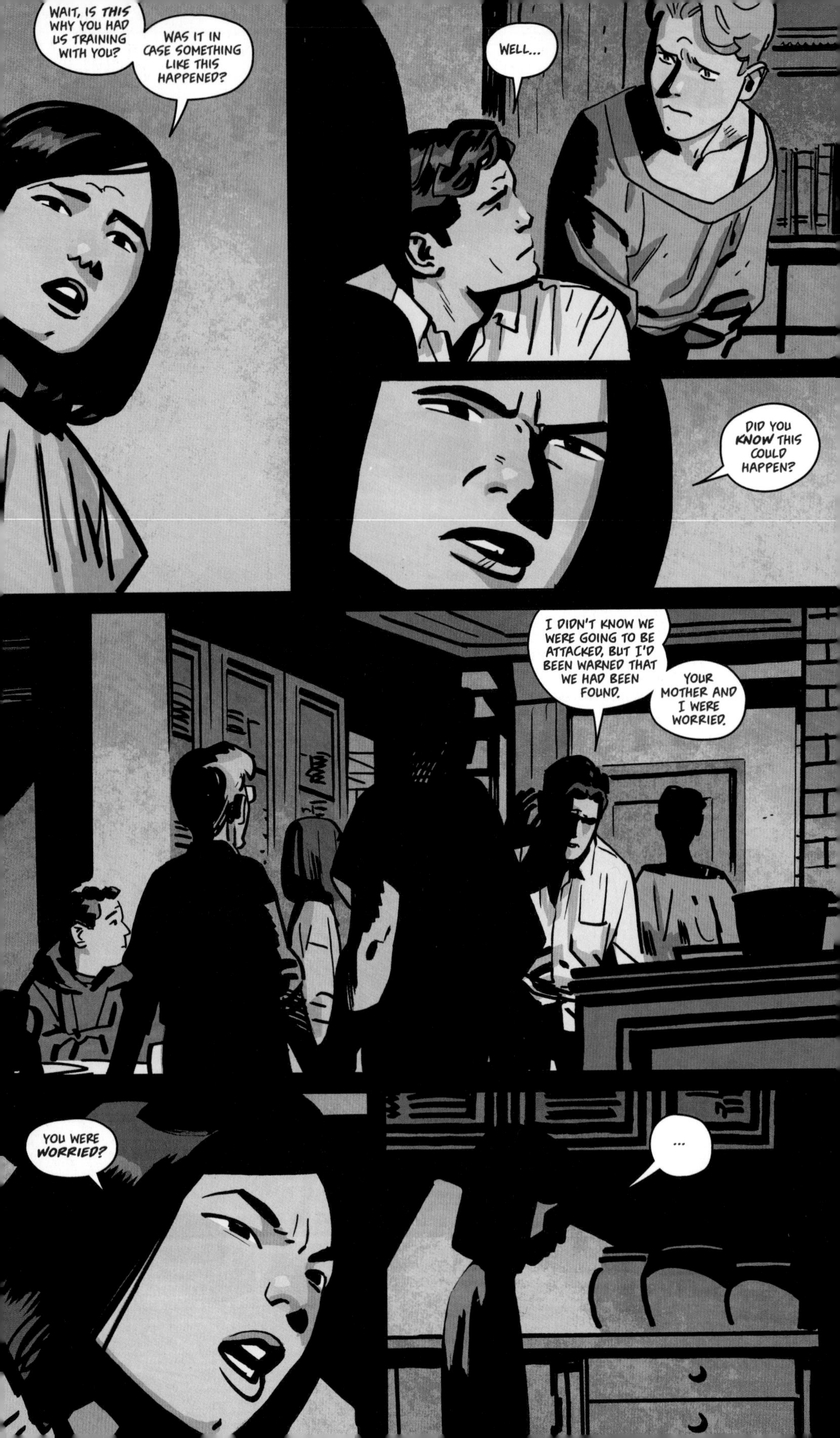
WAIT, IS THIS WHY YOU HAD US TRAINING WITH YOU?
WAS IT IN CASE SOMETHING LIKE THIS HAPPENED?
WELL...
DID YOU KNOW THIS COULD HAPPEN?
I DIDN'T KNOW WE WERE GOING TO BE ATTACKED, BUT I'D BEEN WARNED THAT WE HAD BEEN FOUND.
YOUR MOTHER AND I WERE WORRIED.
YOU WERE WORRIED?
...

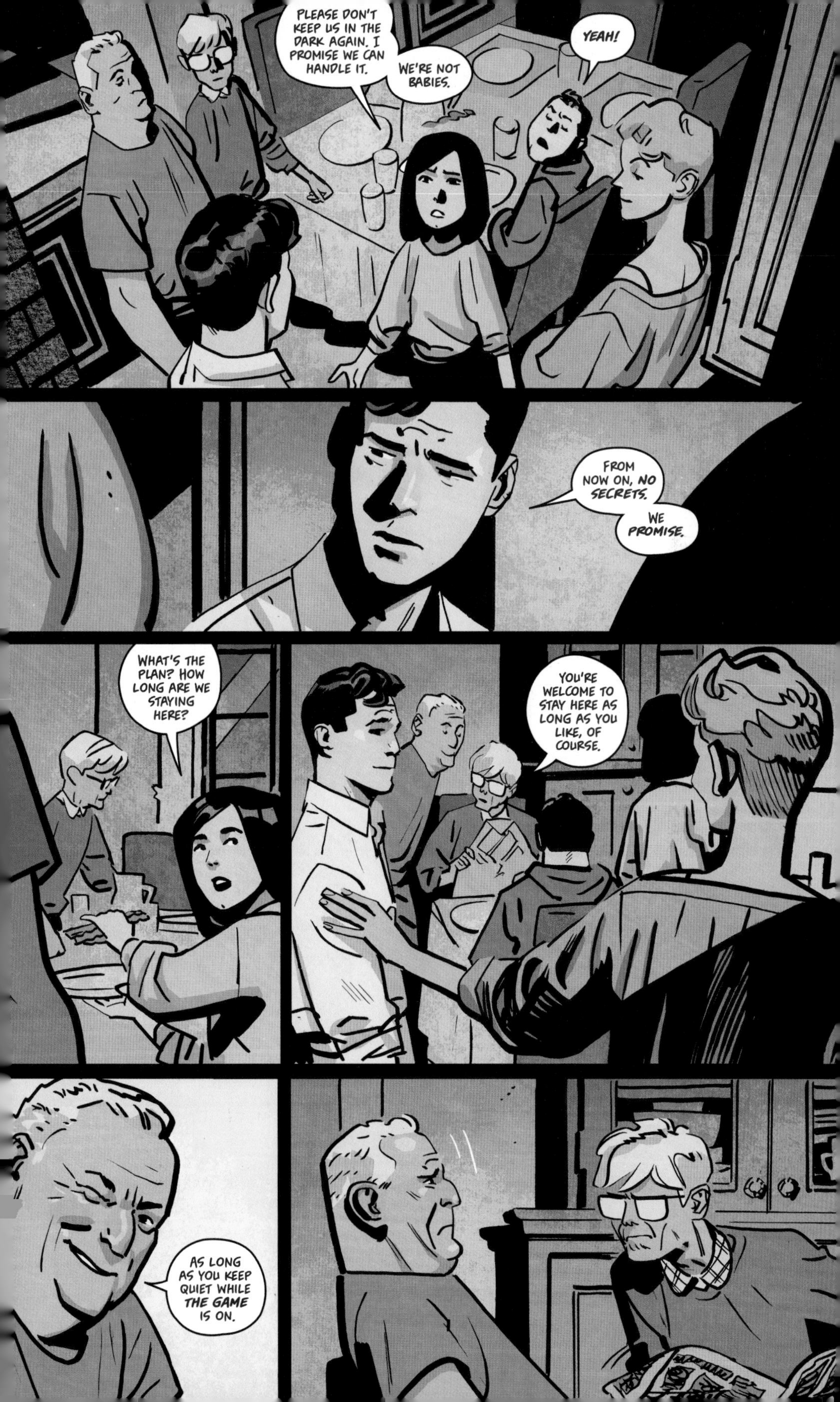
PLEASE DON'T KEEP US IN THE DARK AGAIN. I PROMISE WE CAN HANDLE IT.
WE'RE NOT BABIES.
YEAH!
FROM NOW ON, NO SECRETS.
WE PROMISE.
WHAT'S THE PLAN? HOW LONG ARE WE STAYING HERE?
YOU'RE WELCOME TO STAY HERE AS LONG AS YOU LIKE, OF COURSE.
AS LONG AS YOU KEEP QUIET WHILE THE GAME IS ON.

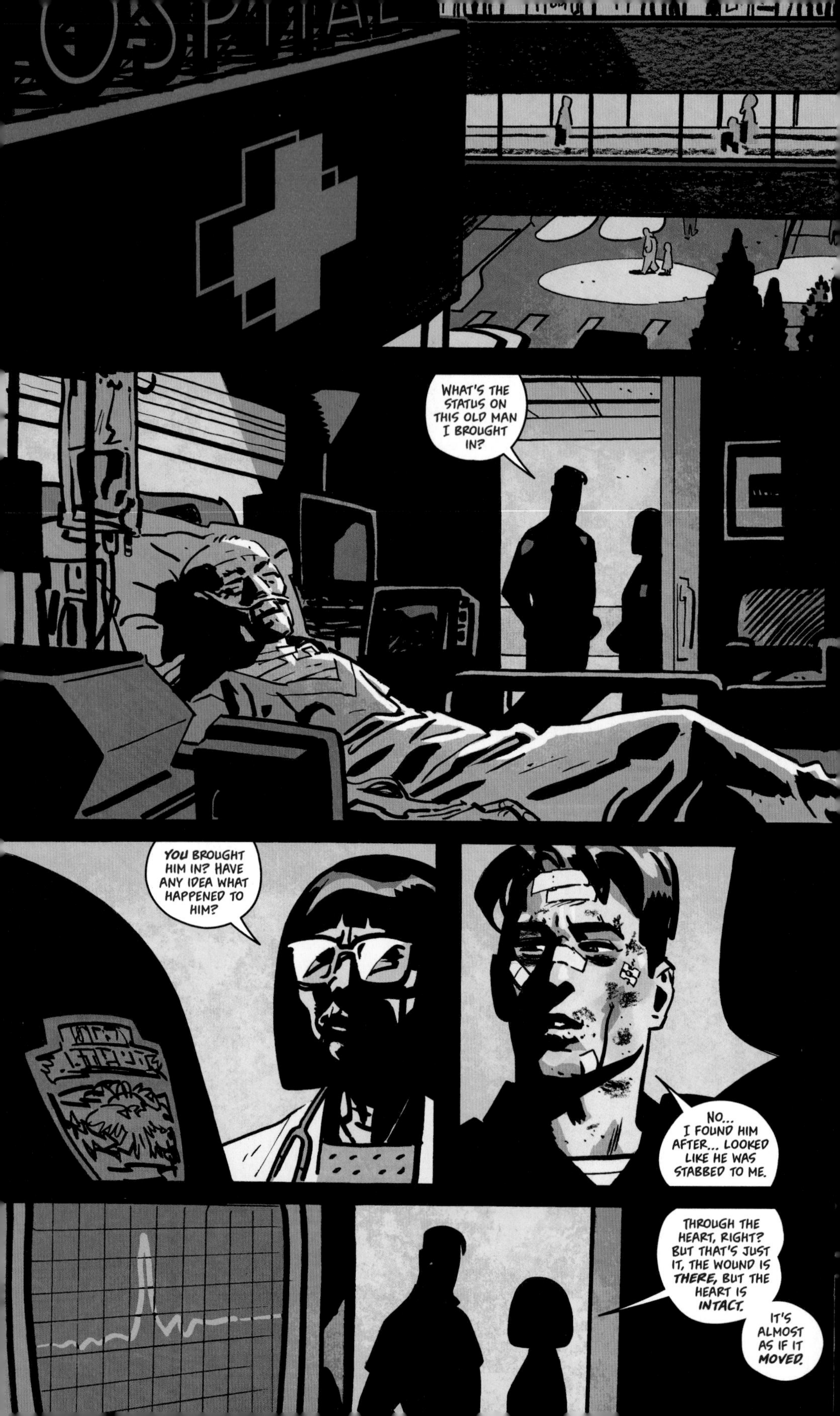
OSPITAL
WHAT'S THE STATUS ON THIS OLD MAN I BROUGHT IN?
YOU BROUGHT HIM IN? HAVE ANY IDEA WHAT HAPPENED TO HIM?
NO... I FOUND HIM AFTER... LOOKED LIKE HE WAS STABBED TO ME.
THROUGH THE HEART, RIGHT? BUT THAT'S JUST IT, THE WOUND IS THERE, BUT THE HEART IS INTACT.
IT'S ALMOST AS IF IT MOVED.

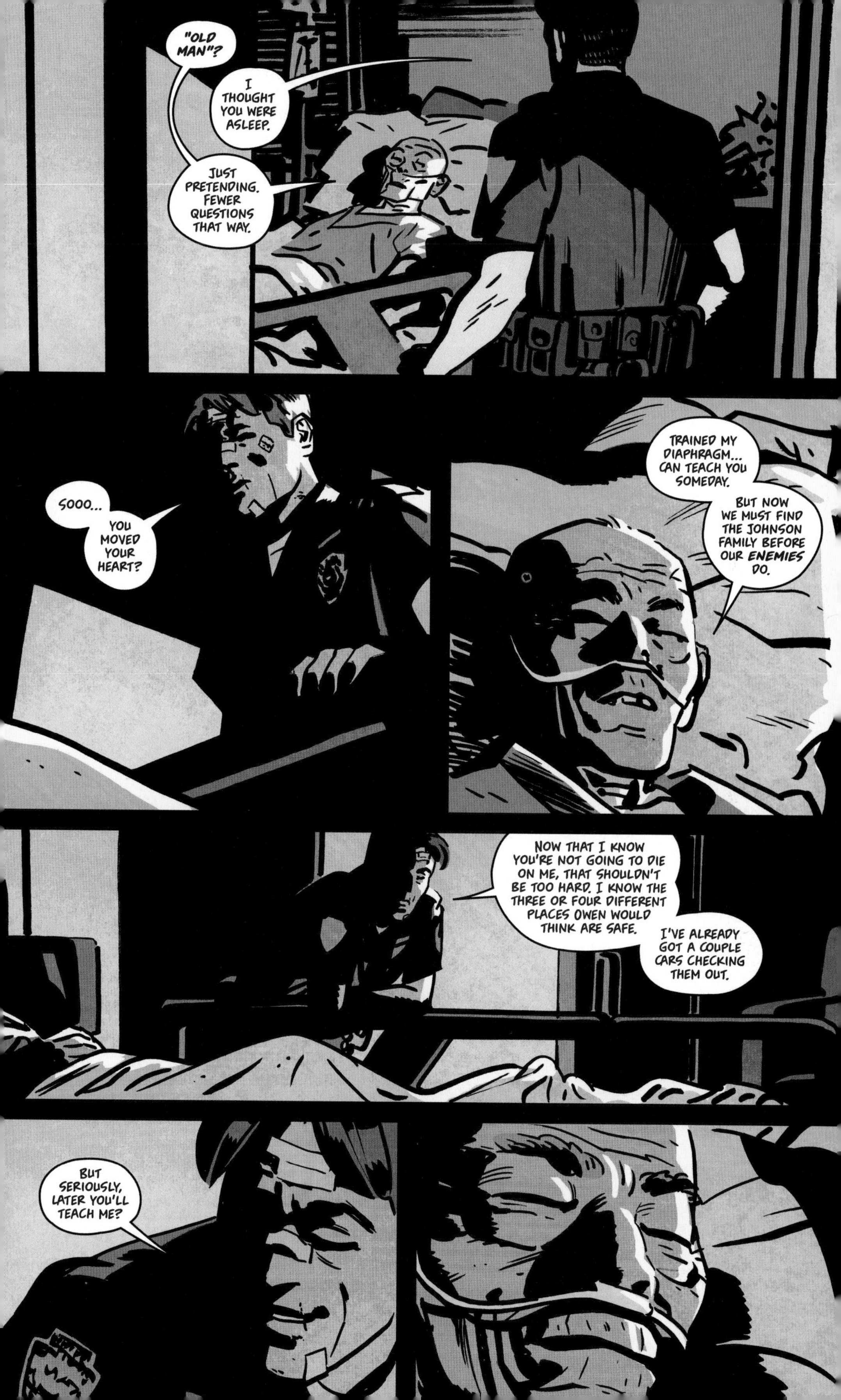
"OLD MAN"?
I THOUGHT YOU WERE ASLEEP.
JUST PRETENDING. FEWER QUESTIONS THAT WAY.
SOOO... YOU MOVED YOUR HEART?
TRAINED MY DIAPHRAGM... CAN TEACH YOU SOMEDAY.
BUT NOW WE MUST FIND THE JOHNSON FAMILY BEFORE OUR ENEMIES DO.
NOW THAT I KNOW YOU'RE NOT GOING TO DIE ON ME, THAT SHOULDN'T BE TOO HARD. I KNOW THE THREE OR FOUR DIFFERENT PLACES OWEN WOULD THINK ARE SAFE.
I'VE ALREADY GOT A COUPLE CARS CHECKING THEM OUT.
BUT SERIOUSLY, LATER YOU'LL TEACH ME?

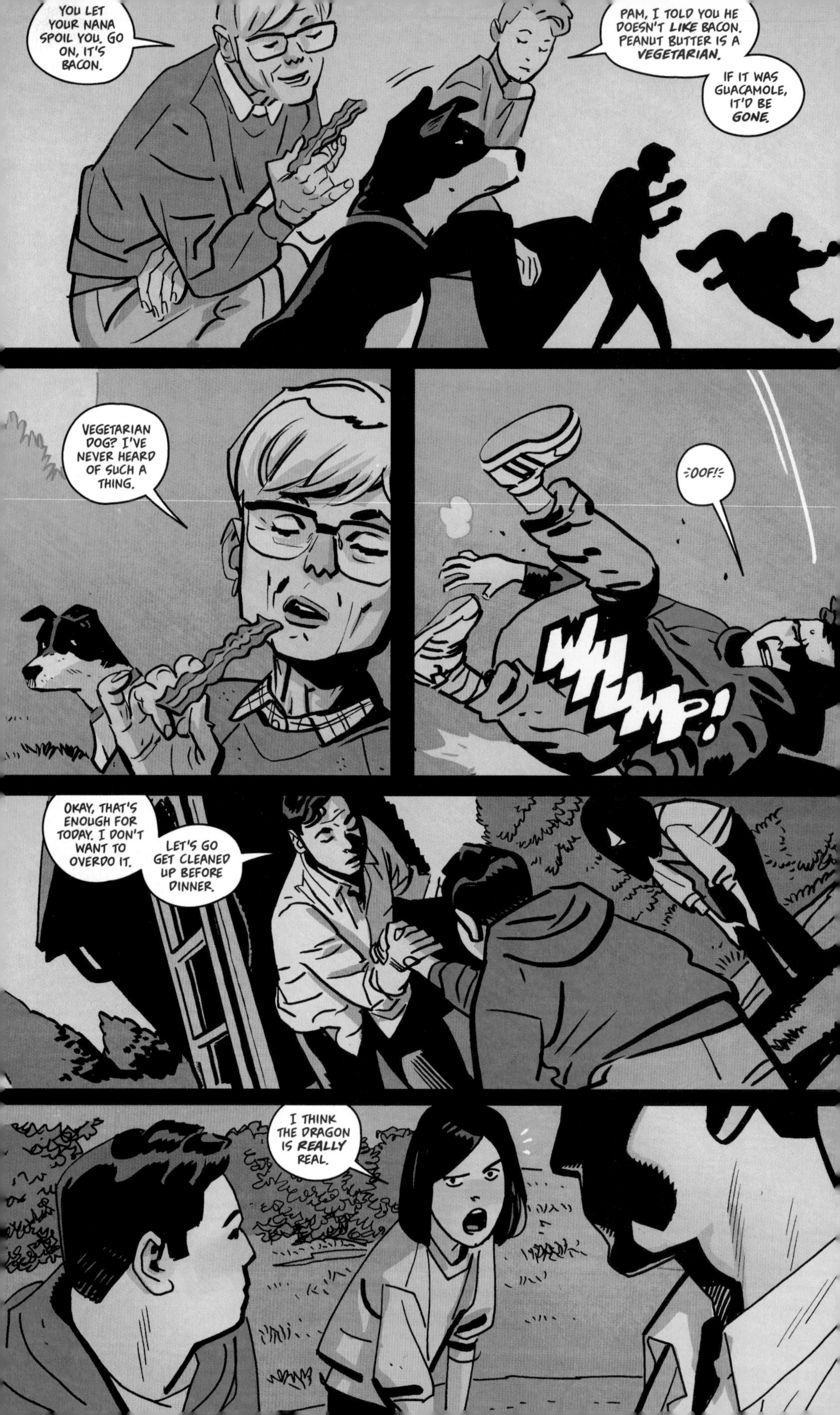
YOU LET YOUR NANA SPOIL YOU. GO ON, IT'S BACON.
PAM, I TOLD YOU HE DOESN'T LIKE BACON. PEANUT BUTTER IS A VEGETARIAN.
IF IT WAS GUACAMOLE, IT'D BE GONE.
VEGETARIAN DOG? I'VE NEVER HEARD OF SUCH A THING.
OOF!
WHUMP!
OKAY, THAT'S ENOUGH FOR TODAY. I DON'T WANT TO OVERDO IT.
LET'S GO GET CLEANED UP BEFORE DINNER.
I THINK THE DRAGON IS REALLY REAL.

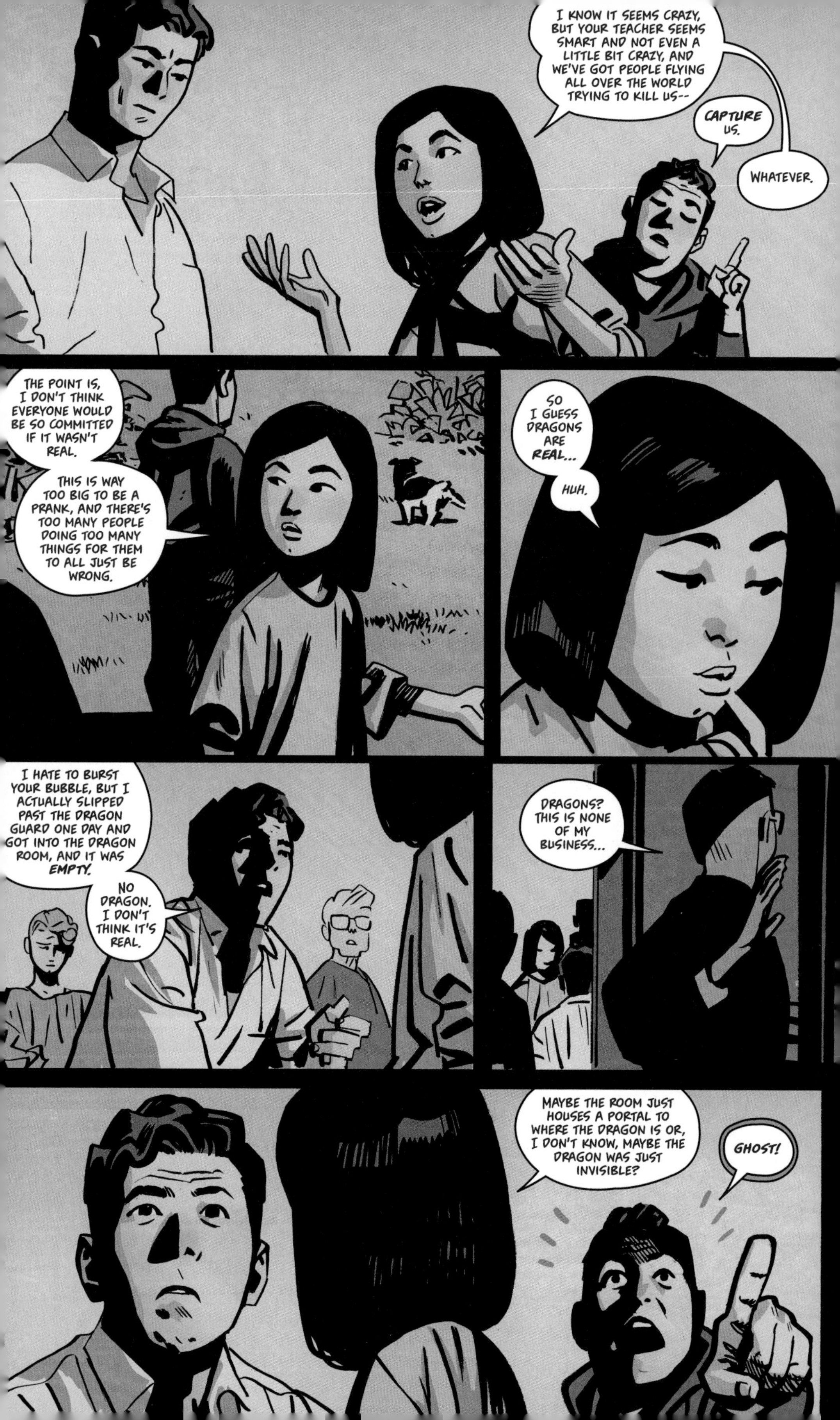
I KNOW IT SEEMS CRAZY, BUT YOUR TEACHER SEEMS SMART AND NOT EVEN A LITTLE BIT CRAZY, AND WE'VE GOT PEOPLE FLYING ALL OVER THE WORLD TRYING TO KILL US--
CAPTURE US.
WHATEVER.
THE POINT IS, I DON'T THINK EVERYONE WOULD BE SO COMMITTED IF IT WASN'T REAL.
THIS IS WAY TOO BIG TO BE A PRANK, AND THERE'S TOO MANY PEOPLE DOING TOO MANY THINGS FOR THEM TO ALL JUST BE WRONG.
SO I GUESS DRAGONS ARE REAL...
HUH.
I HATE TO BURST YOUR BUBBLE, BUT I ACTUALLY SLIPPED PAST THE DRAGON GUARD ONE DAY AND GOT INTO THE DRAGON ROOM, AND IT WAS EMPTY.
NO DRAGON. I DON'T THINK IT'S REAL.
DRAGONS? THIS IS NONE OF MY BUSINESS...
MAYBE THE ROOM JUST HOUSES A PORTAL TO WHERE THE DRAGON IS OR, I DON'T KNOW, MAYBE THE DRAGON WAS JUST INVISIBLE?
GHOST!

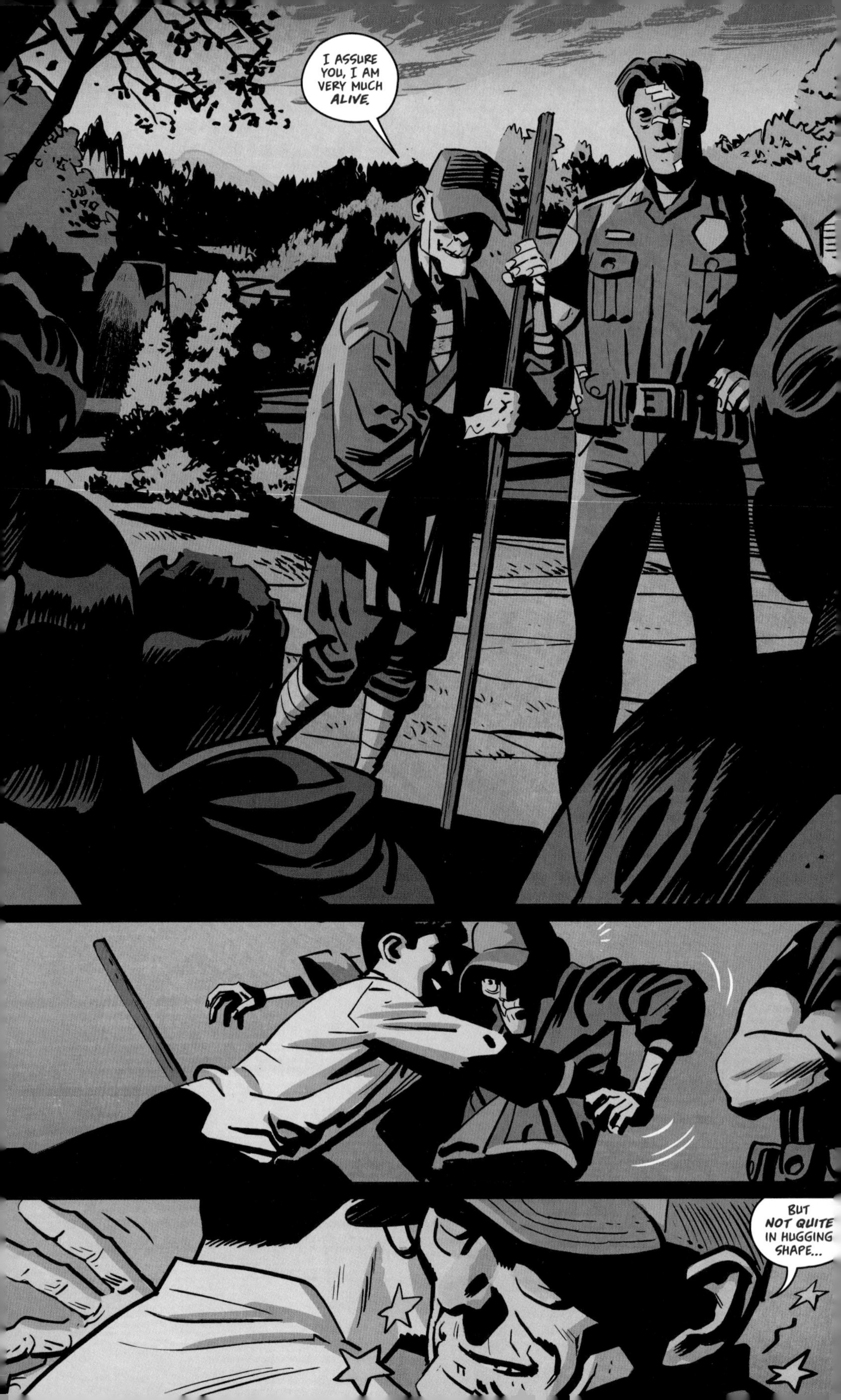
I ASSURE YOU, I AM VERY MUCH ALIVE.
BUT NOT QUITE IN HUGGING SHAPE...

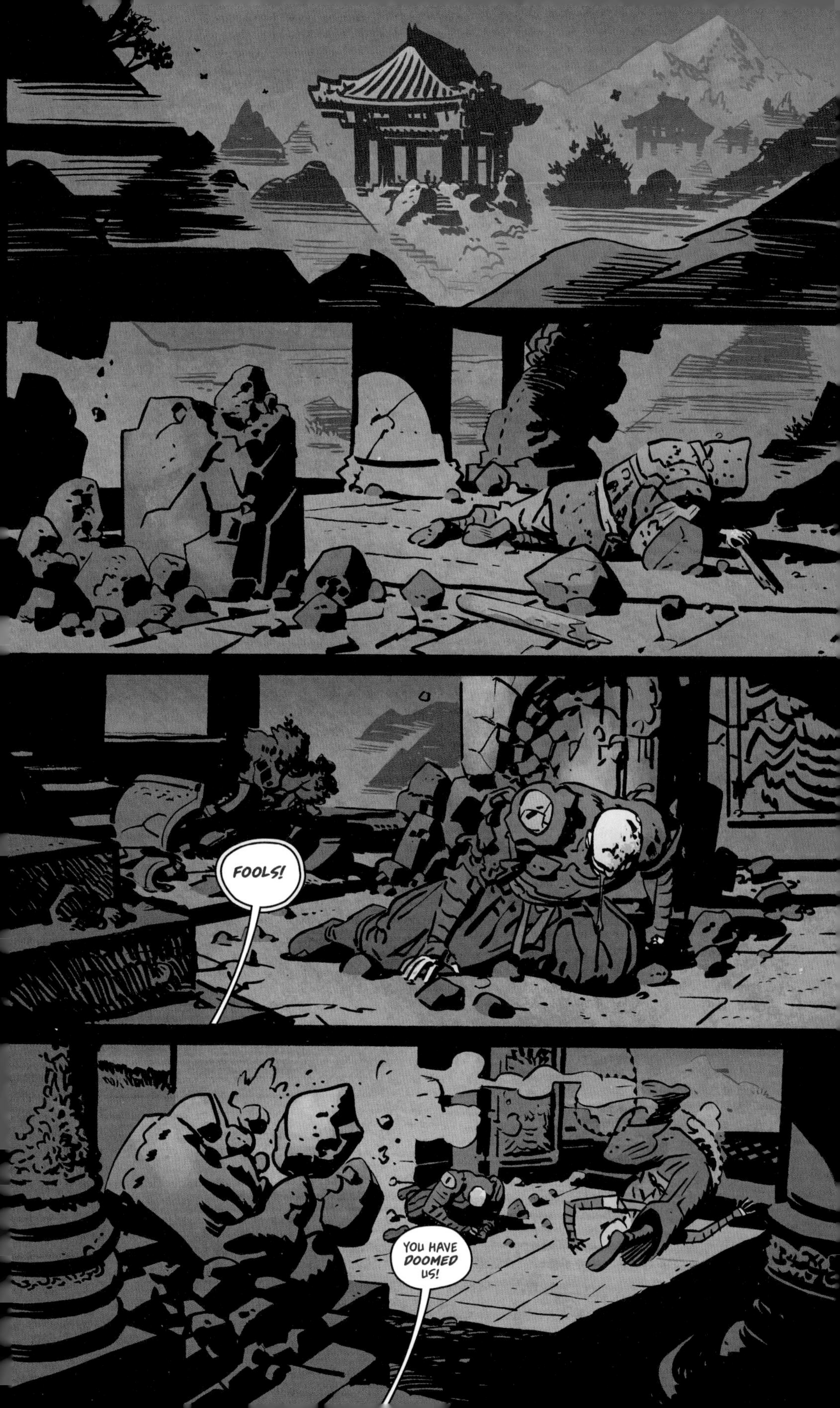
FOOLS!
YOU HAVE DOOMED US!

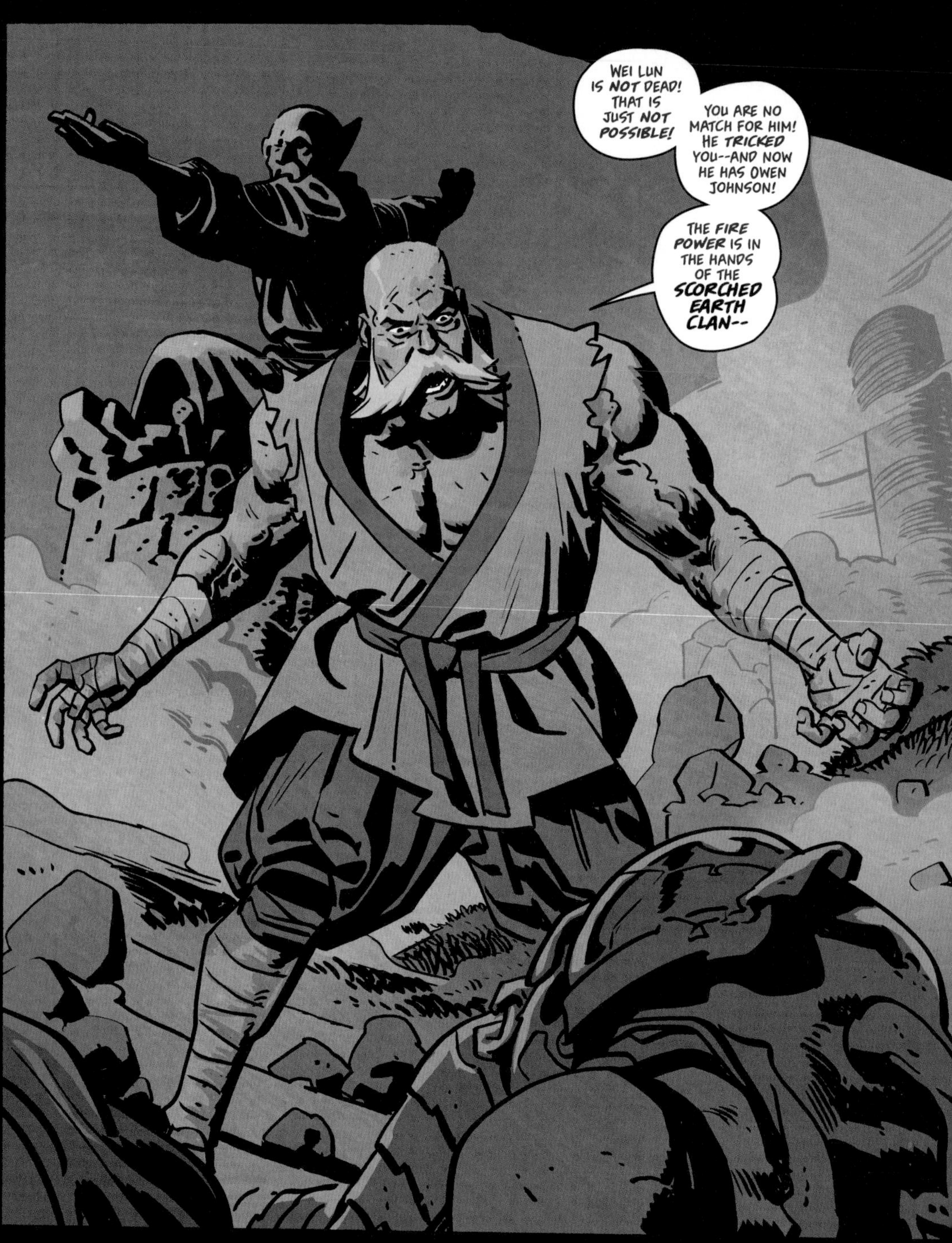
WEI LUN IS NOT DEAD! THAT IS JUST NOT POSSIBLE!
YOU ARE NO MATCH FOR HIM! HE TRICKED YOU--AND NOW HE HAS OWEN JOHNSON!
THE FIRE POWER IS IN THE HANDS OF THE SCORCHED EARTH CLAN--
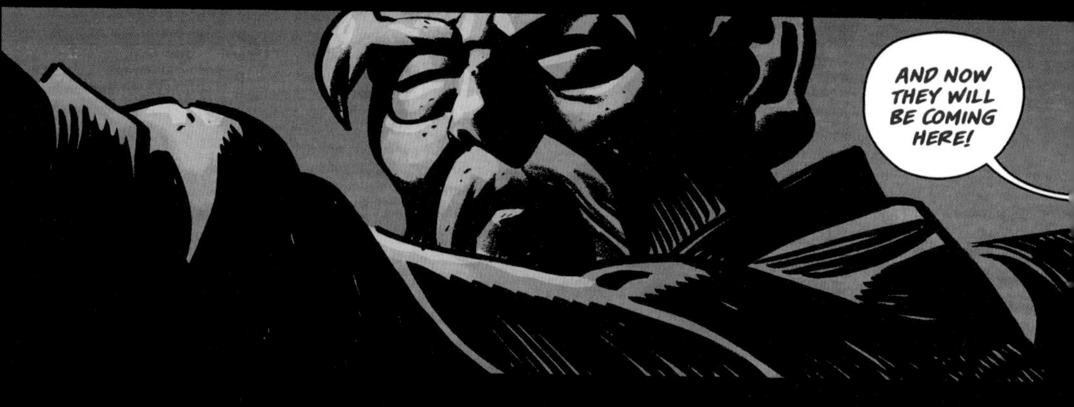
AND NOW THEY WILL BE COMING HERE!

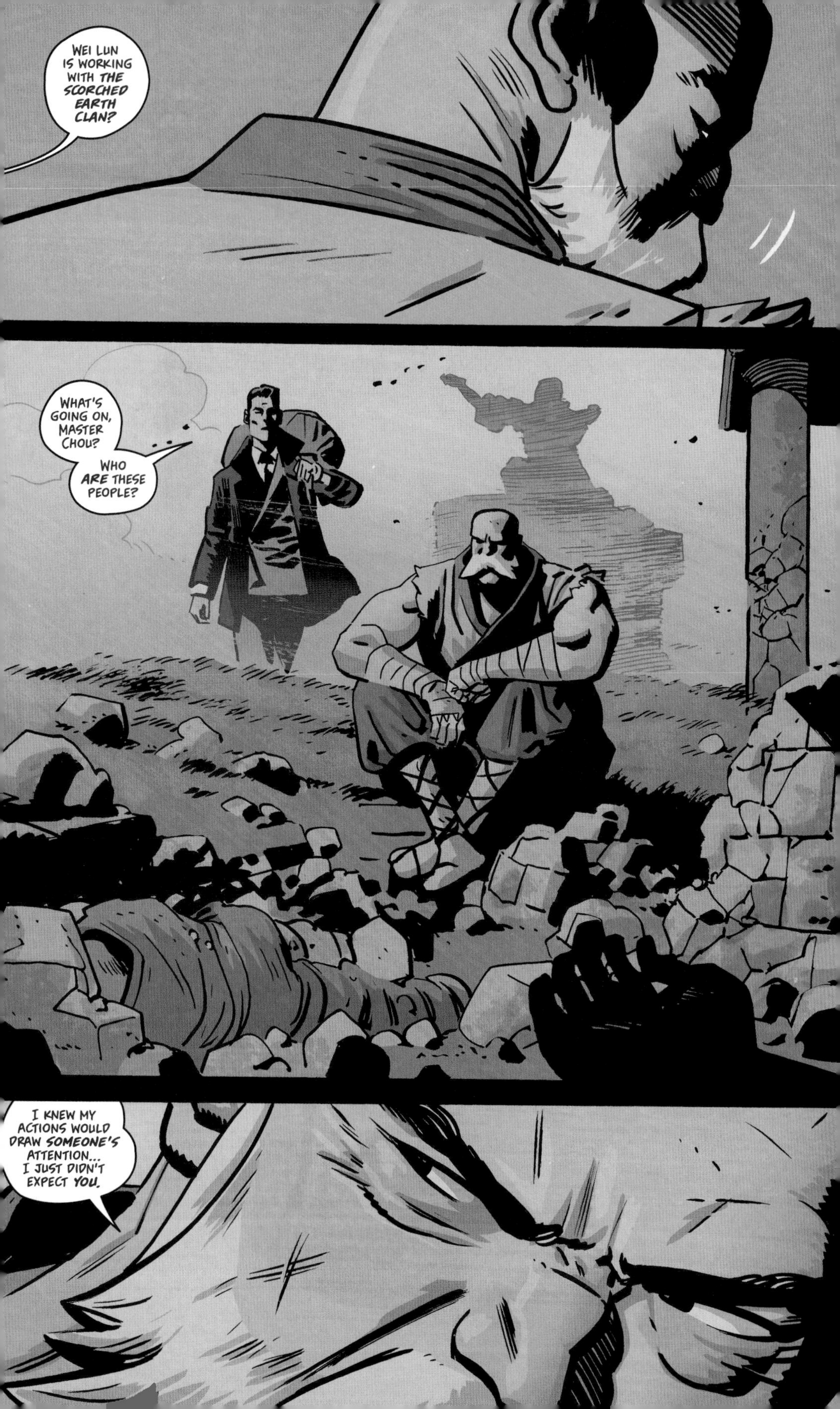
WEI LUN IS WORKING WITH THE SCORCHED EARTH CLAN?
WHAT'S GOING ON, MASTER CHOU?
WHO ARE THESE PEOPLE?
I KNEW MY ACTIONS WOULD DRAW SOMEONE'S ATTENTION... I JUST DIDN'T EXPECT YOU.

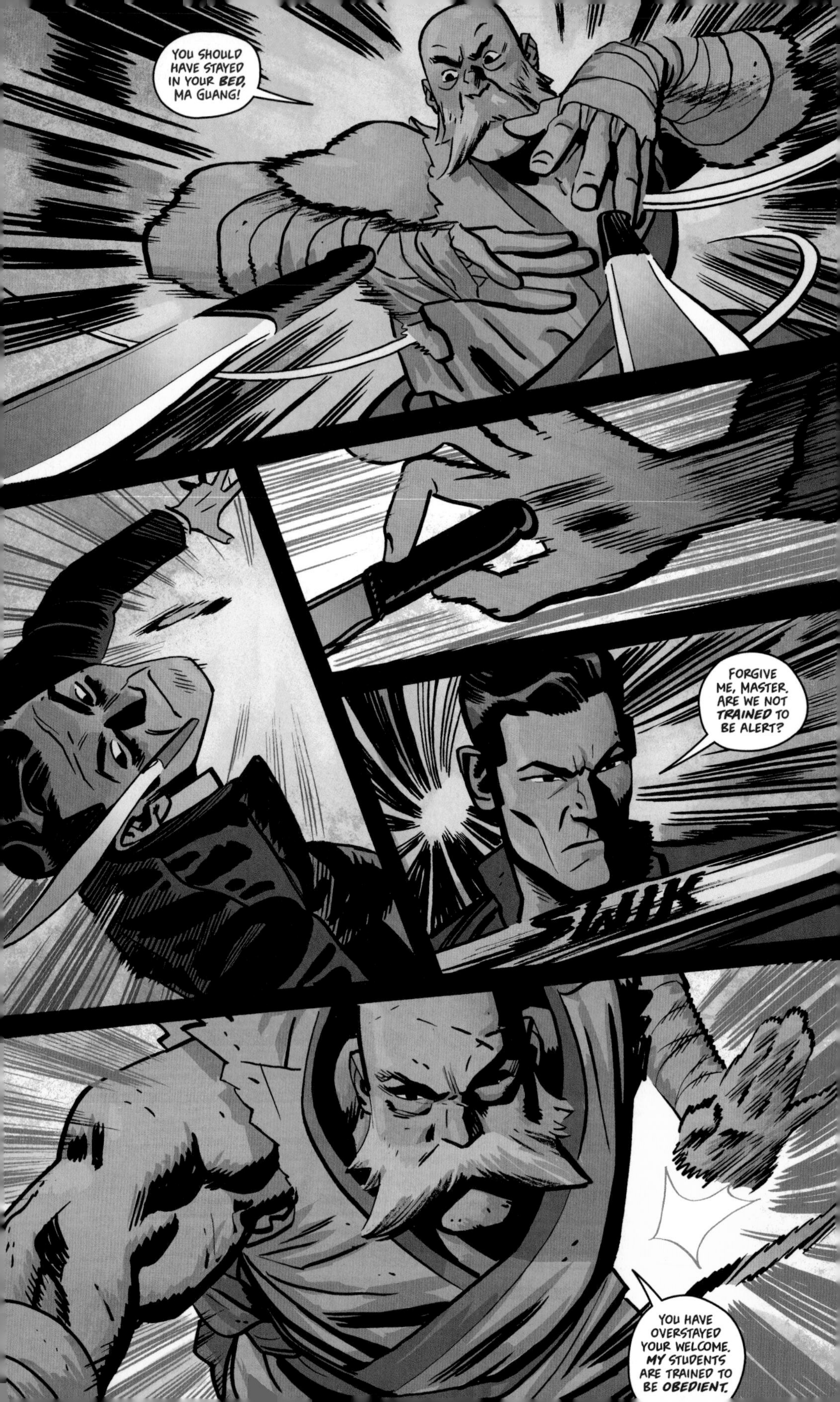
YOU SHOULD HAVE STAYED IN YOUR BED, MA GUANG!
FORGIVE ME, MASTER. ARE WE NOT TRAINED TO BE ALERT?
SHNK
YOU HAVE OVERSTAYED YOUR WELCOME. MY STUDENTS ARE TRAINED TO BE OBEDIENT.

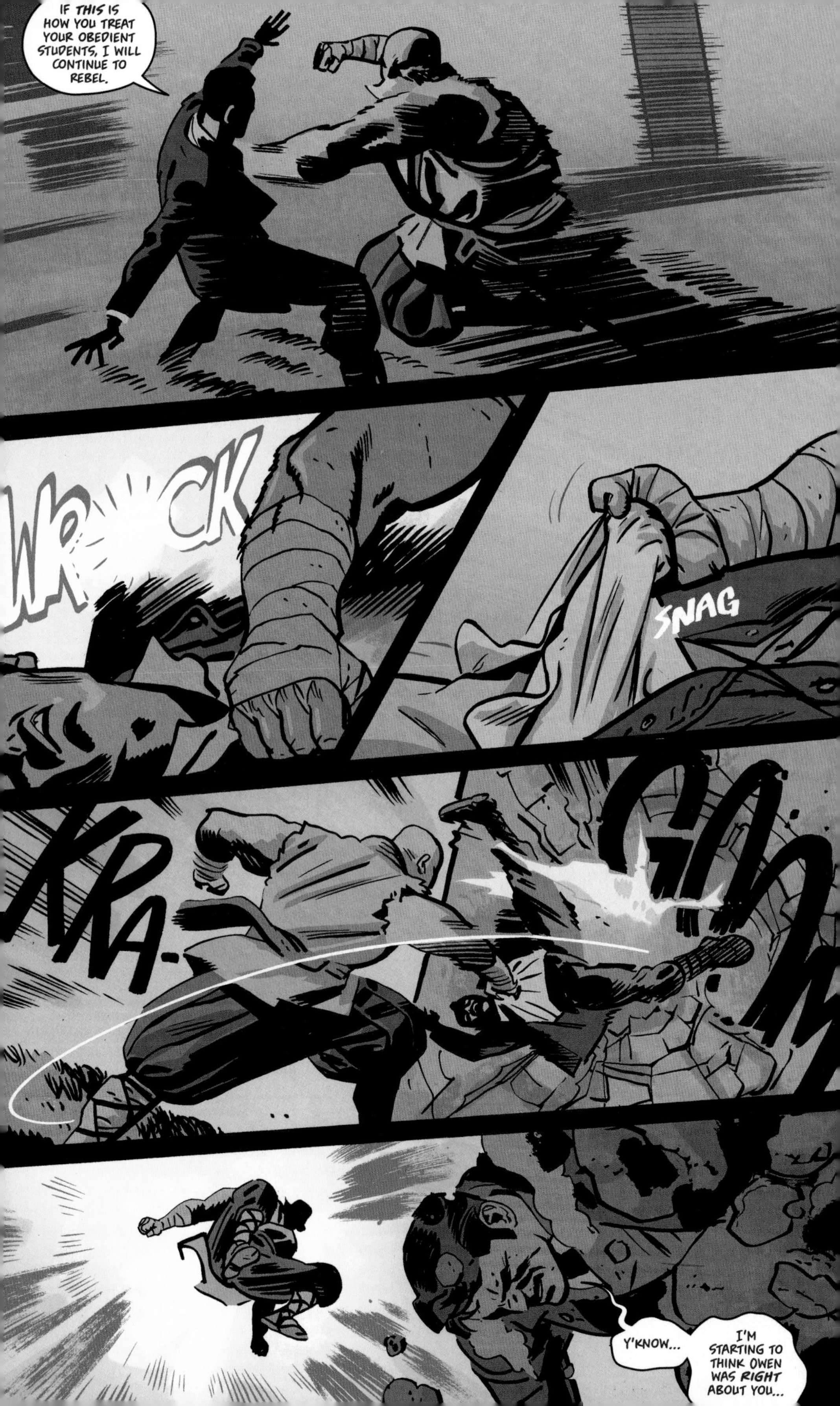
IF THIS IS HOW YOU TREAT YOUR OBEDIENT STUDENTS, I WILL CONTINUE TO REBEL.
WR- CK
SNAG
KRA-
Y'KNOW...
I'M STARTING TO THINK OWEN WAS RIGHT ABOUT YOU...

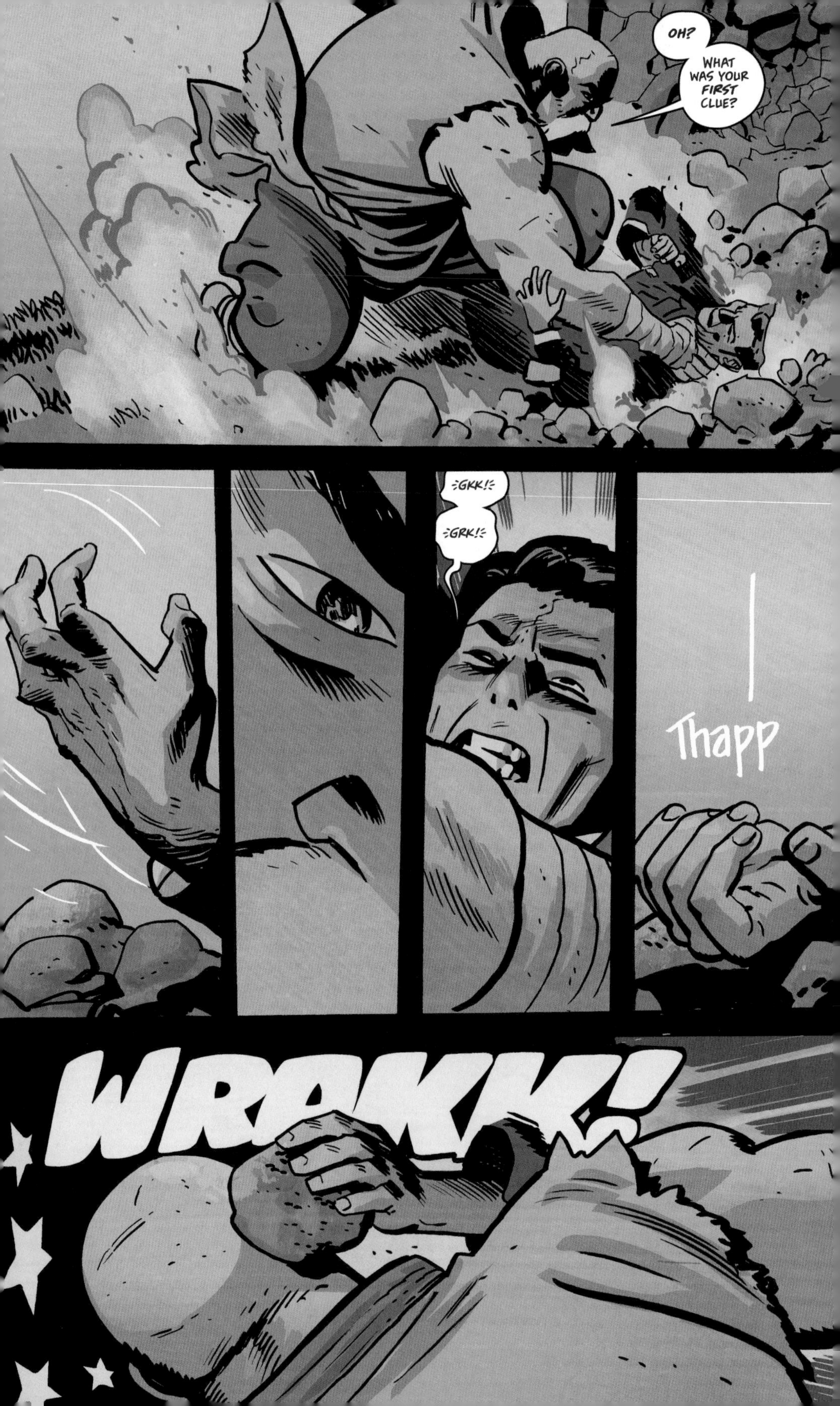
OH?
WHAT WAS YOUR FIRST CLUE?
GKK!
GRK!
Thapp
WRAKK!

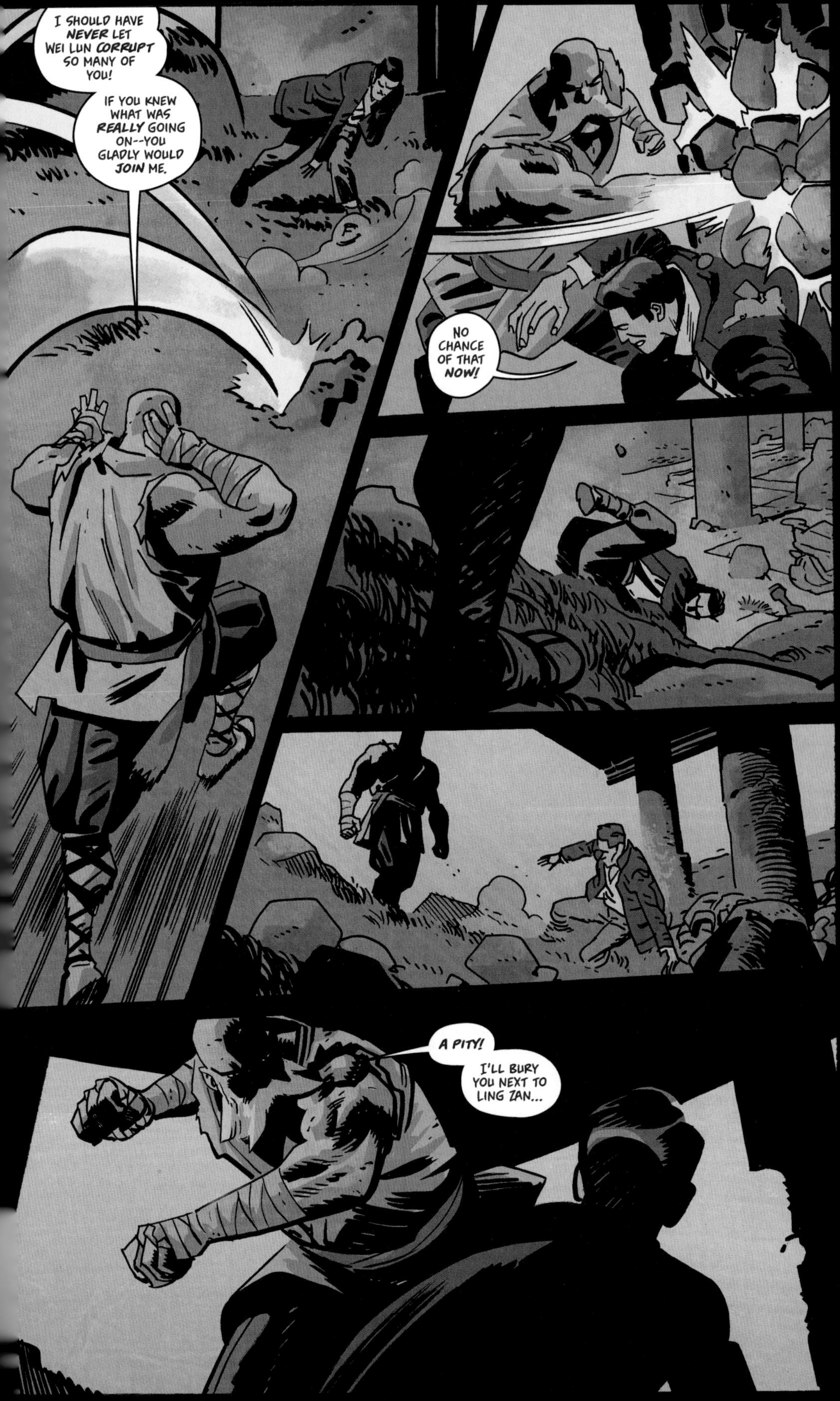
I SHOULD HAVE NEVER LET WEI LUN CORRUPT SO MANY OF YOU!
IF YOU KNEW WHAT WAS REALLY GOING ON--YOU GLADLY WOULD JOIN ME.
NO CHANCE OF THAT NOW!
A PITY!
I'LL BURY YOU NEXT TO LING ZAN...

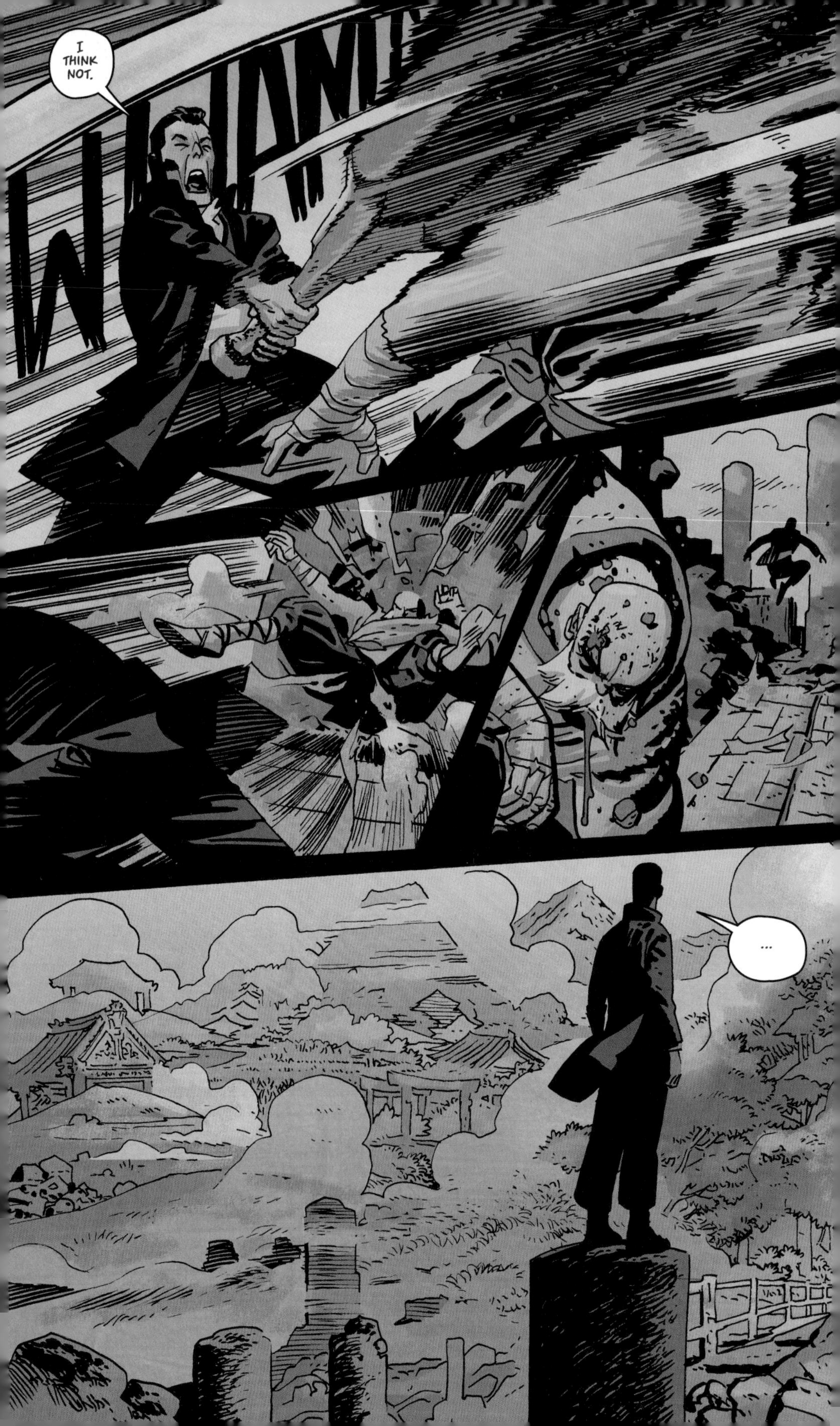
I THINK NOT.
...

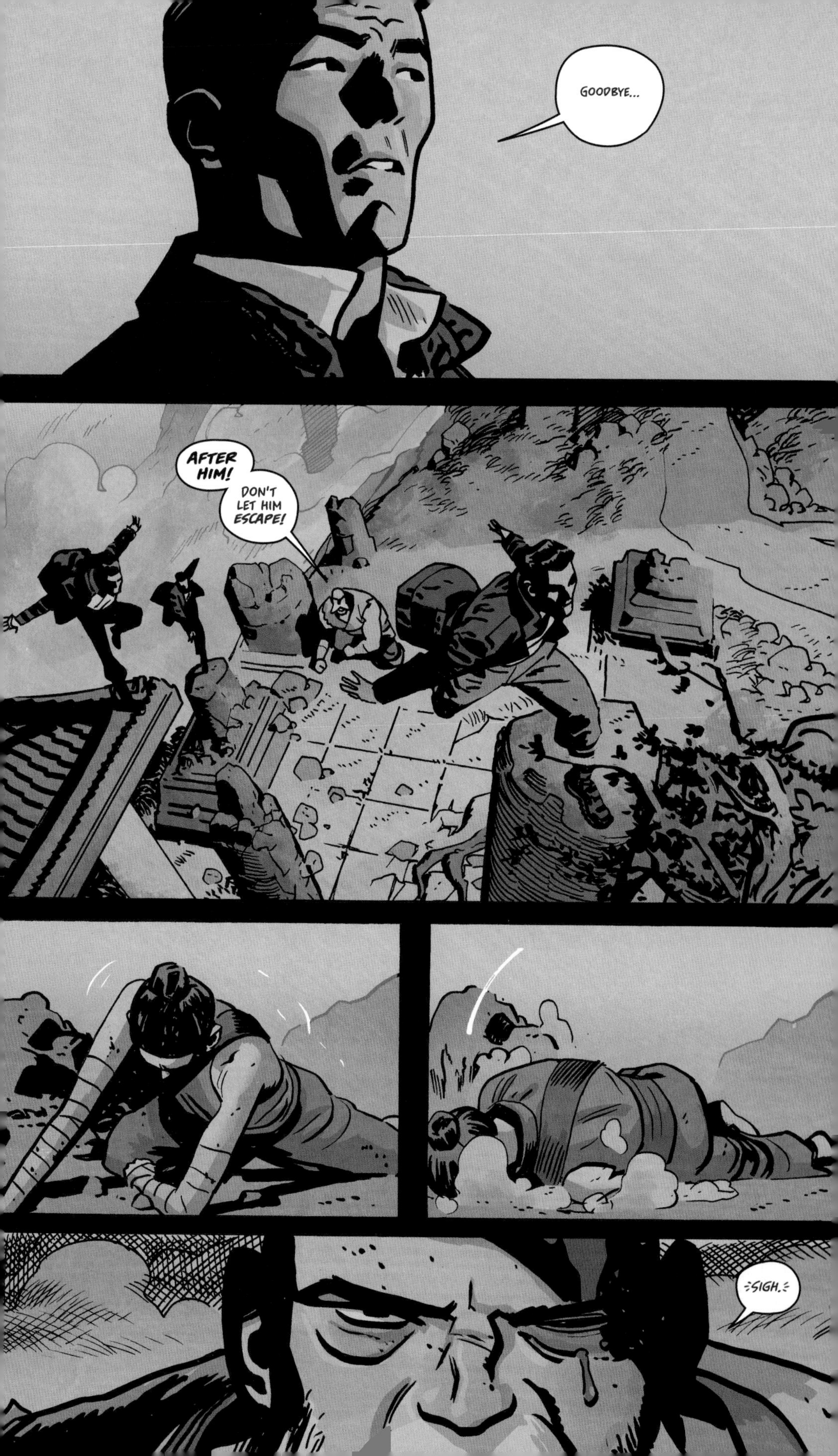

GOODBYE...
AFTER HIM!
DON'T LET HIM ESCAPE!
SIGH.

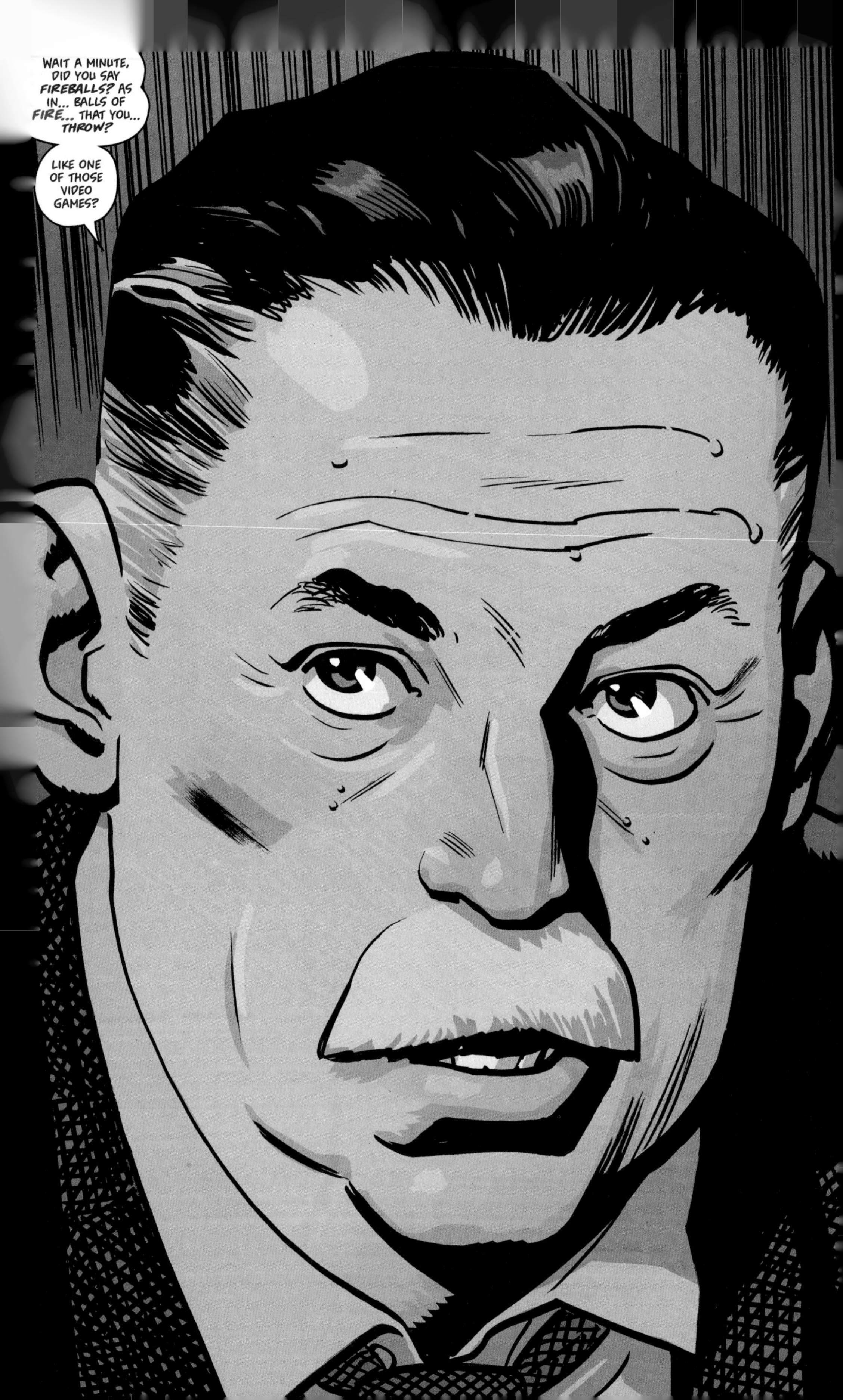
WAIT A MINUTE, DID YOU SAY FIREBALLS? AS IN... BALLS OF FIRE... THAT YOU... THROW?
LIKE ONE OF THOSE VIDEO GAMES?

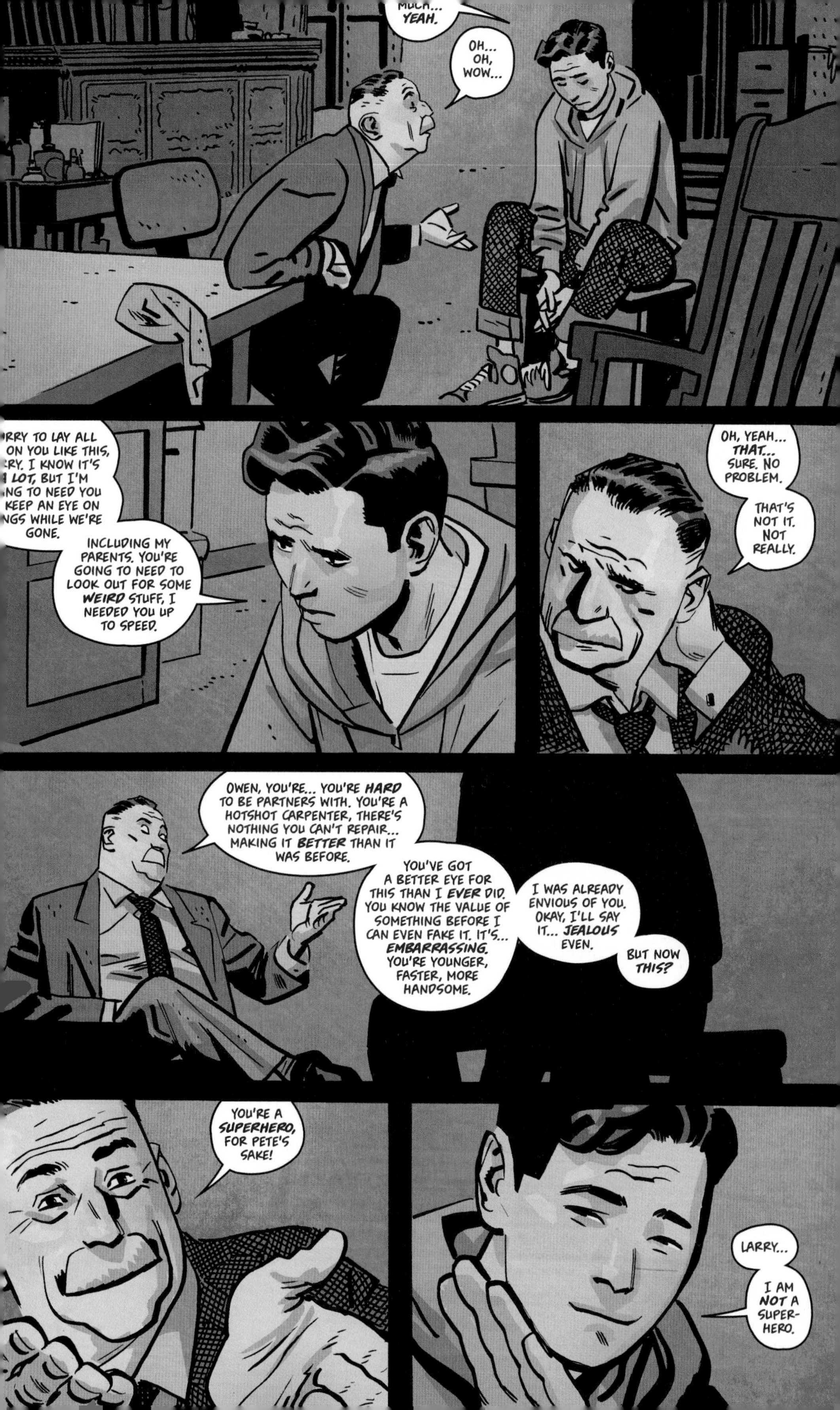
MUCH... YEAH.
OH... OH, WOW...
RRY TO LAY ALL ON YOU LIKE THIS, RY. I KNOW IT'S LOT, BUT I'M NG TO NEED YOU KEEP AN EYE ON NGS WHILE WE'RE GONE.
INCLUDING MY PARENTS. YOU'RE GOING TO NEED TO LOOK OUT FOR SOME WEIRD STUFF, I NEEDED YOU UP TO SPEED.
OH, YEAH... THAT... SURE. NO PROBLEM.
THAT'S NOT IT. NOT REALLY.
OWEN, YOU'RE... YOU'RE HARD TO BE PARTNERS WITH. YOU'RE A HOTSHOT CARPENTER, THERE'S NOTHING YOU CAN'T REPAIR... MAKING IT BETTER THAN IT WAS BEFORE.
YOU'VE GOT A BETTER EYE FOR THIS THAN I EVER DID. YOU KNOW THE VALUE OF SOMETHING BEFORE I CAN EVEN FAKE IT. IT'S... EMBARRASSING. YOU'RE YOUNGER, FASTER, MORE HANDSOME.
I WAS ALREADY ENVIOUS OF YOU. OKAY, I'LL SAY IT... JEALOUS EVEN.
BUT NOW THIS?
YOU'RE A SUPERHERO, FOR PETE'S SAKE!
LARRY...
I AM NOT A SUPER-HERO.

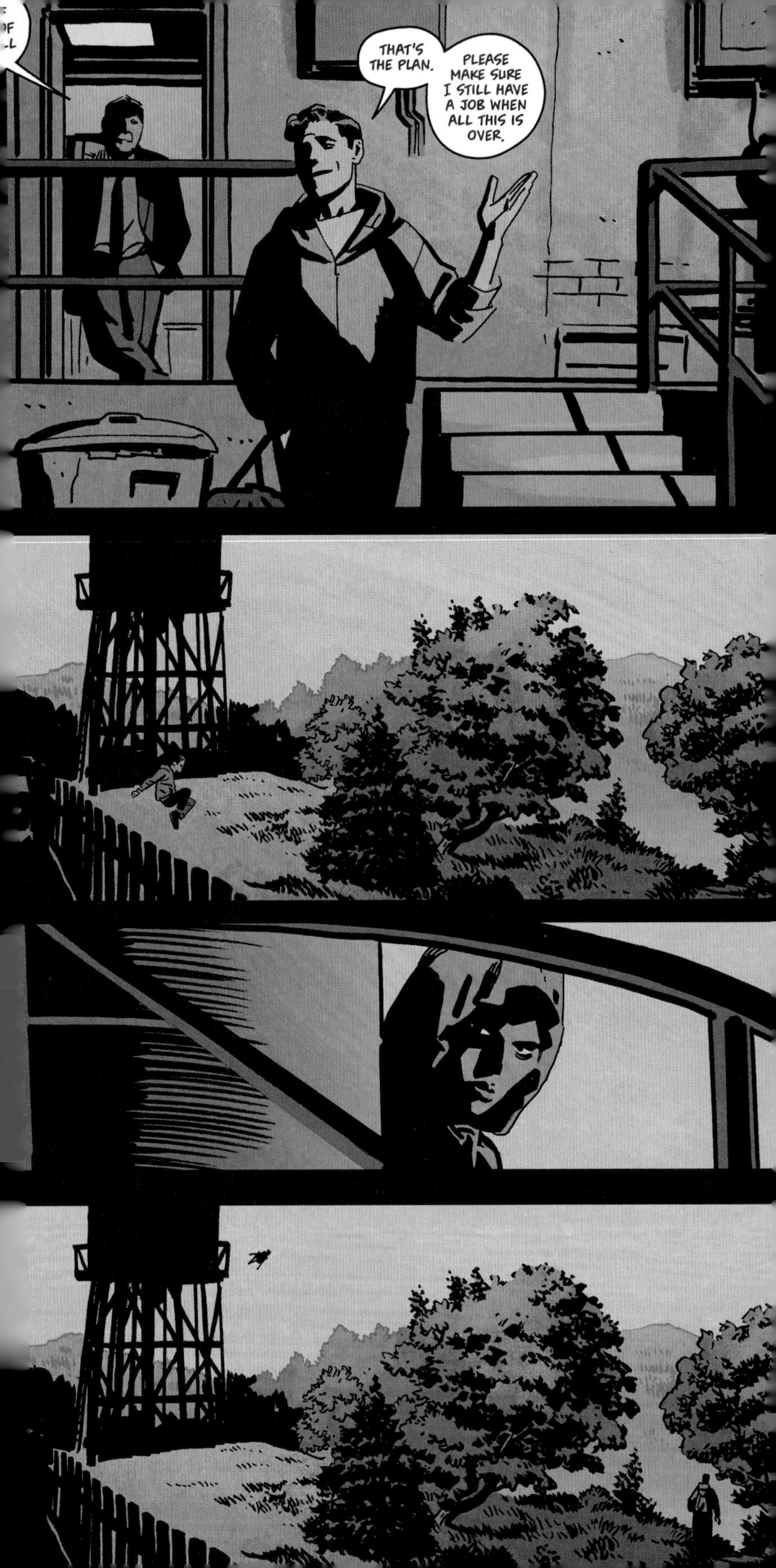
THAT'S THE PLAN.
PLEASE MAKE SURE I STILL HAVE A JOB WHEN ALL THIS IS OVER.

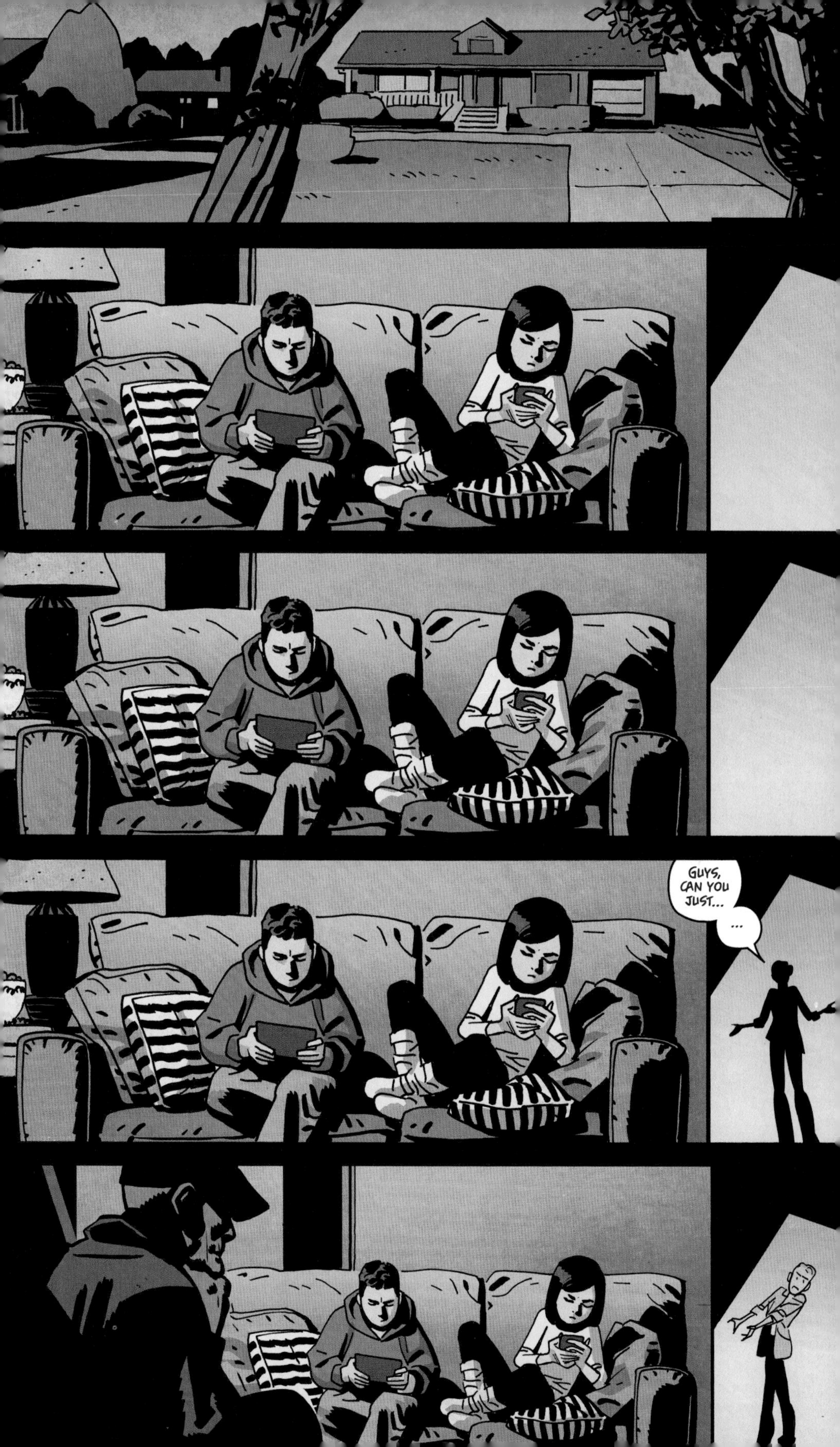
GUYS, CAN YOU JUST...
...

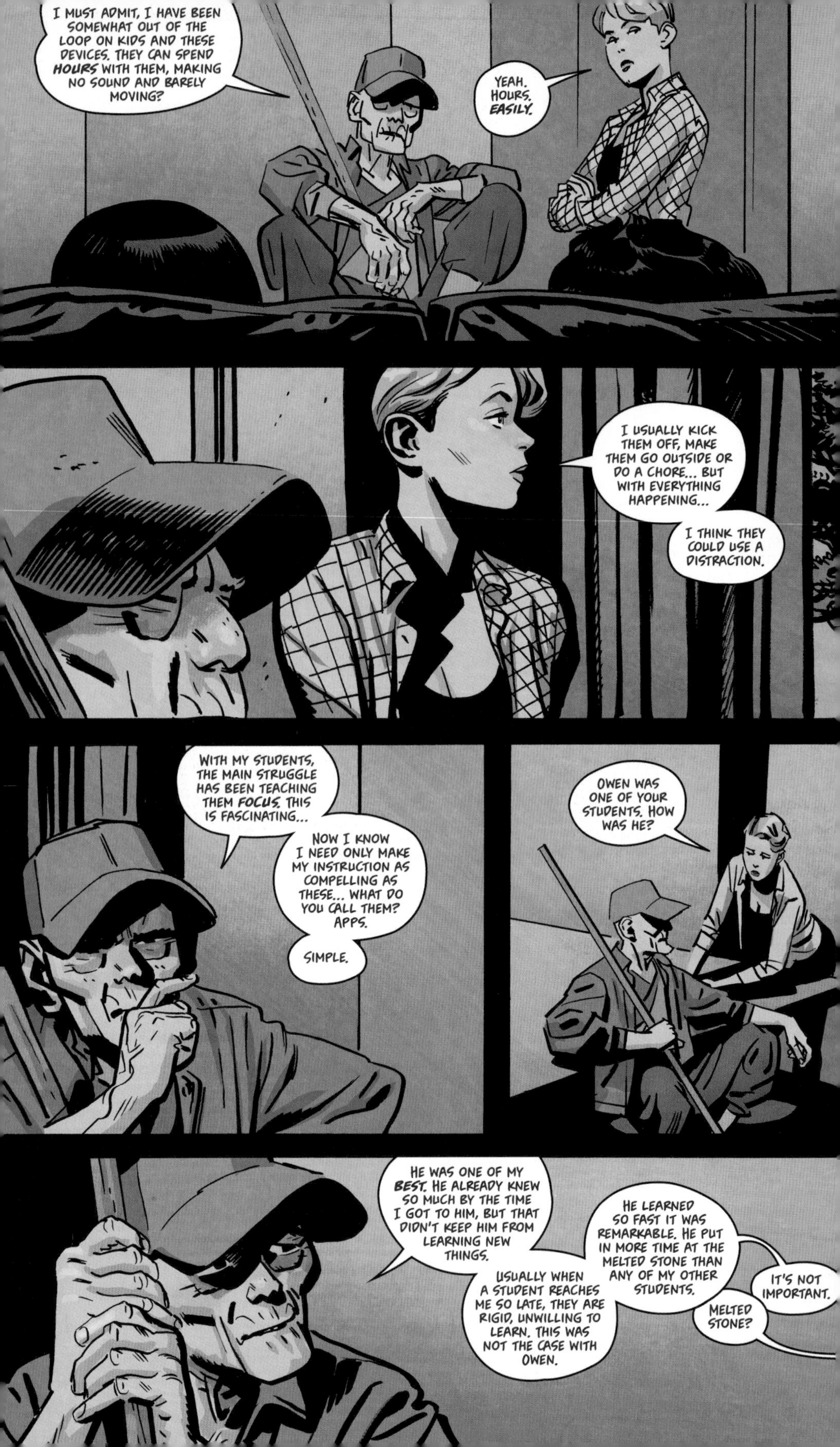
I MUST ADMIT, I HAVE BEEN SOMEWHAT OUT OF THE LOOP ON KIDS AND THESE DEVICES. THEY CAN SPEND *HOURS* WITH THEM, MAKING NO SOUND AND BARELY MOVING?
YEAH. HOURS. *EASILY.*
I USUALLY KICK THEM OFF, MAKE THEM GO OUTSIDE OR DO A CHORE... BUT WITH EVERYTHING HAPPENING...
I THINK THEY COULD USE A DISTRACTION.
WITH MY STUDENTS, THE MAIN STRUGGLE HAS BEEN TEACHING THEM *FOCUS*. THIS IS FASCINATING...
NOW I KNOW I NEED ONLY MAKE MY INSTRUCTION AS COMPELLING AS THESE... WHAT DO YOU CALL THEM? APPS.
SIMPLE.
OWEN WAS ONE OF YOUR STUDENTS. HOW WAS HE?
HE WAS ONE OF MY *BEST*. HE ALREADY KNEW SO MUCH BY THE TIME I GOT TO HIM, BUT THAT DIDN'T KEEP HIM FROM LEARNING NEW THINGS.
USUALLY WHEN A STUDENT REACHES ME SO LATE, THEY ARE RIGID, UNWILLING TO LEARN. THIS WAS NOT THE CASE WITH OWEN.
HE LEARNED SO FAST IT WAS REMARKABLE. HE PUT IN MORE TIME AT THE MELTED STONE THAN ANY OF MY OTHER STUDENTS.
MELTED STONE?
IT'S NOT IMPORTANT.

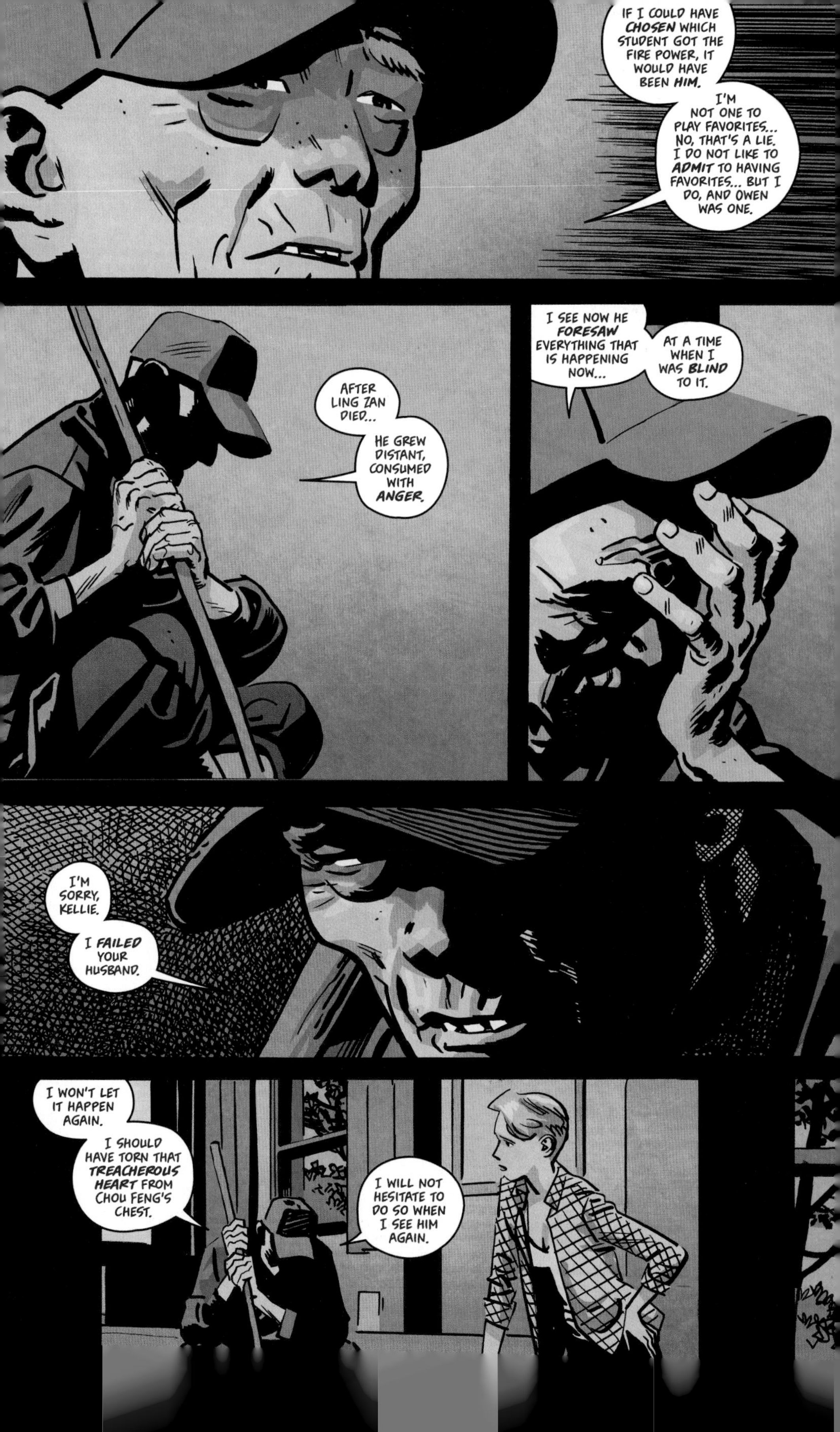
IF I COULD HAVE CHOSEN WHICH STUDENT GOT THE FIRE POWER, IT WOULD HAVE BEEN HIM.
I'M NOT ONE TO PLAY FAVORITES... NO, THAT'S A LIE. I DO NOT LIKE TO ADMIT TO HAVING FAVORITES... BUT I DO, AND OWEN WAS ONE.
AFTER LING ZAN DIED...
HE GREW DISTANT, CONSUMED WITH ANGER.
I SEE NOW HE FORESAW EVERYTHING THAT IS HAPPENING NOW...
AT A TIME WHEN I WAS BLIND TO IT.
I'M SORRY, KELLIE.
I FAILED YOUR HUSBAND.
I WON'T LET IT HAPPEN AGAIN.
I SHOULD HAVE TORN THAT TREACHEROUS HEART FROM CHOU FENG'S CHEST.
I WILL NOT HESITATE TO DO SO WHEN I SEE HIM AGAIN.

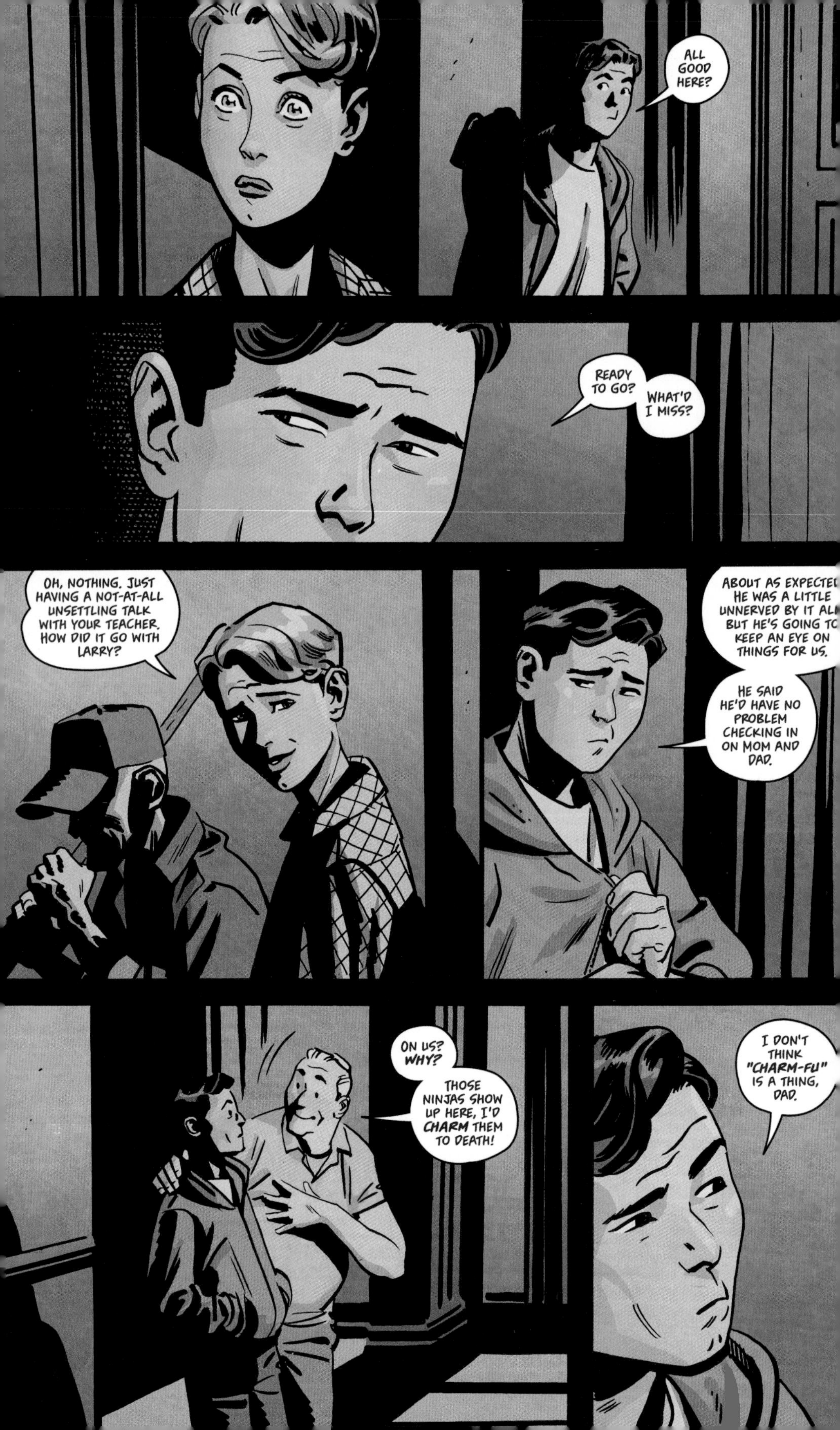
ALL GOOD HERE?
READY TO GO?
WHAT'D I MISS?
OH, NOTHING. JUST HAVING A NOT-AT-ALL UNSETTLING TALK WITH YOUR TEACHER. HOW DID IT GO WITH LARRY?
ABOUT AS EXPECTED HE WAS A LITTLE UNNERVED BY IT ALL BUT HE'S GOING TO KEEP AN EYE ON THINGS FOR US.
HE SAID HE'D HAVE NO PROBLEM CHECKING IN ON MOM AND DAD.
ON US? *WHY?*
THOSE NINJAS SHOW UP HERE, I'D *CHARM* THEM TO DEATH!
I DON'T THINK *"CHARM-FU"* IS A THING, DAD.

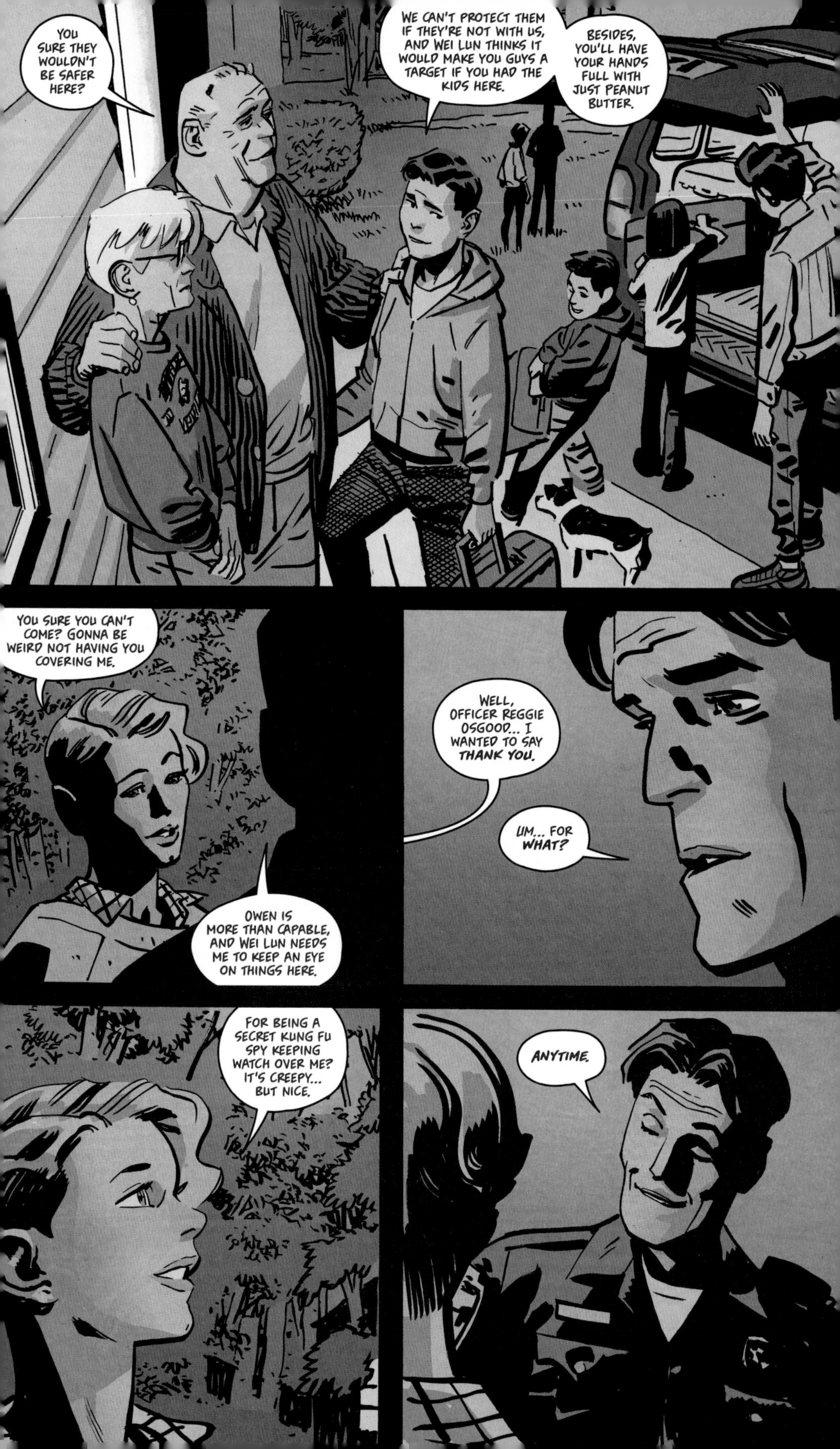
YOU SURE THEY WOULDN'T BE SAFER HERE?
WE CAN'T PROTECT THEM IF THEY'RE NOT WITH US, AND WEI LUN THINKS IT WOULD MAKE YOU GUYS A TARGET IF YOU HAD THE KIDS HERE.
BESIDES, YOU'LL HAVE YOUR HANDS FULL WITH JUST PEANUT BUTTER.
YOU SURE YOU CAN'T COME? GONNA BE WEIRD NOT HAVING YOU COVERING ME.
OWEN IS MORE THAN CAPABLE, AND WEI LUN NEEDS ME TO KEEP AN EYE ON THINGS HERE.
WELL, OFFICER REGGIE OSGOOD... I WANTED TO SAY *THANK YOU.*
UM... FOR *WHAT?*
FOR BEING A SECRET KUNG FU SPY KEEPING WATCH OVER ME? IT'S CREEPY... BUT NICE.
ANYTIME.

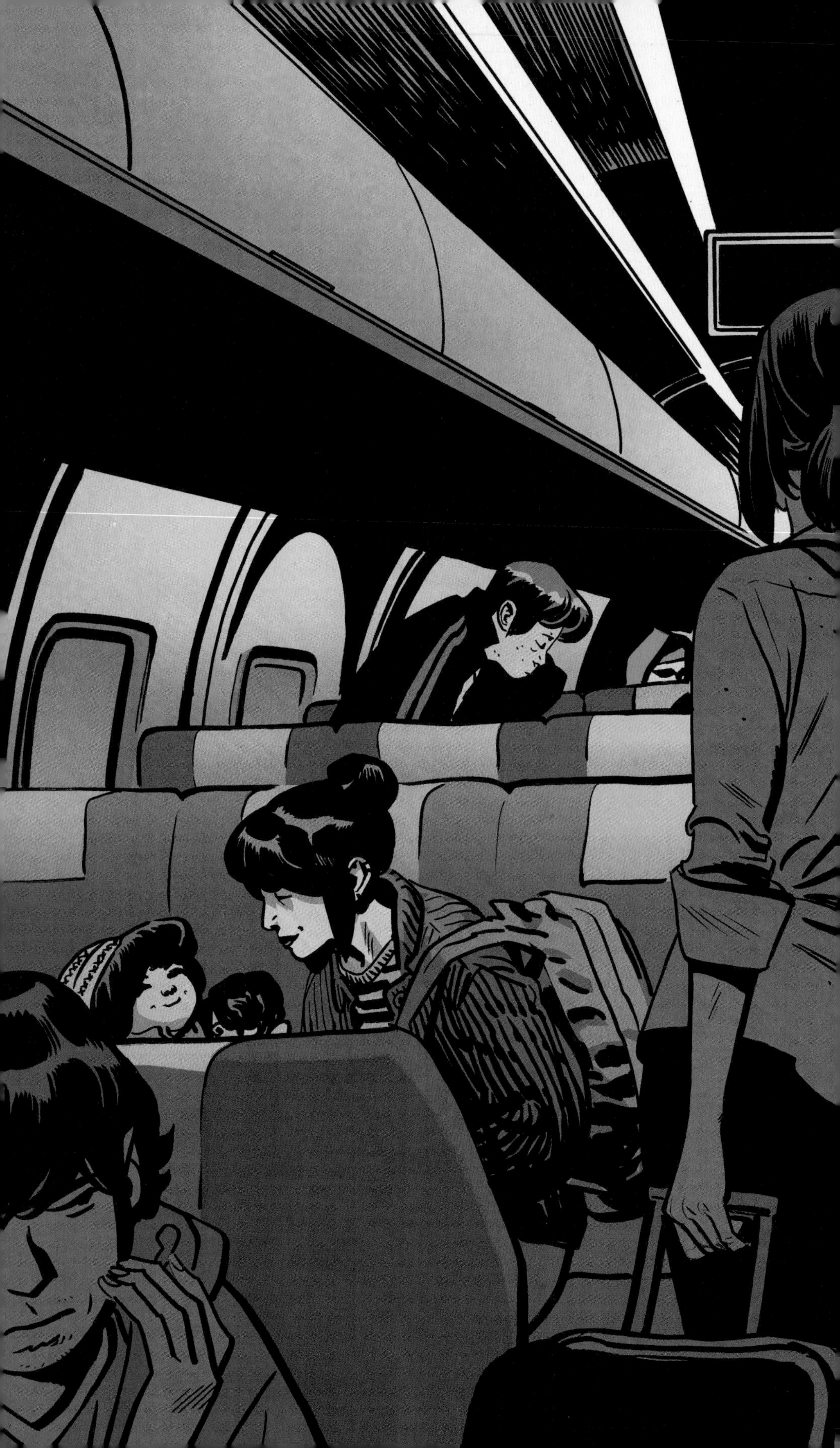

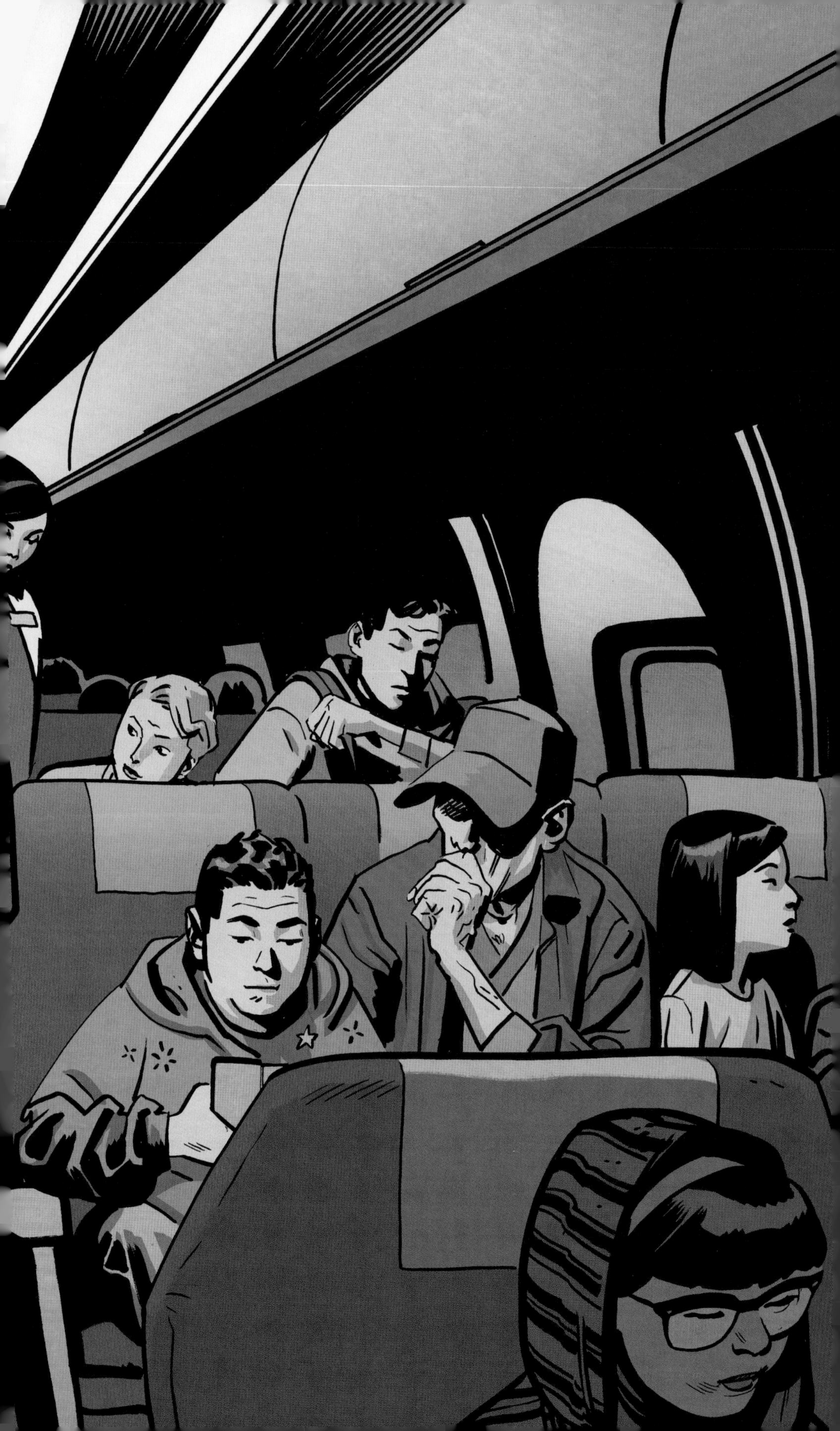

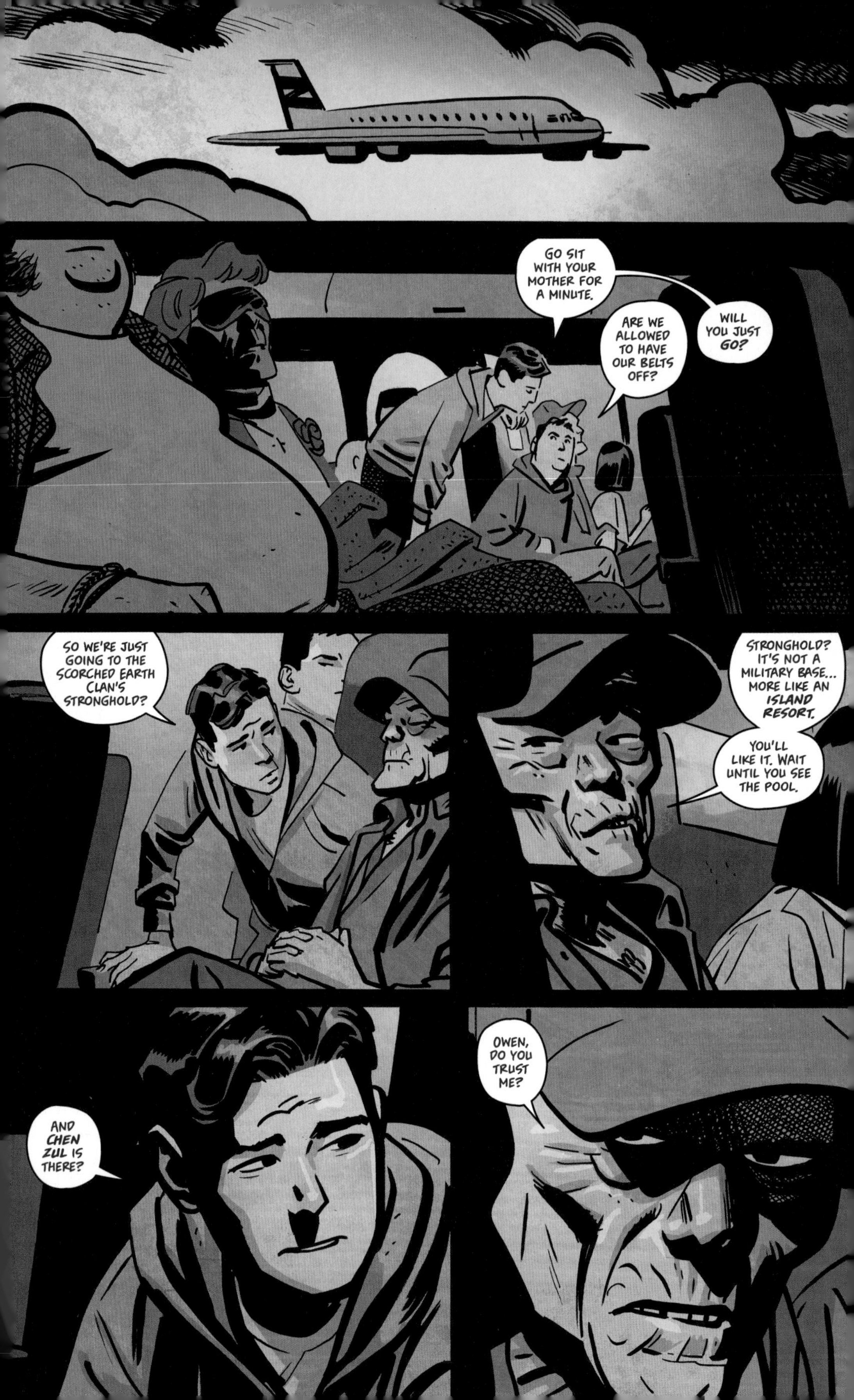
GO SIT WITH YOUR MOTHER FOR A MINUTE.
ARE WE ALLOWED TO HAVE OUR BELTS OFF?
WILL YOU JUST GO?
SO WE'RE JUST GOING TO THE SCORCHED EARTH CLAN'S STRONGHOLD?
STRONGHOLD? IT'S NOT A MILITARY BASE... MORE LIKE AN ISLAND RESORT.
YOU'LL LIKE IT. WAIT UNTIL YOU SEE THE POOL.
AND CHEN ZUL IS THERE?
OWEN, DO YOU TRUST ME?

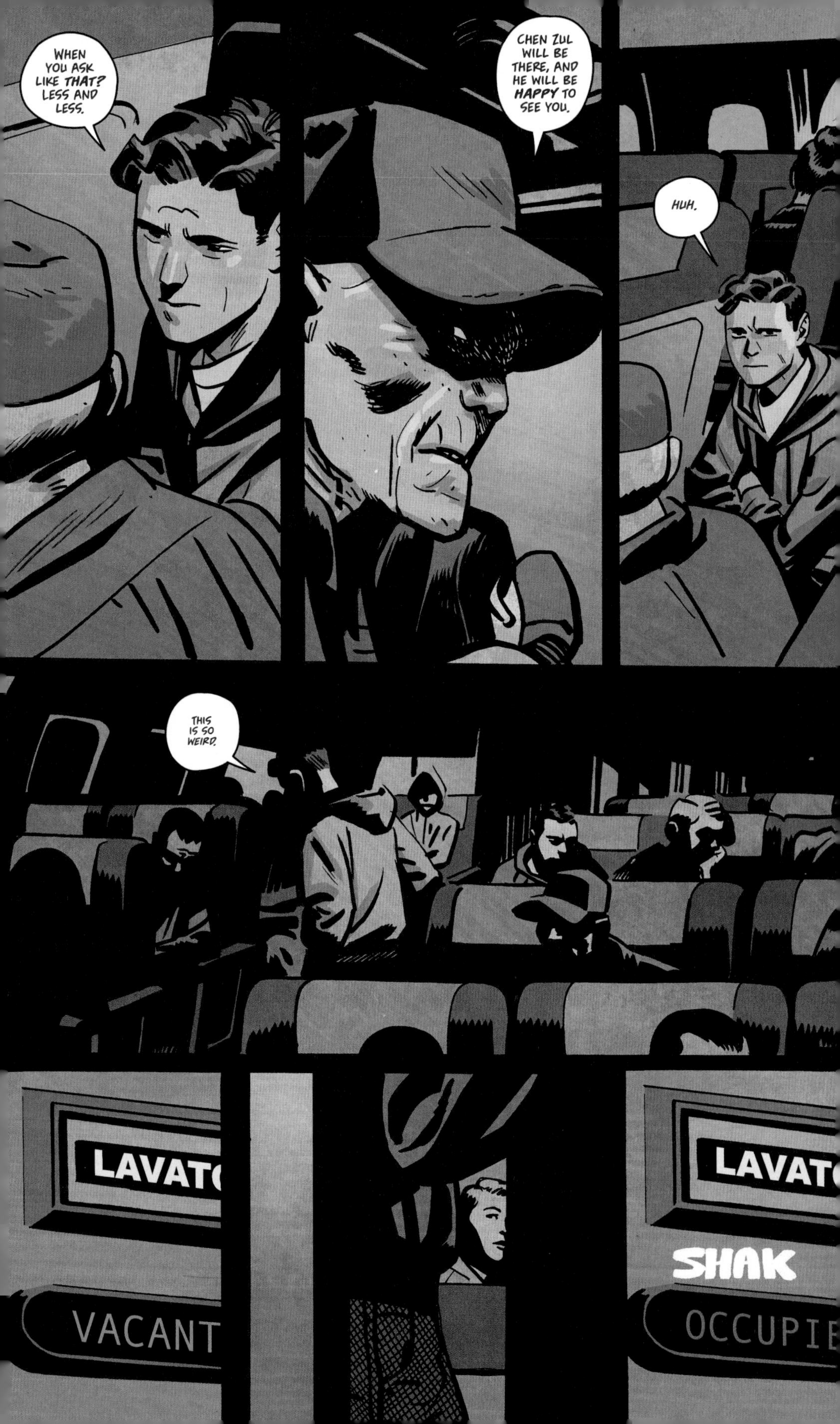
WHEN YOU ASK LIKE *THAT?* LESS AND LESS.
CHEN ZUL WILL BE THERE, AND HE WILL BE *HAPPY* TO SEE YOU.
HUH.
THIS IS SO WEIRD.
LAVATO
VACANT
LAVATO
SHAK
OCCUPIE

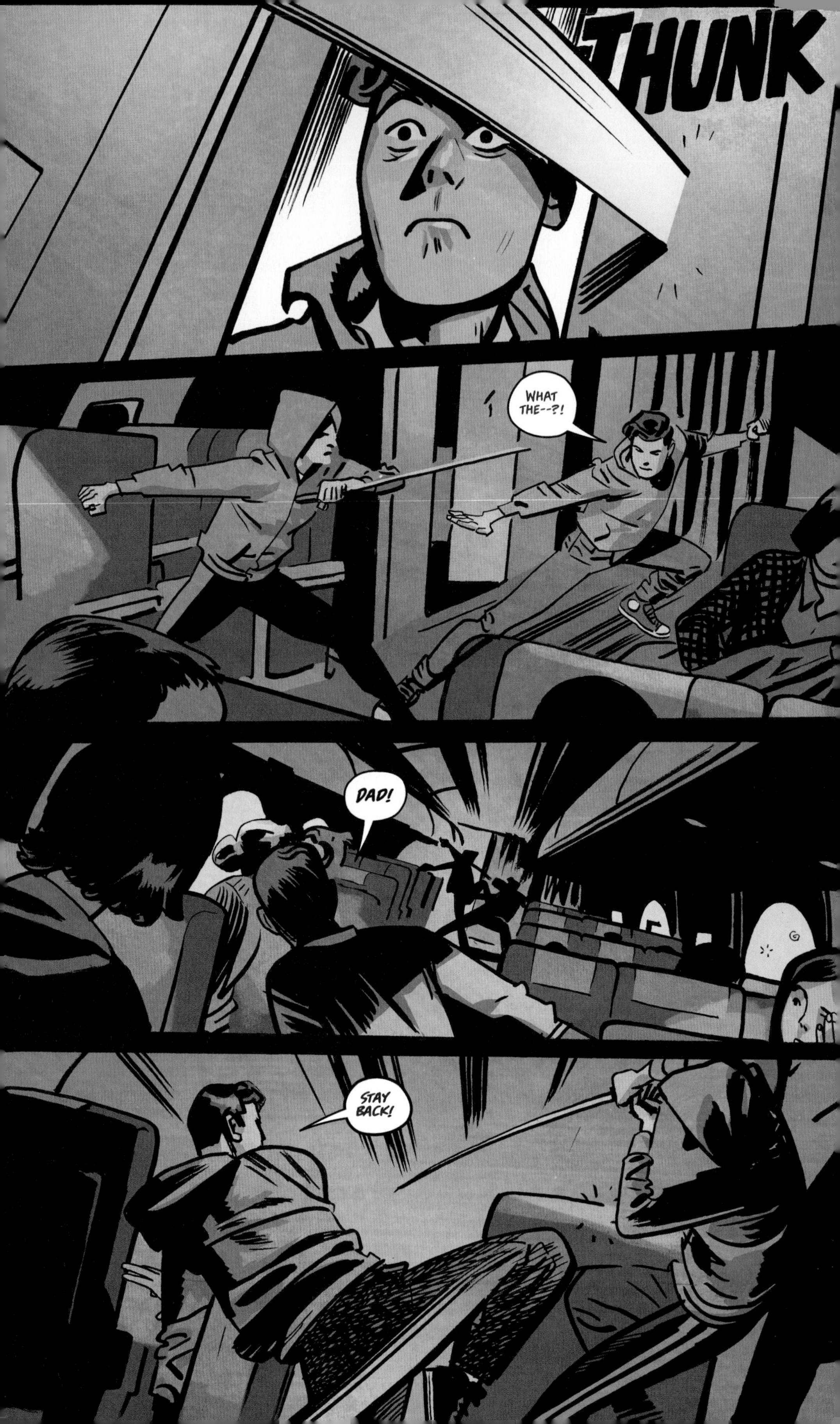
THUNK
WHAT THE--?!
DAD!
STAY BACK!

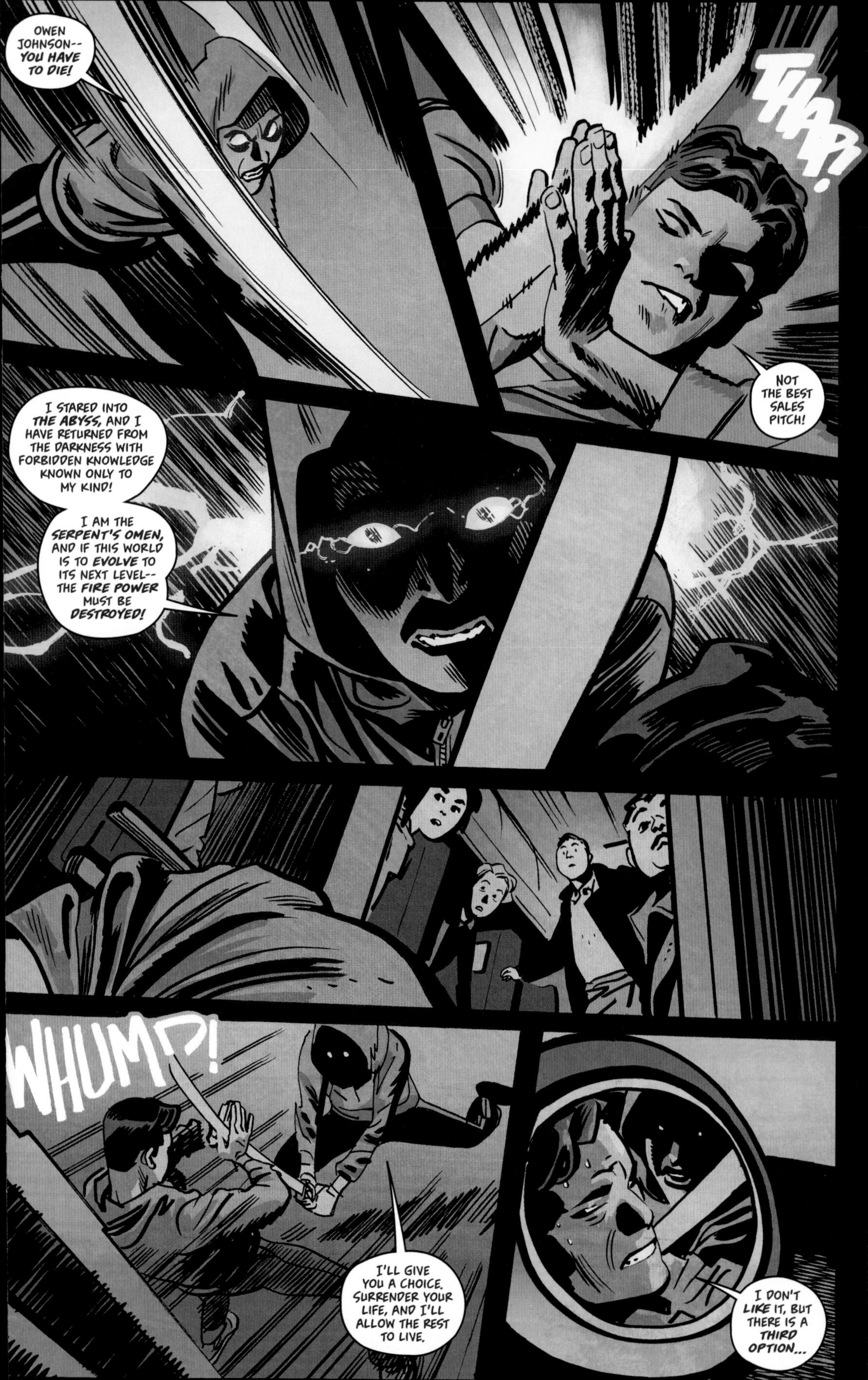
OWEN JOHNSON-- YOU HAVE TO DIE!
THAP!
NOT THE BEST SALES PITCH!
I STARED INTO THE ABYSS, AND I HAVE RETURNED FROM THE DARKNESS WITH FORBIDDEN KNOWLEDGE KNOWN ONLY TO MY KIND!
I AM THE SERPENT'S OMEN, AND IF THIS WORLD IS TO EVOLVE TO ITS NEXT LEVEL-- THE FIRE POWER MUST BE DESTROYED!
WHUMP!
I'LL GIVE YOU A CHOICE. SURRENDER YOUR LIFE, AND I'LL ALLOW THE REST TO LIVE.
I DON'T LIKE IT, BUT THERE IS A THIRD OPTION...

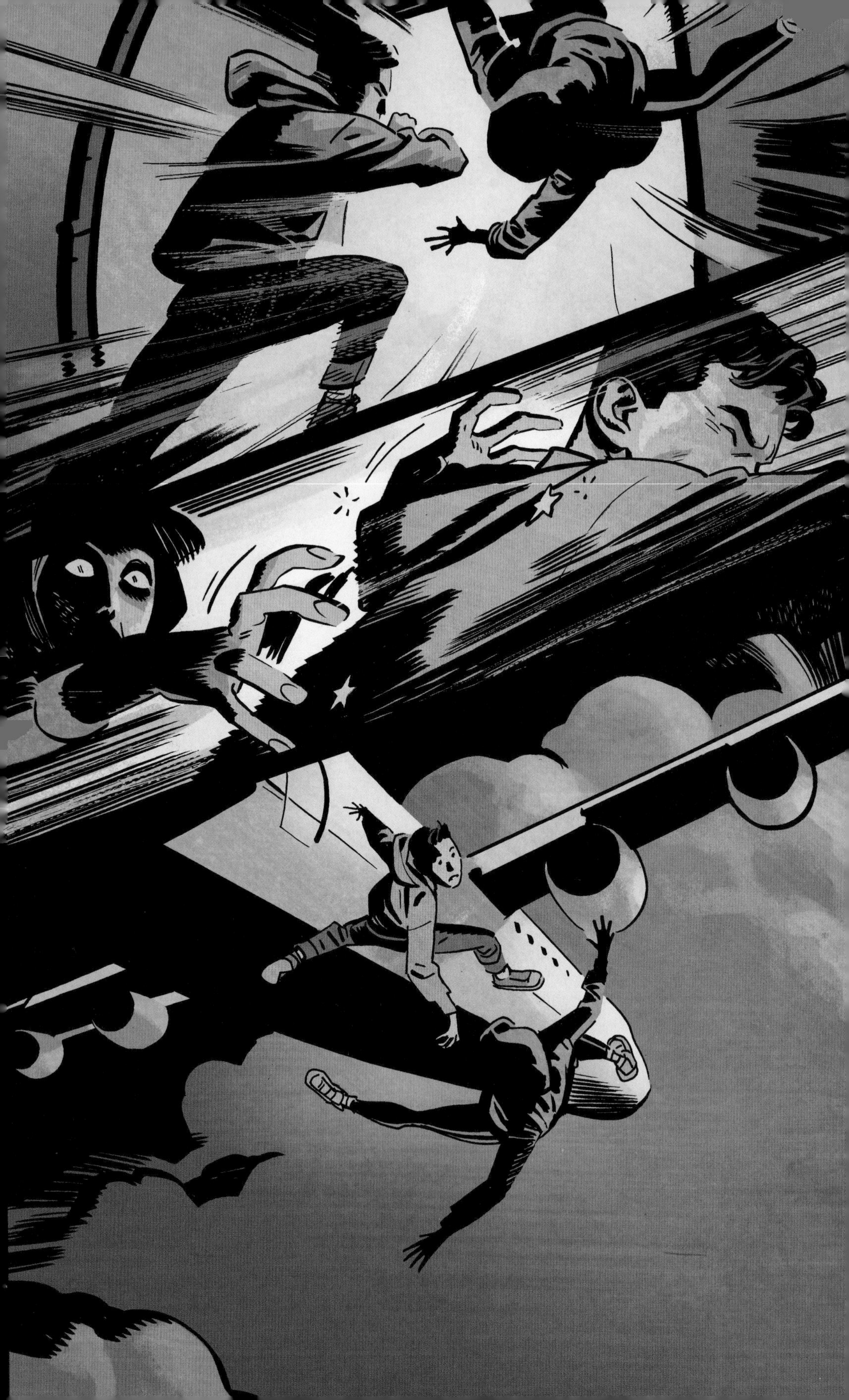

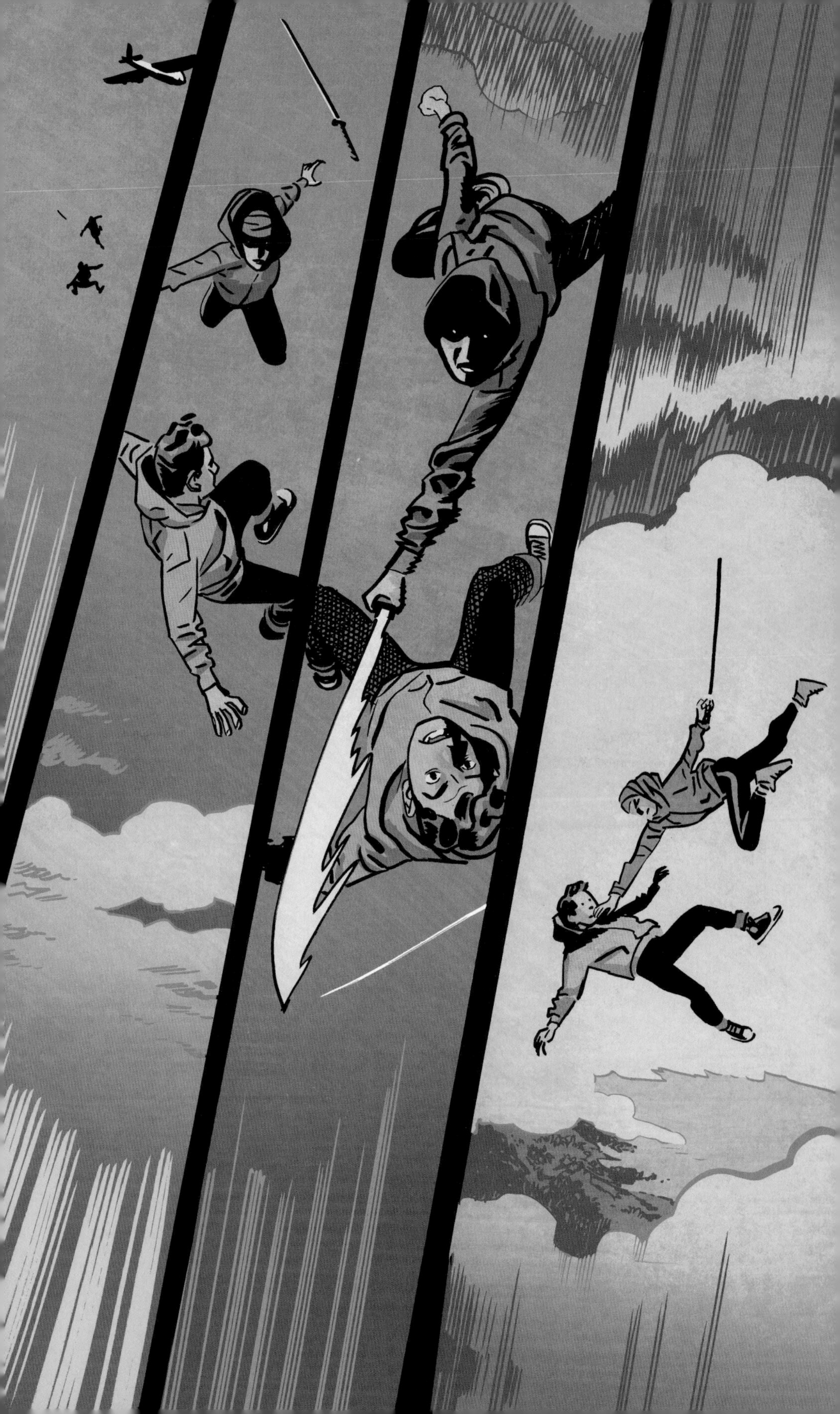

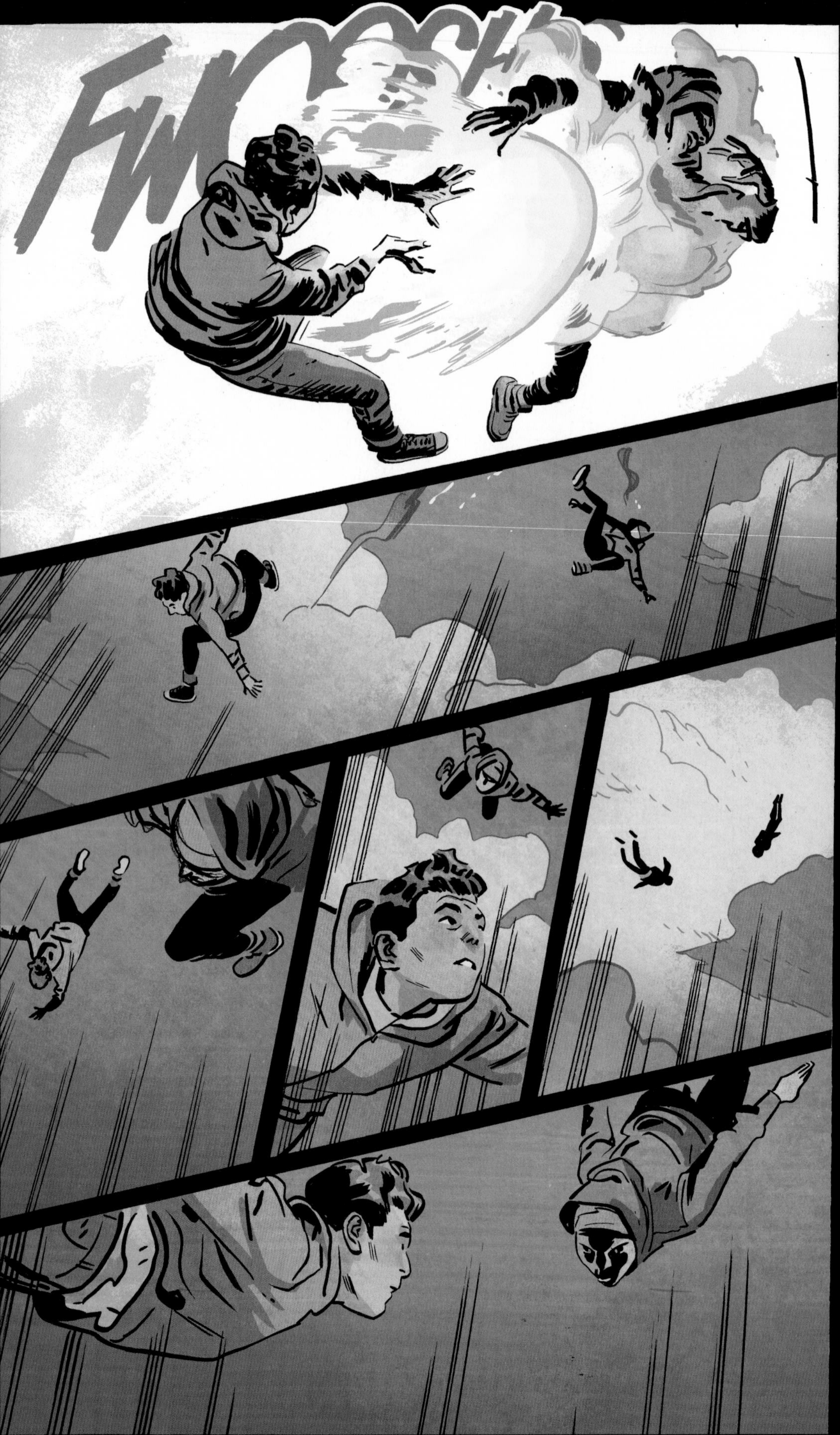
FWOOSH

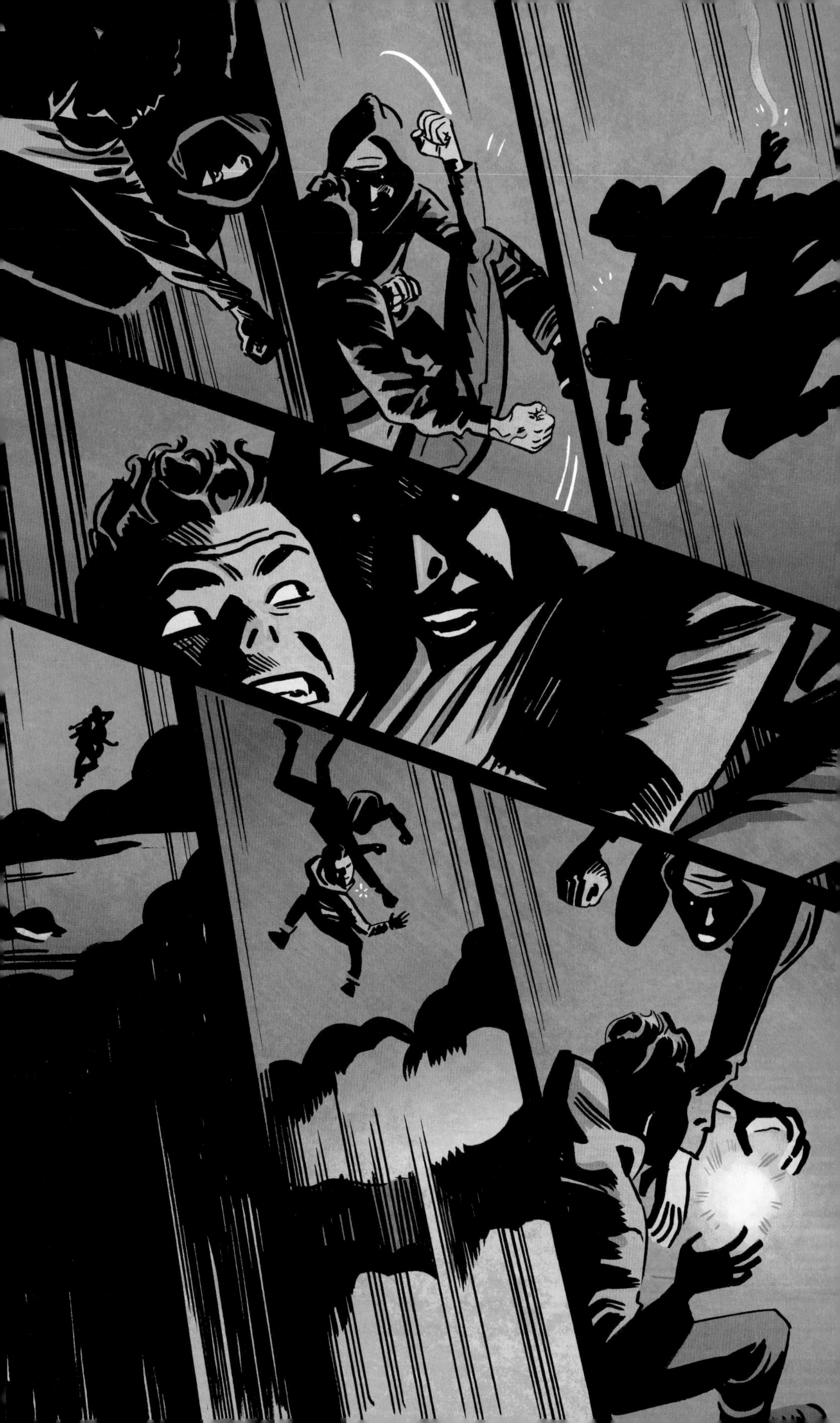

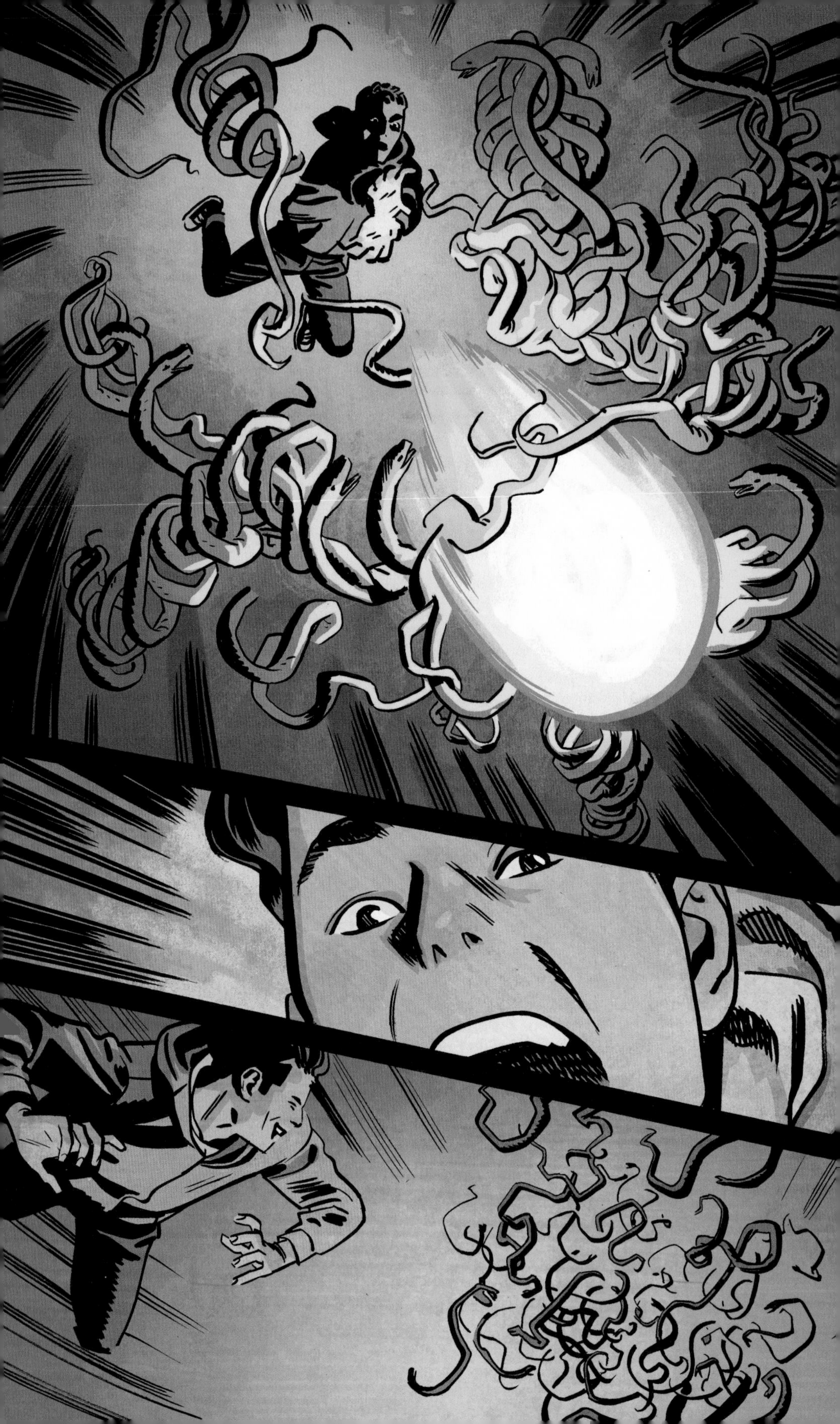

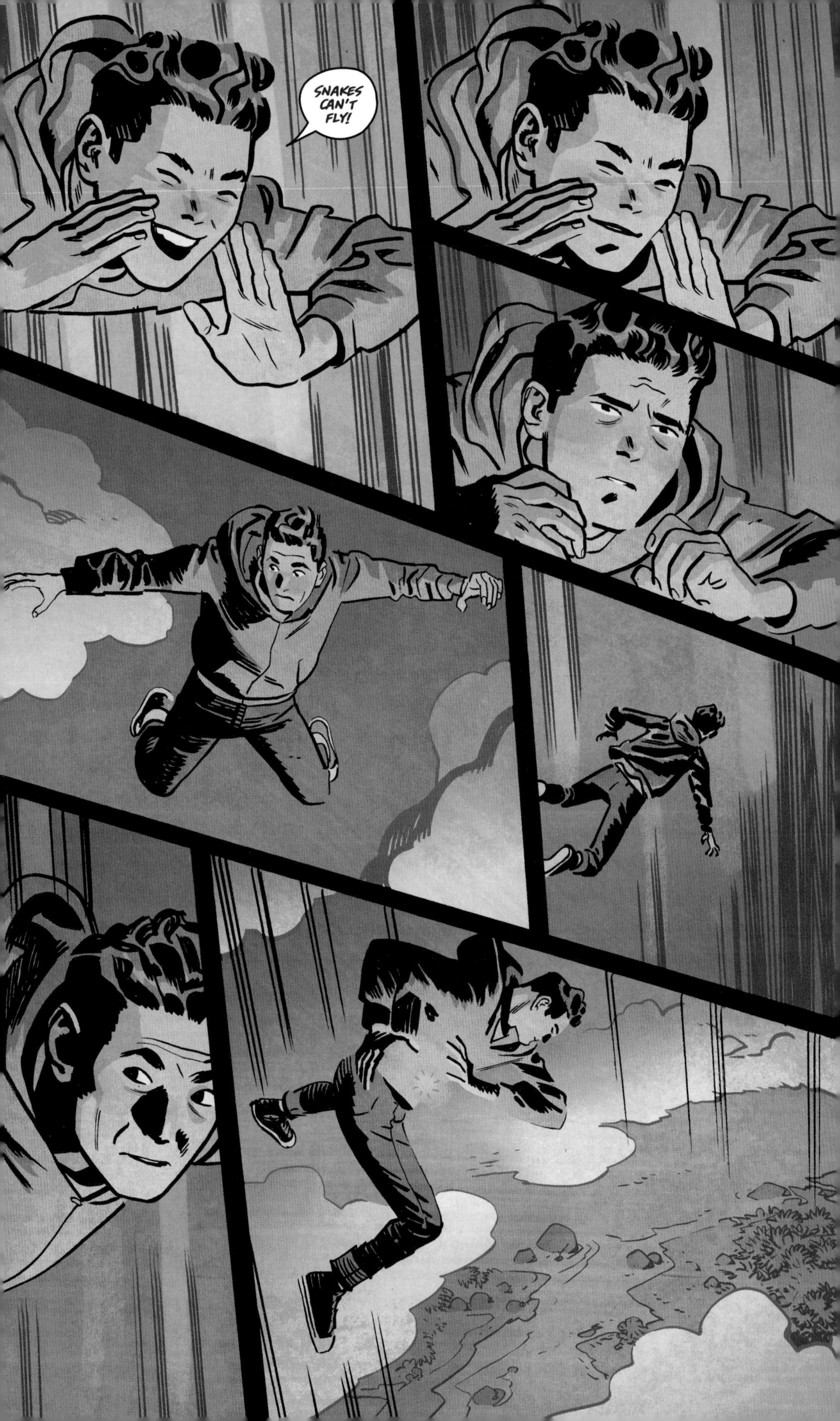
SNAKES CAN'T FLY!

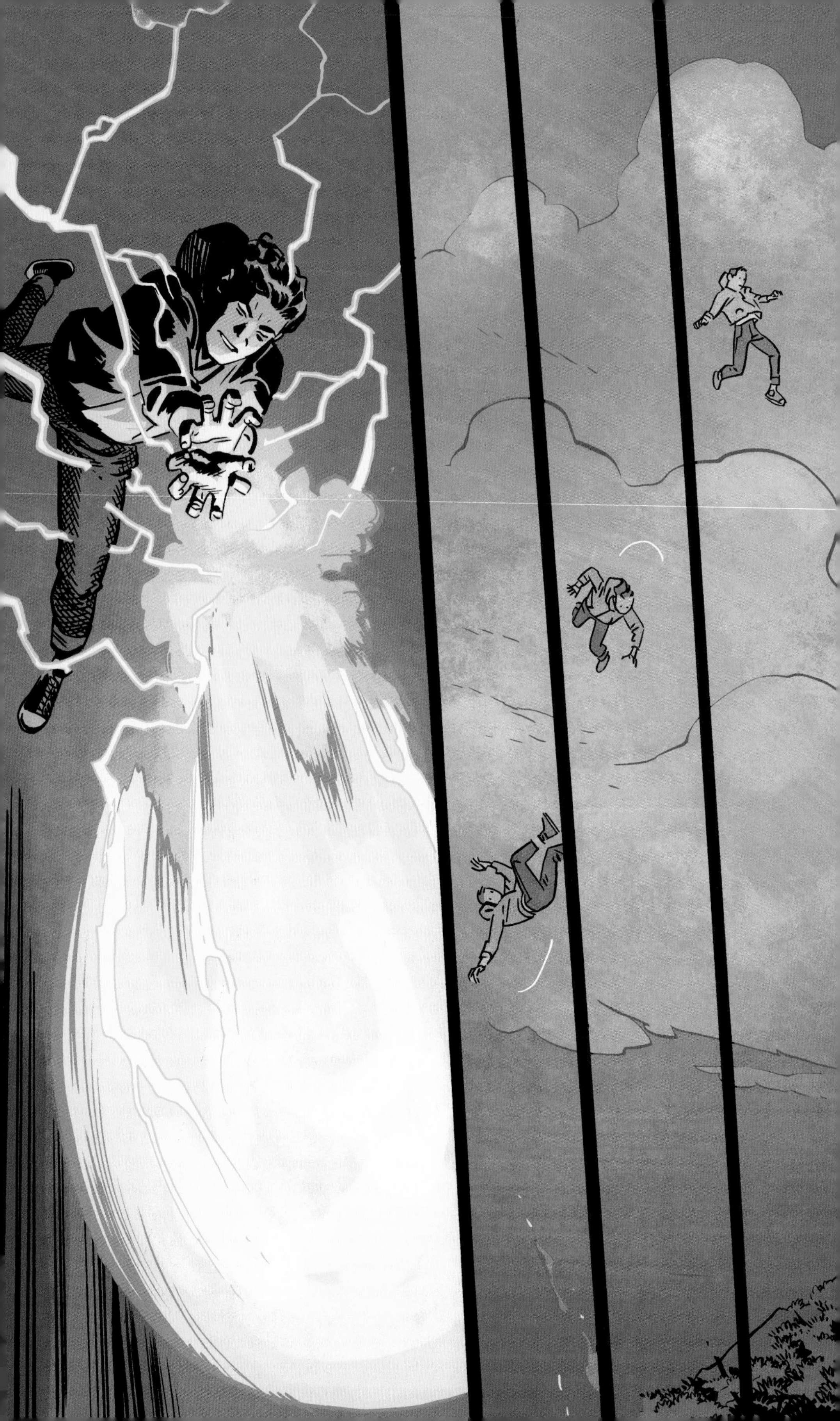

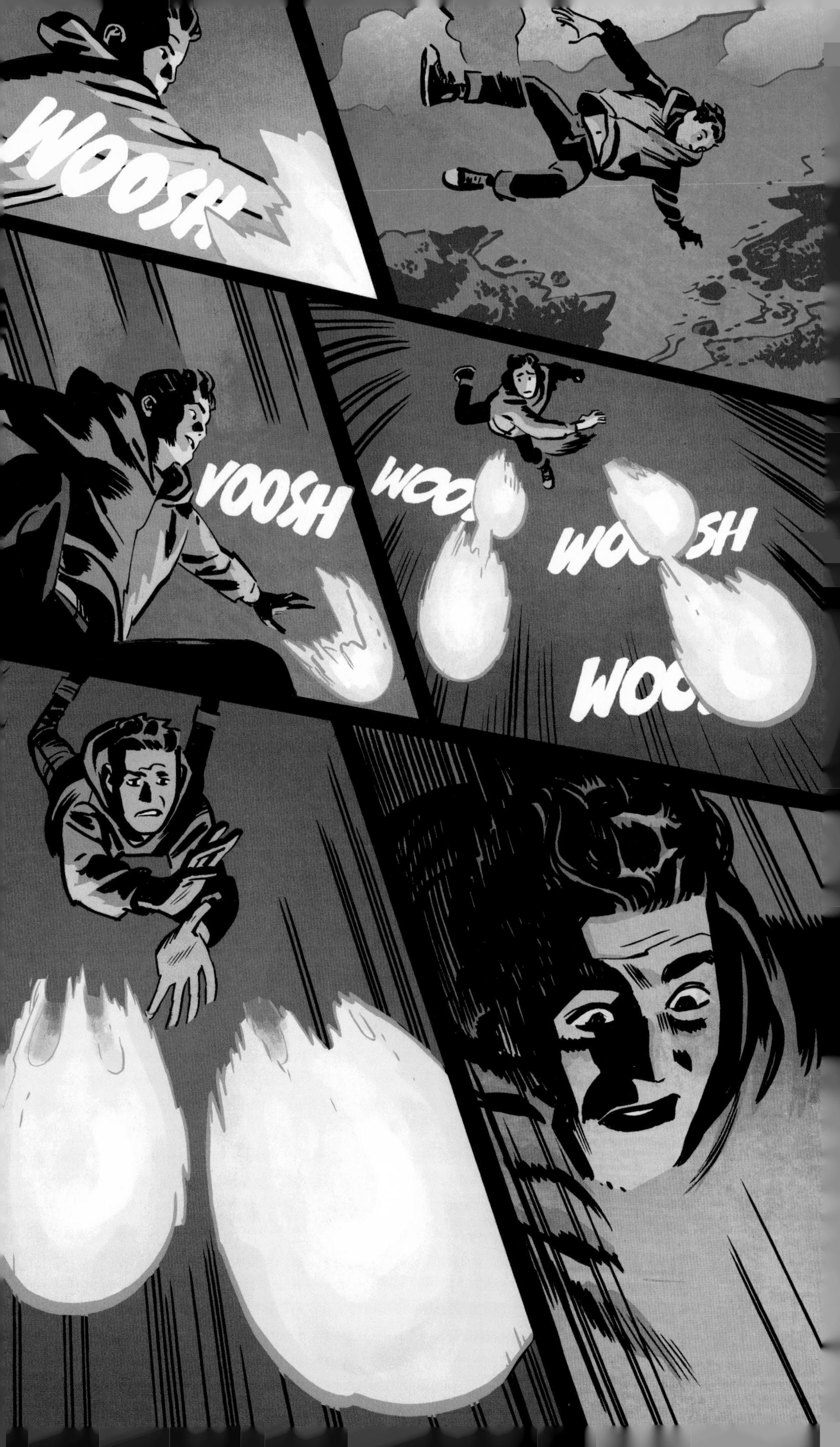
WOOSH!
WOOSH
WOOSH

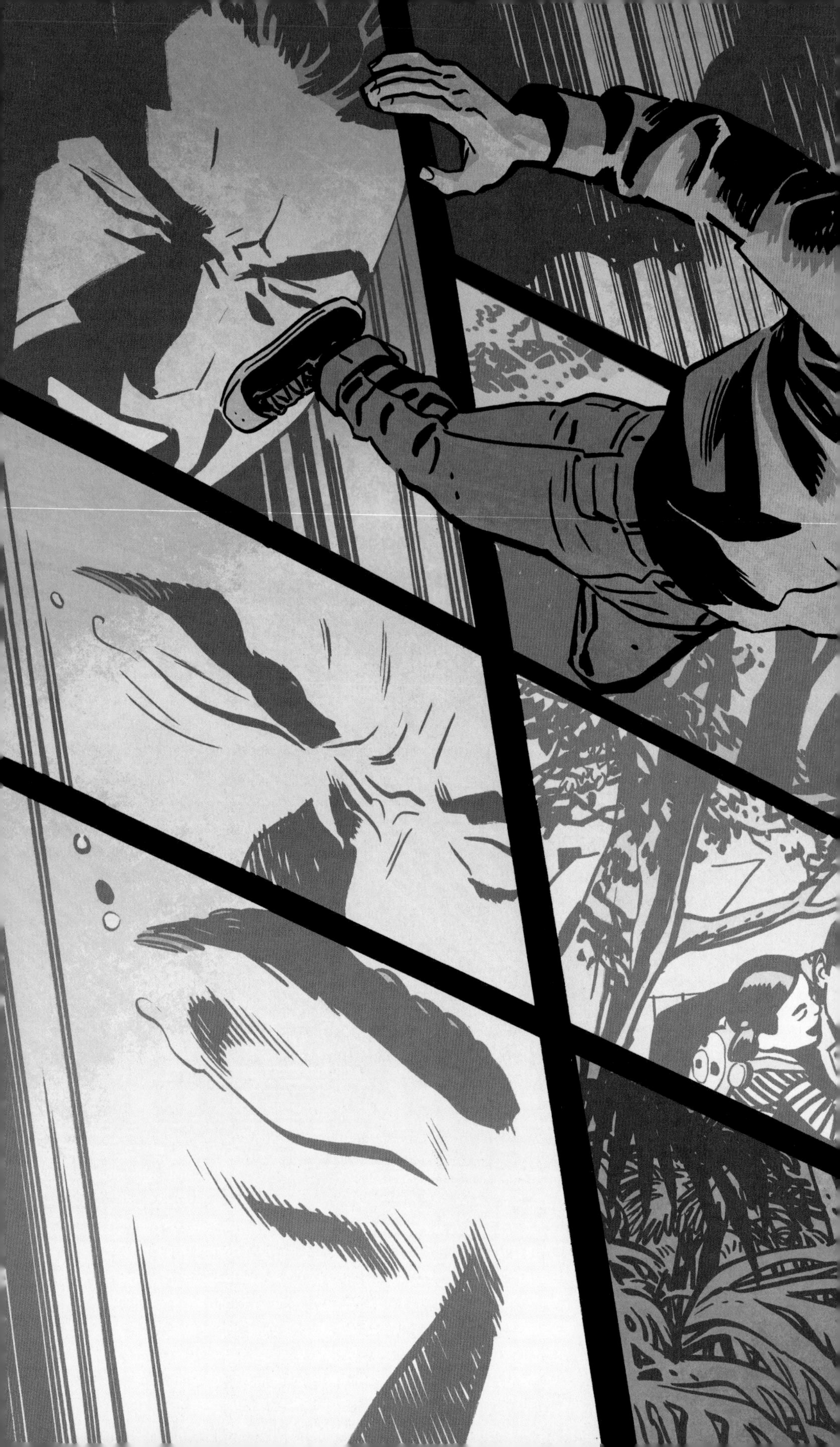

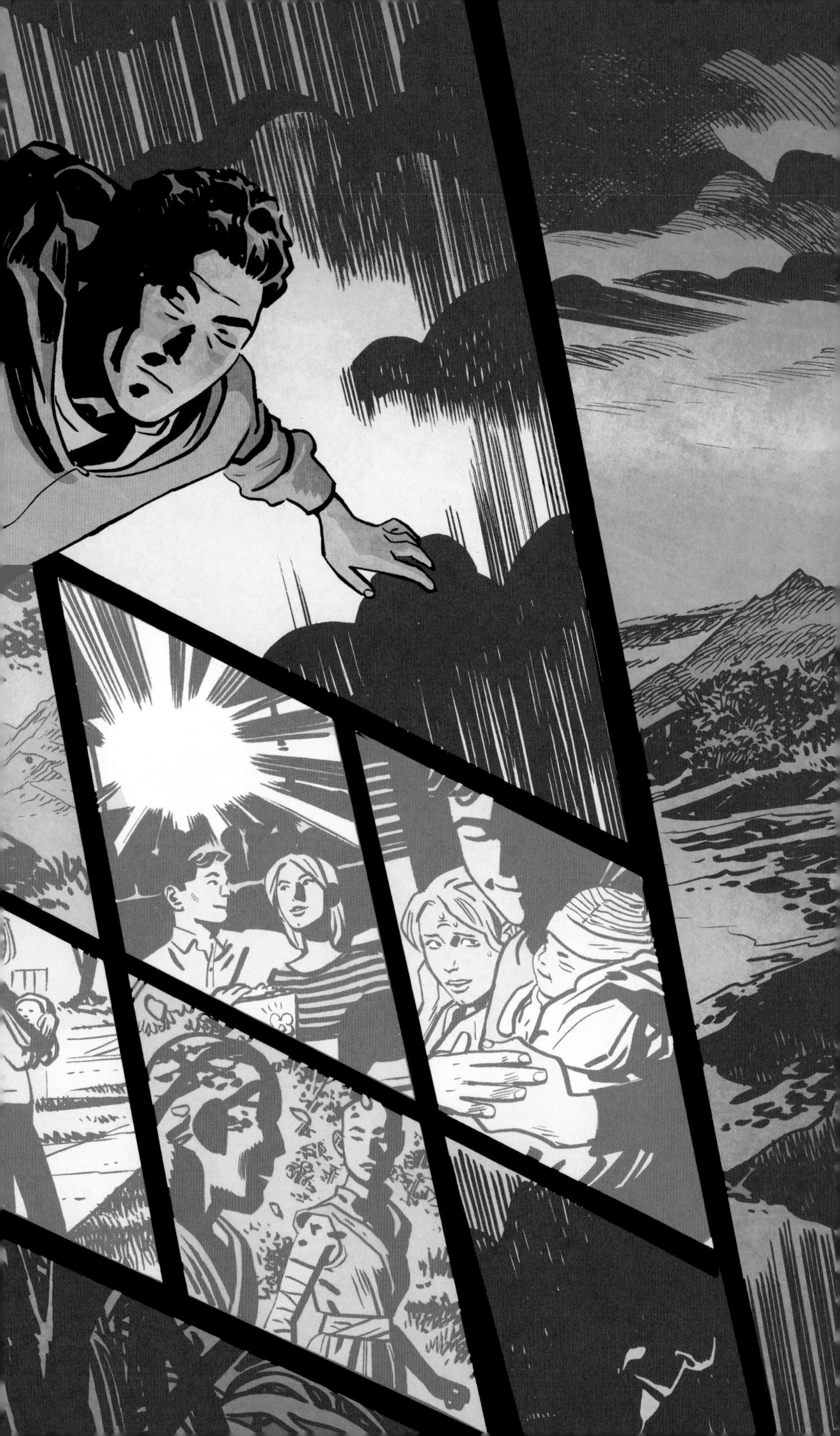

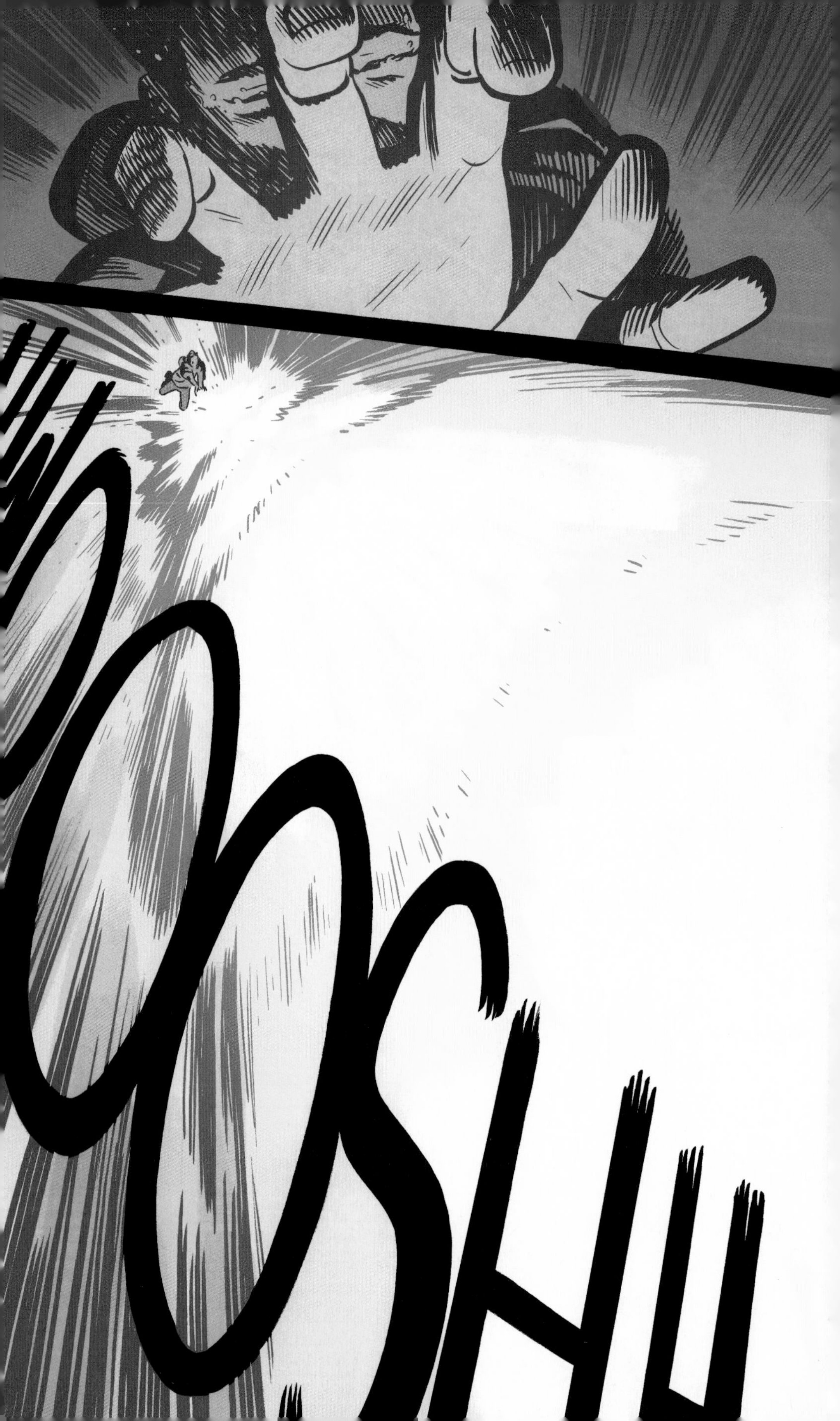
WOOOSH

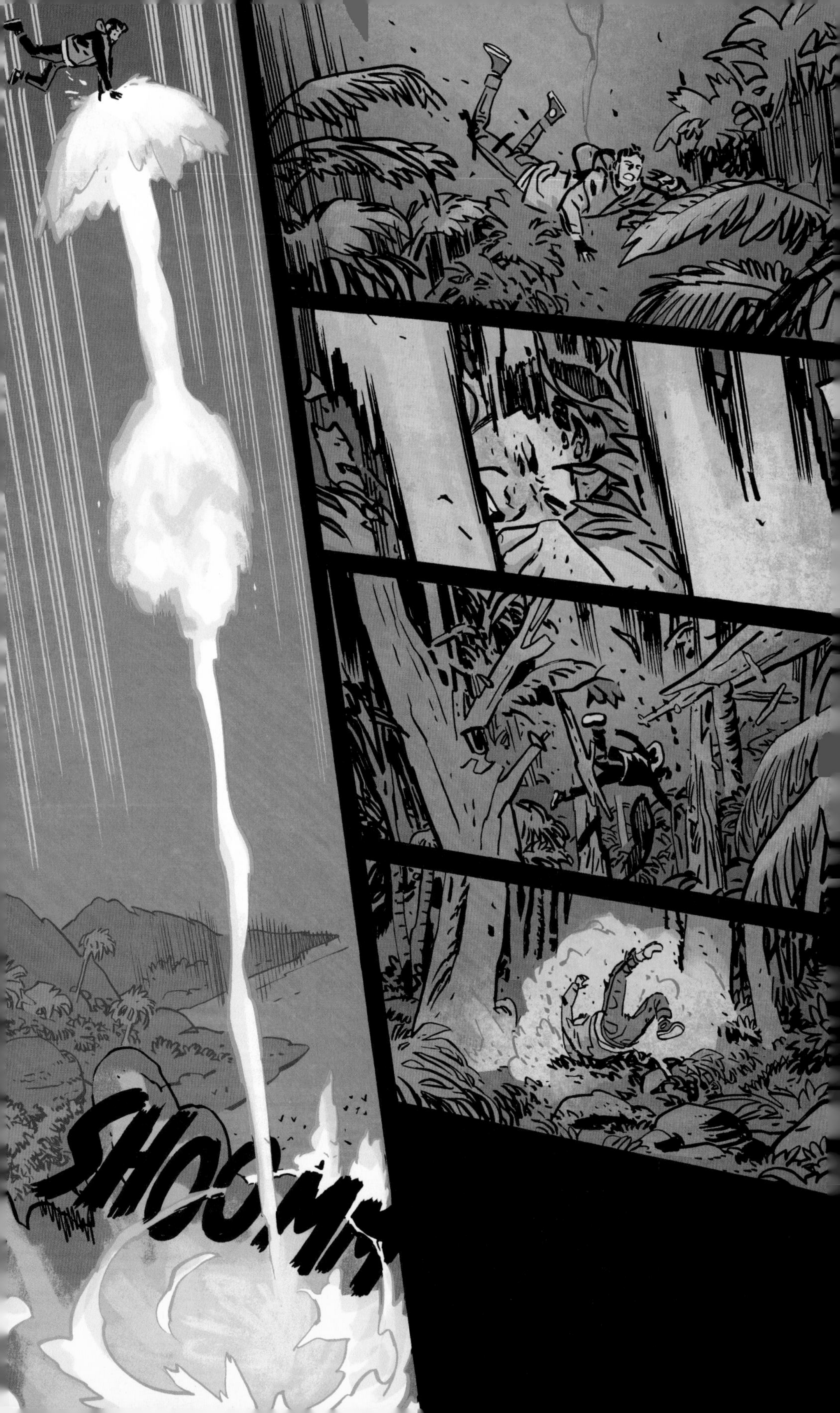
SHOOM

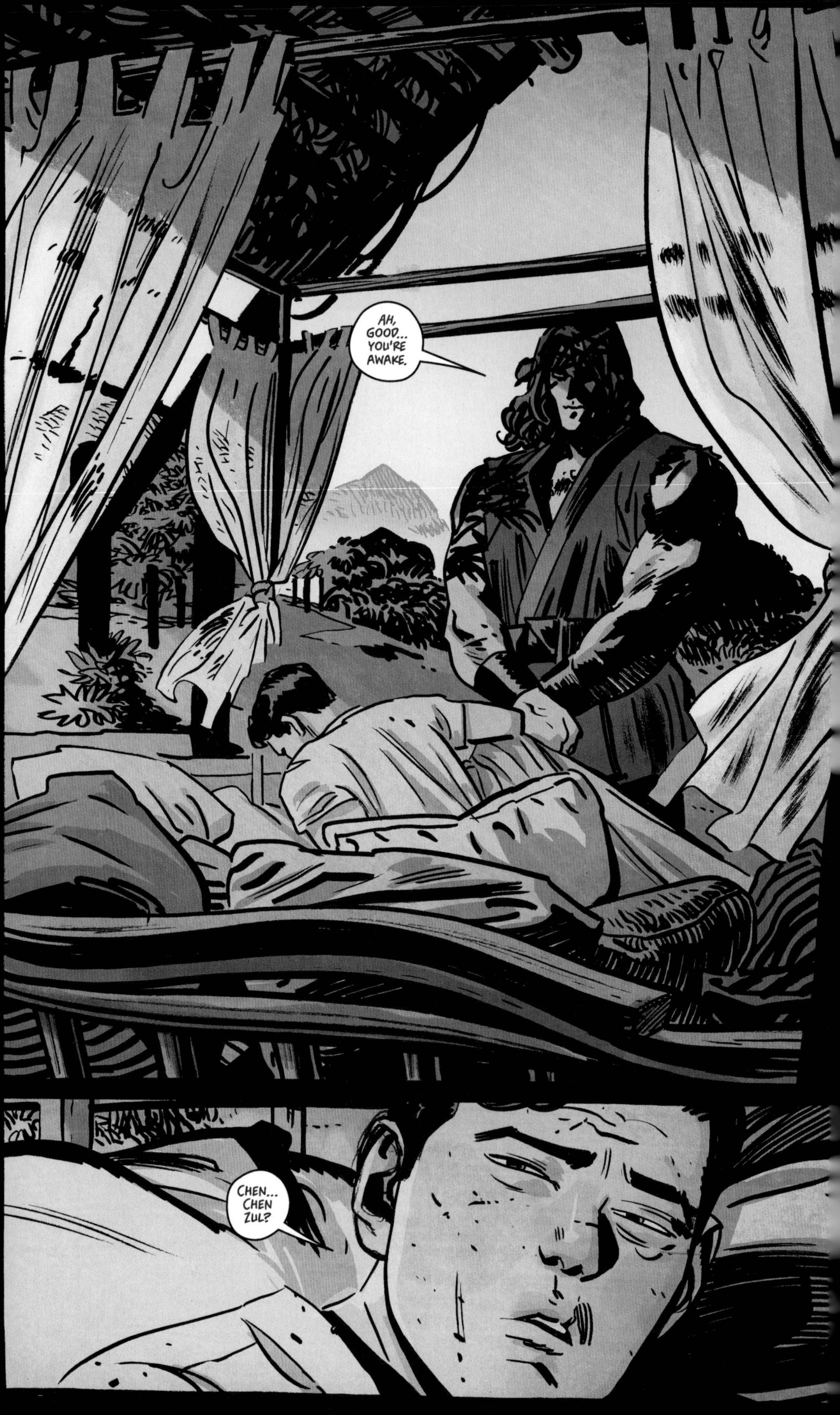
AH, GOOD... YOU'RE AWAKE.
CHEN... CHEN ZUL?

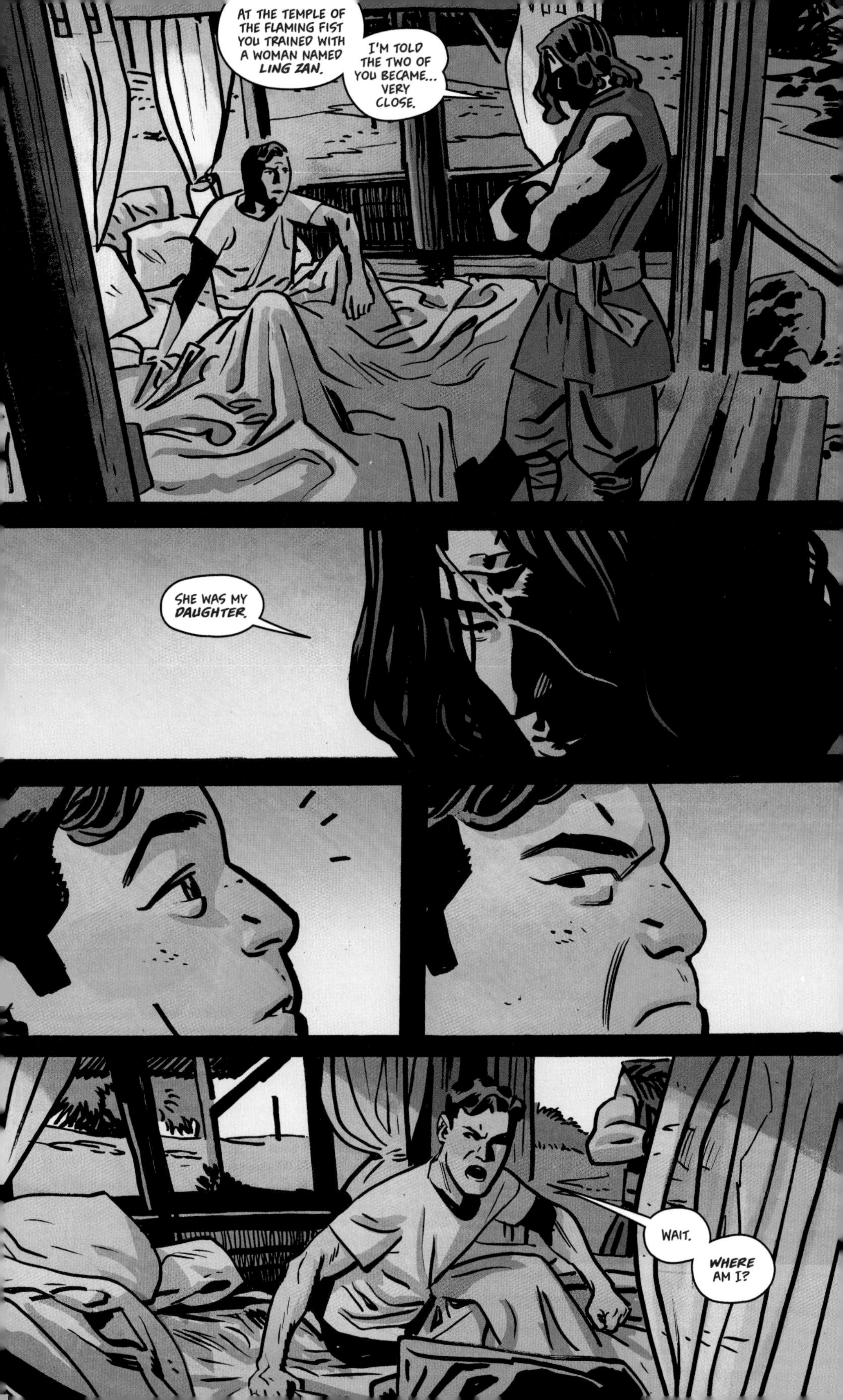
AT THE TEMPLE OF THE FLAMING FIST YOU TRAINED WITH A WOMAN NAMED LING ZAN.
I'M TOLD THE TWO OF YOU BECAME... VERY CLOSE.
SHE WAS MY DAUGHTER.
WAIT.
WHERE AM I?

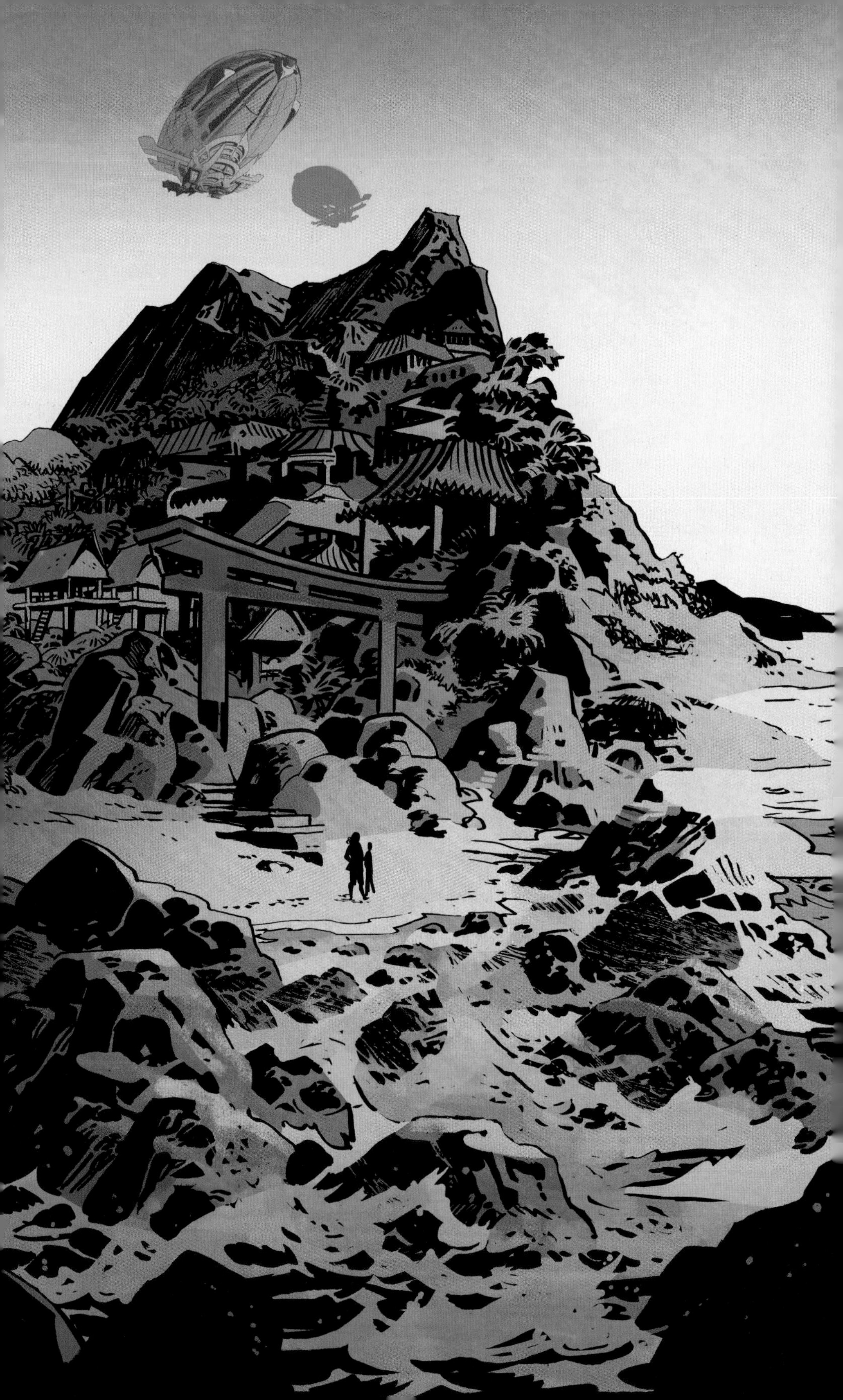

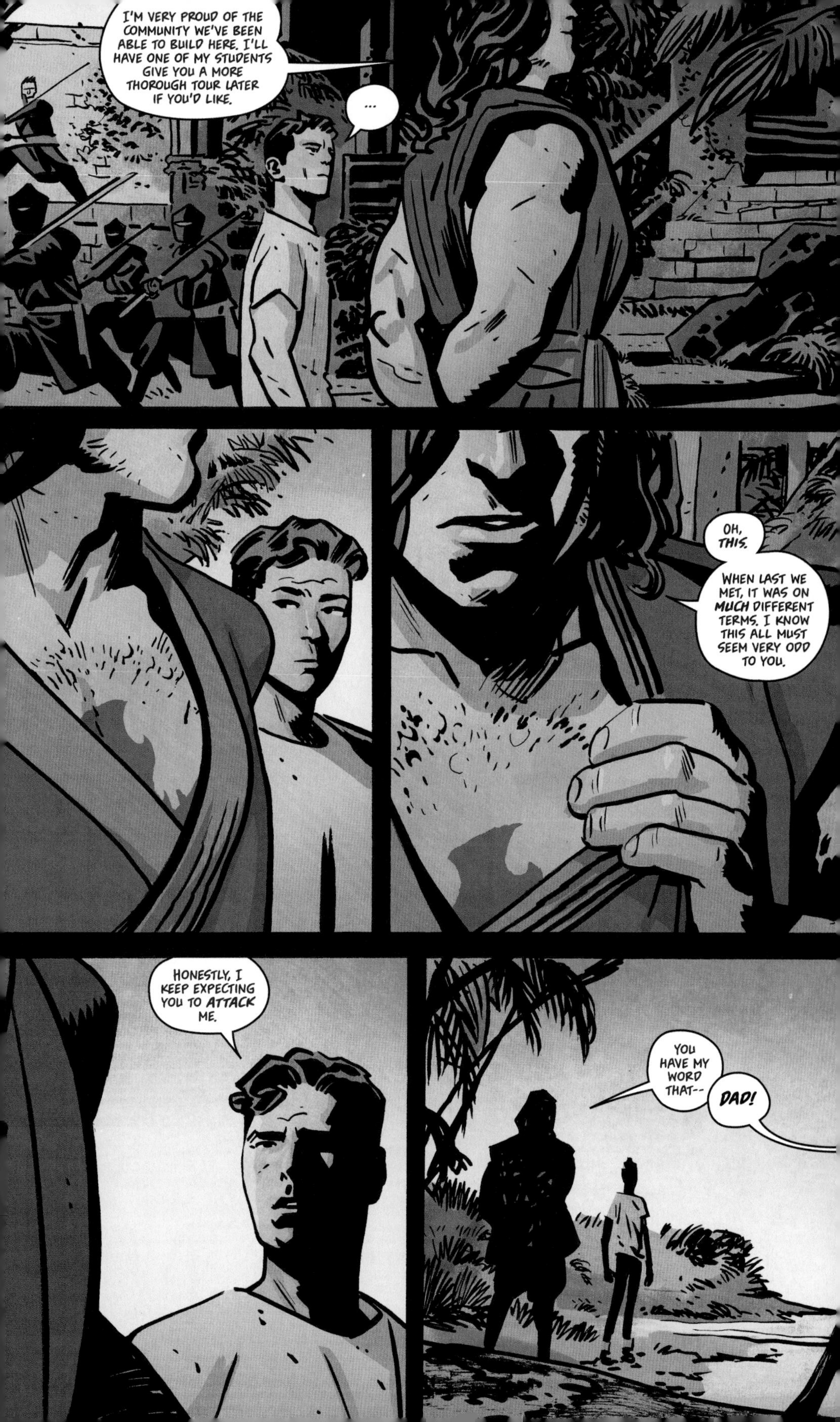
I'M VERY PROUD OF THE COMMUNITY WE'VE BEEN ABLE TO BUILD HERE. I'LL HAVE ONE OF MY STUDENTS GIVE YOU A MORE THOROUGH TOUR LATER IF YOU'D LIKE.
...
OH, THIS.
WHEN LAST WE MET, IT WAS ON MUCH DIFFERENT TERMS. I KNOW THIS ALL MUST SEEM VERY ODD TO YOU.
HONESTLY, I KEEP EXPECTING YOU TO ATTACK ME.
YOU HAVE MY WORD THAT--
DAD!

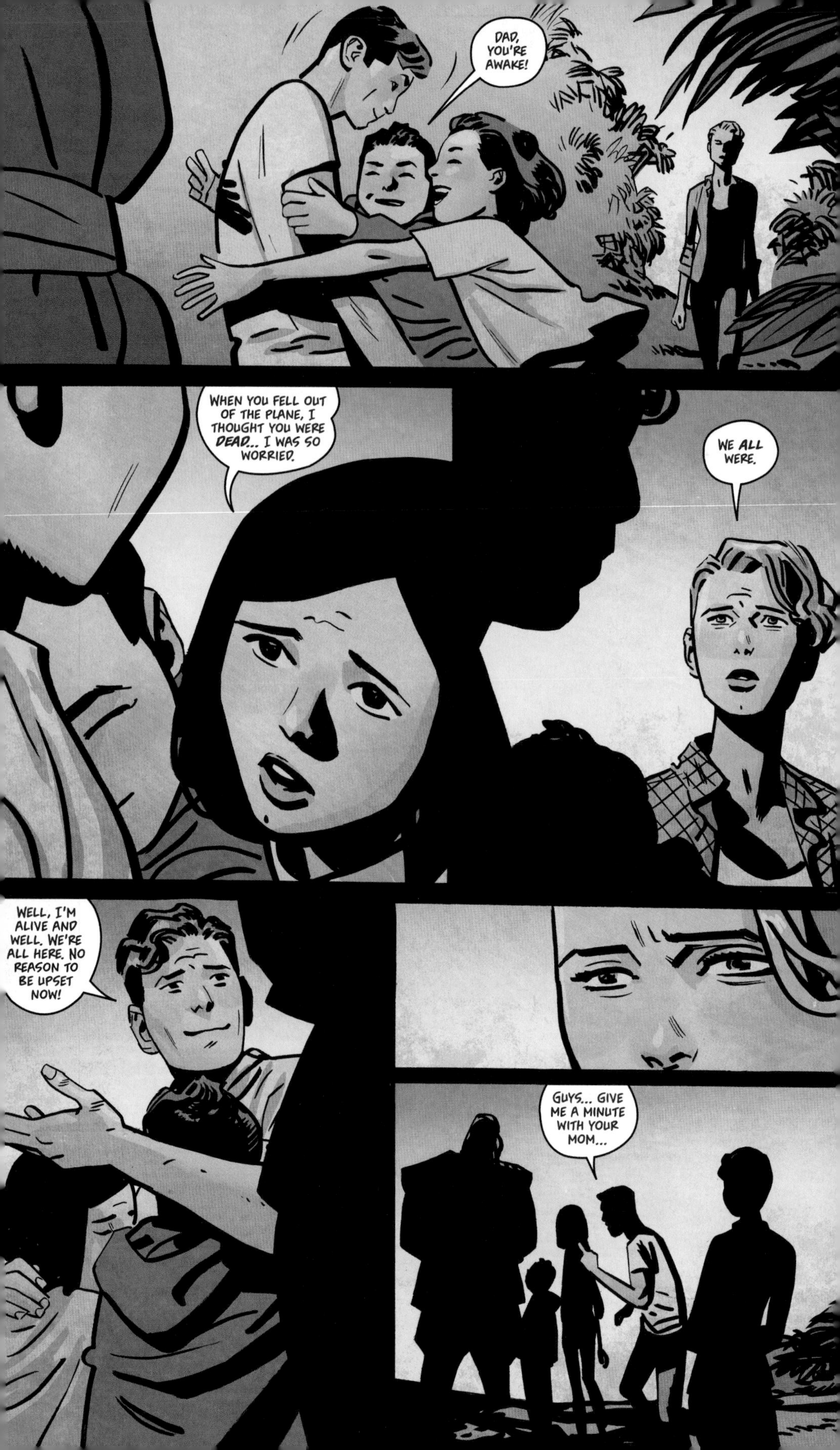
DAD, YOU'RE AWAKE!
WHEN YOU FELL OUT OF THE PLANE, I THOUGHT YOU WERE DEAD... I WAS SO WORRIED.
WE ALL WERE.
WELL, I'M ALIVE AND WELL. WE'RE ALL HERE. NO REASON TO BE UPSET NOW!
GUYS... GIVE ME A MINUTE WITH YOUR MOM...

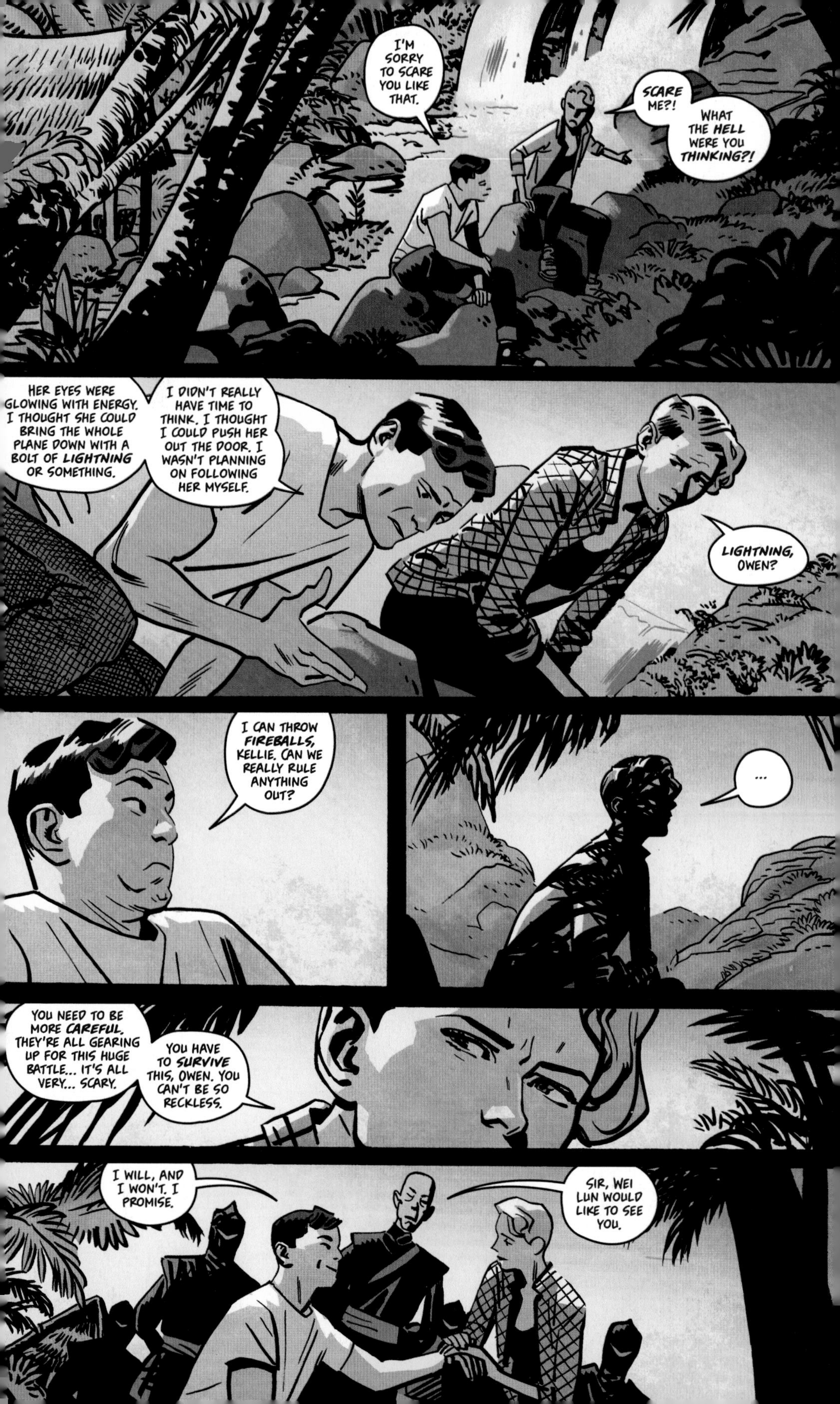
I'M SORRY TO SCARE YOU LIKE THAT.
SCARE ME?!
WHAT THE HELL WERE YOU THINKING?!
HER EYES WERE GLOWING WITH ENERGY. I THOUGHT SHE COULD BRING THE WHOLE PLANE DOWN WITH A BOLT OF LIGHTNING OR SOMETHING.
I DIDN'T REALLY HAVE TIME TO THINK. I THOUGHT I COULD PUSH HER OUT THE DOOR. I WASN'T PLANNING ON FOLLOWING HER MYSELF.
LIGHTNING, OWEN?
I CAN THROW FIREBALLS, KELLIE. CAN WE REALLY RULE ANYTHING OUT?
...
YOU NEED TO BE MORE CAREFUL. THEY'RE ALL GEARING UP FOR THIS HUGE BATTLE... IT'S ALL VERY... SCARY.
YOU HAVE TO SURVIVE THIS, OWEN. YOU CAN'T BE SO RECKLESS.
I WILL, AND I WON'T. I PROMISE.
SIR, WEI LUN WOULD LIKE TO SEE YOU.

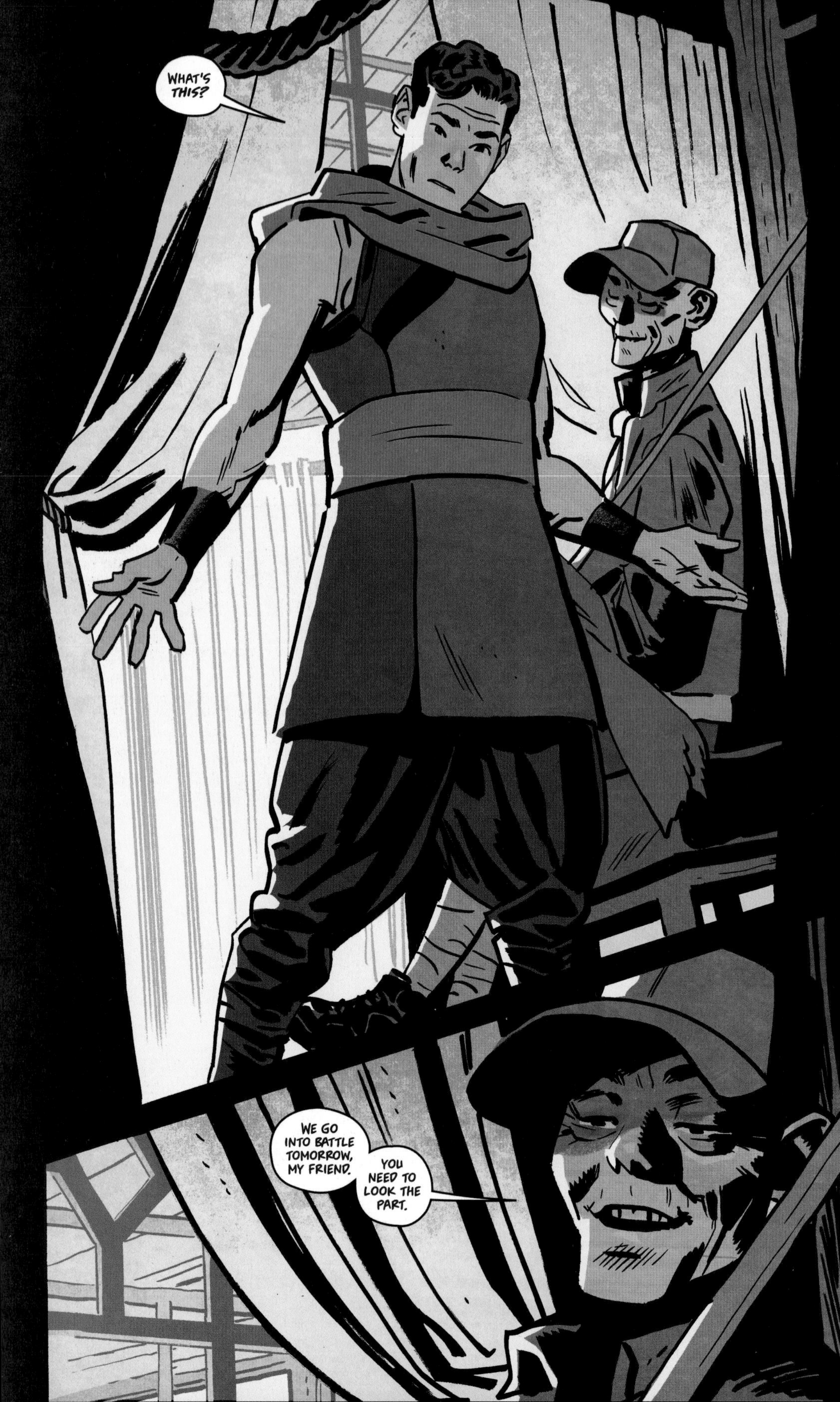
WHAT'S THIS?
WE GO INTO BATTLE TOMORROW, MY FRIEND.
YOU NEED TO LOOK THE PART.

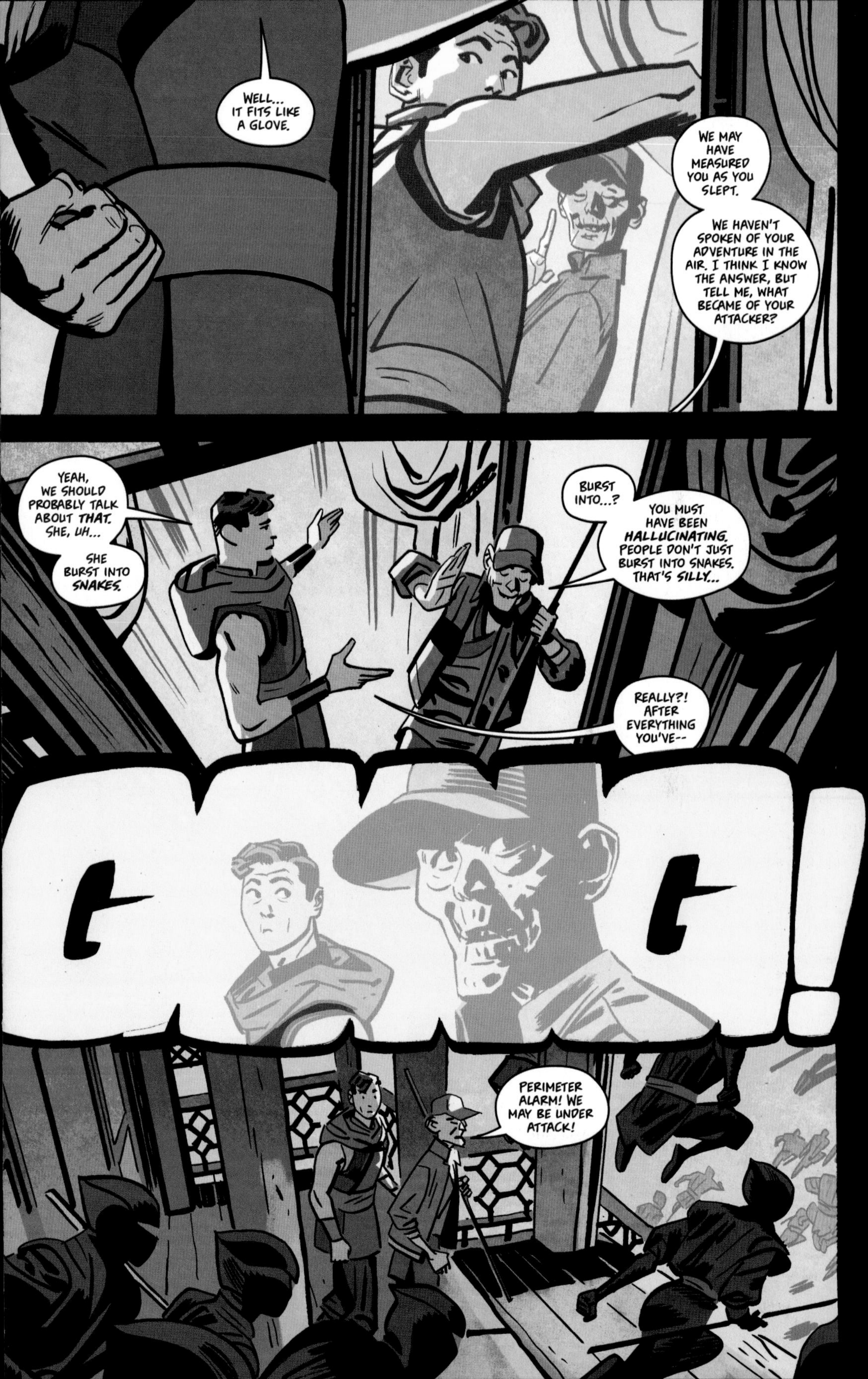
WELL... IT FITS LIKE A GLOVE.
WE MAY HAVE MEASURED YOU AS YOU SLEPT.
WE HAVEN'T SPOKEN OF YOUR ADVENTURE IN THE AIR. I THINK I KNOW THE ANSWER, BUT TELL ME, WHAT BECAME OF YOUR ATTACKER?
YEAH, WE SHOULD PROBABLY TALK ABOUT THAT. SHE, UH...
SHE BURST INTO SNAKES.
BURST INTO...?
YOU MUST HAVE BEEN HALLUCINATING. PEOPLE DON'T JUST BURST INTO SNAKES. THAT'S SILLY...
REALLY?! AFTER EVERYTHING YOU'VE--
PERIMETER ALARM! WE MAY BE UNDER ATTACK!

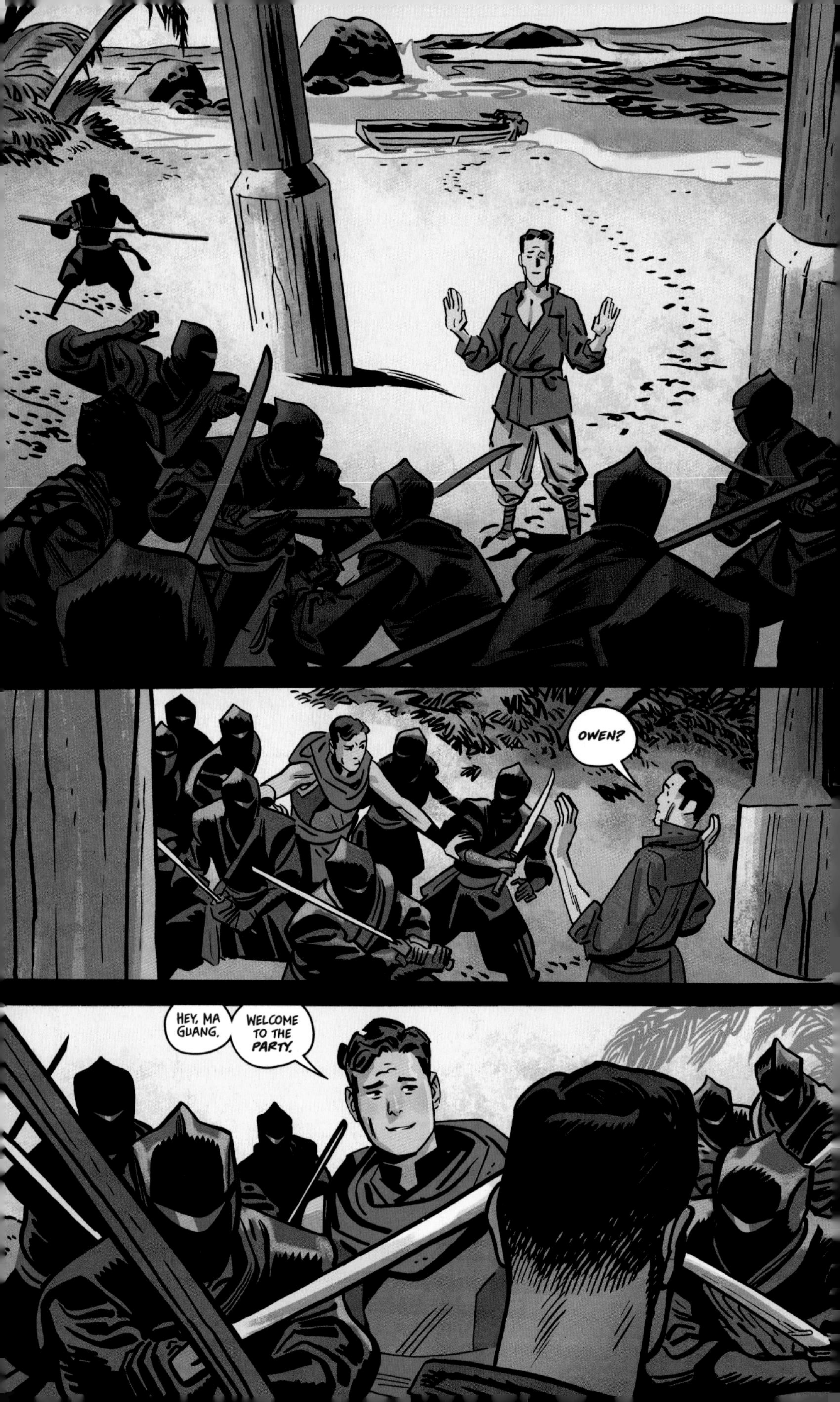
OWEN?
HEY, MA GUANG.
WELCOME TO THE PARTY.

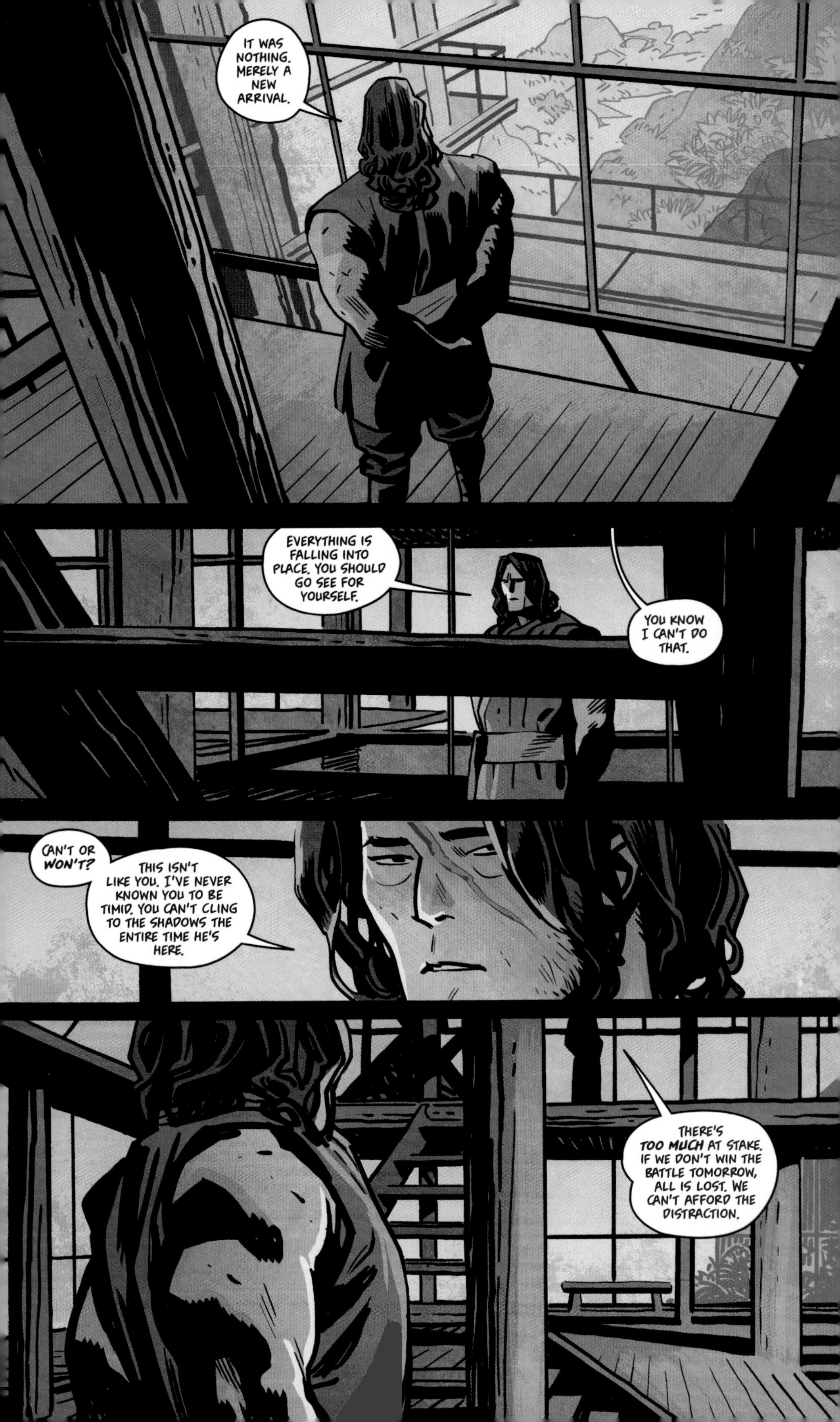
IT WAS NOTHING. MERELY A NEW ARRIVAL.
EVERYTHING IS FALLING INTO PLACE. YOU SHOULD GO SEE FOR YOURSELF.
YOU KNOW I CAN'T DO THAT.
CAN'T OR WON'T?
THIS ISN'T LIKE YOU. I'VE NEVER KNOWN YOU TO BE TIMID. YOU CAN'T CLING TO THE SHADOWS THE ENTIRE TIME HE'S HERE.
THERE'S TOO MUCH AT STAKE. IF WE DON'T WIN THE BATTLE TOMORROW, ALL IS LOST. WE CAN'T AFFORD THE DISTRACTION.

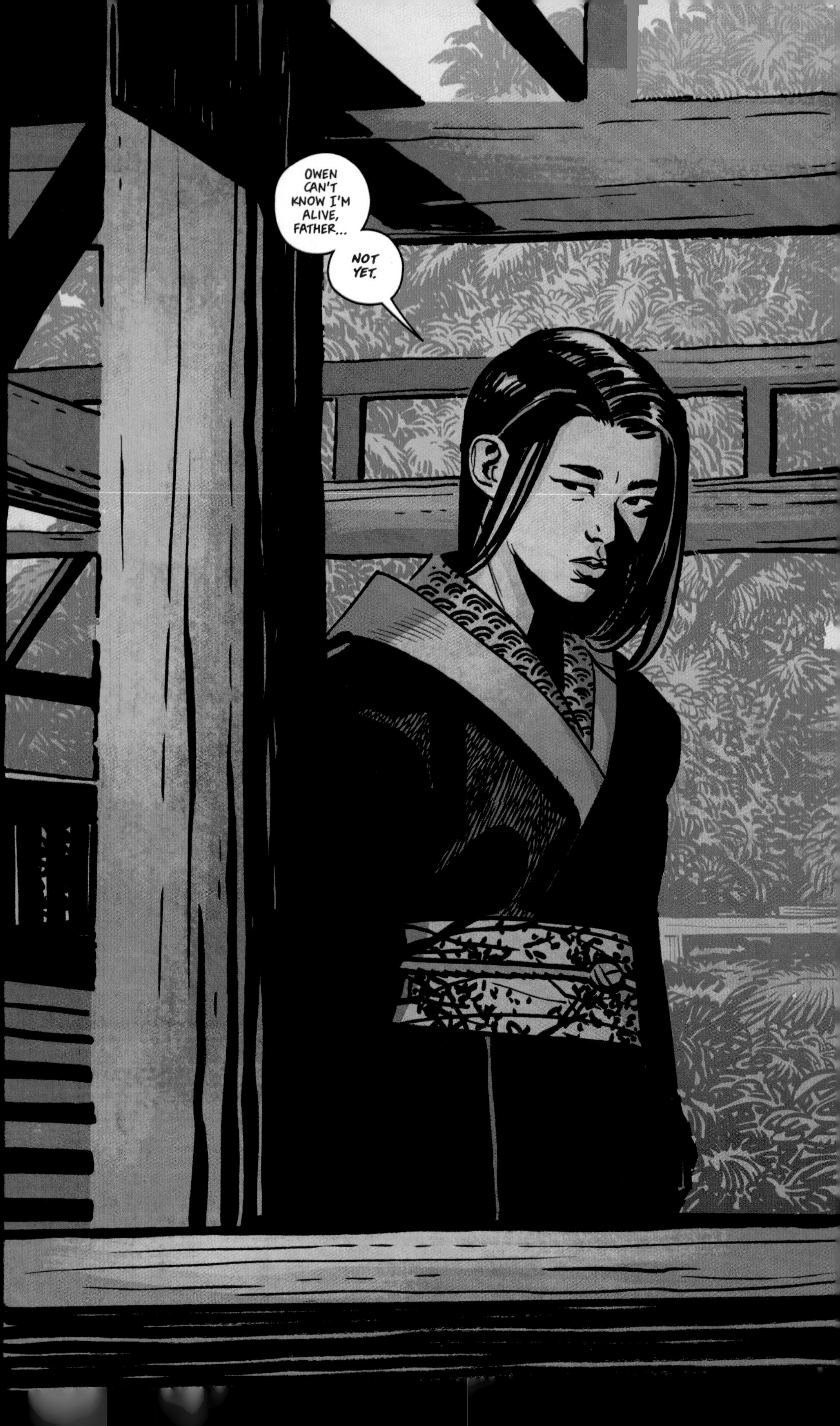
OWEN CAN'T KNOW I'M ALIVE, FATHER...
NOT YET.

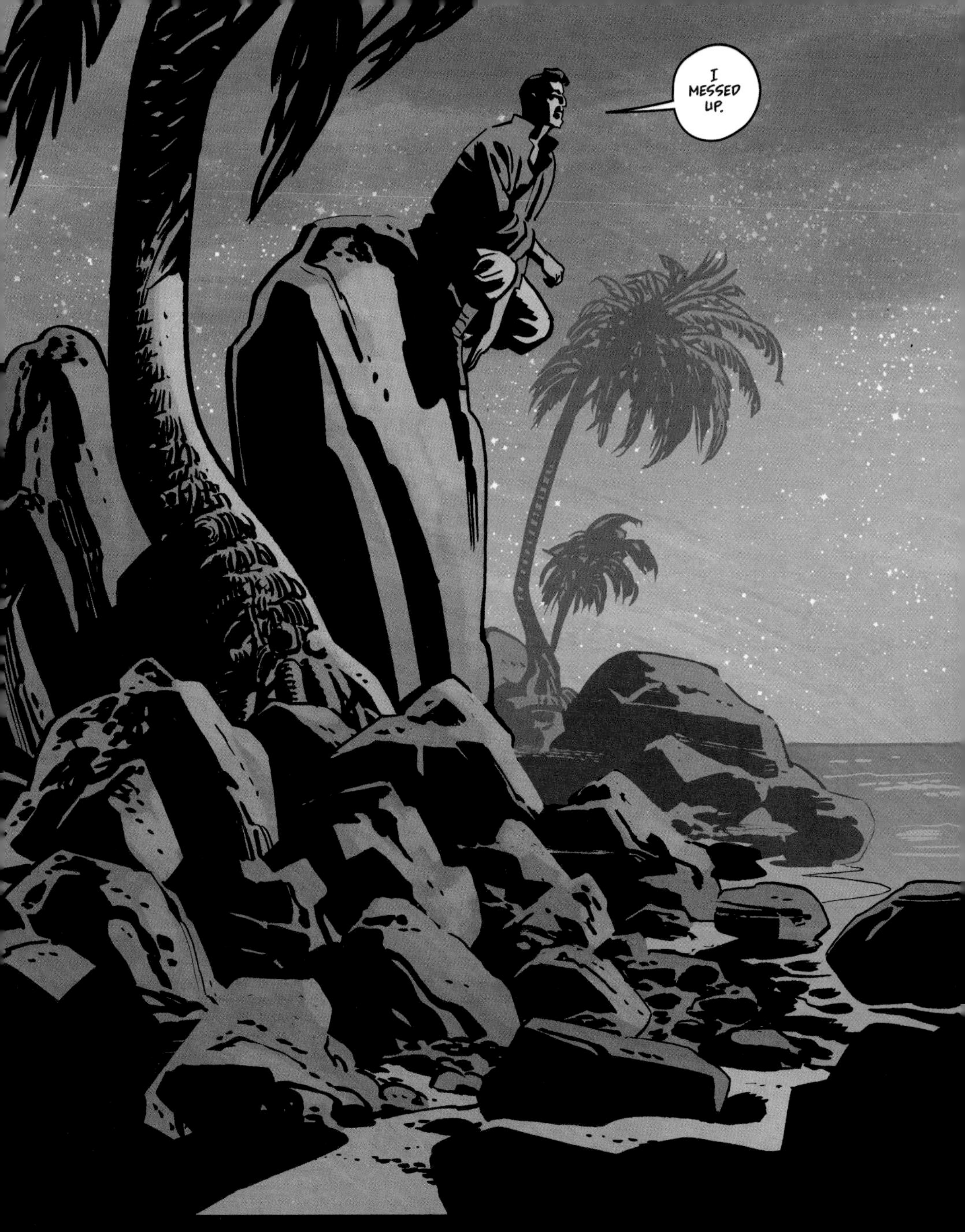
I MESSED UP.

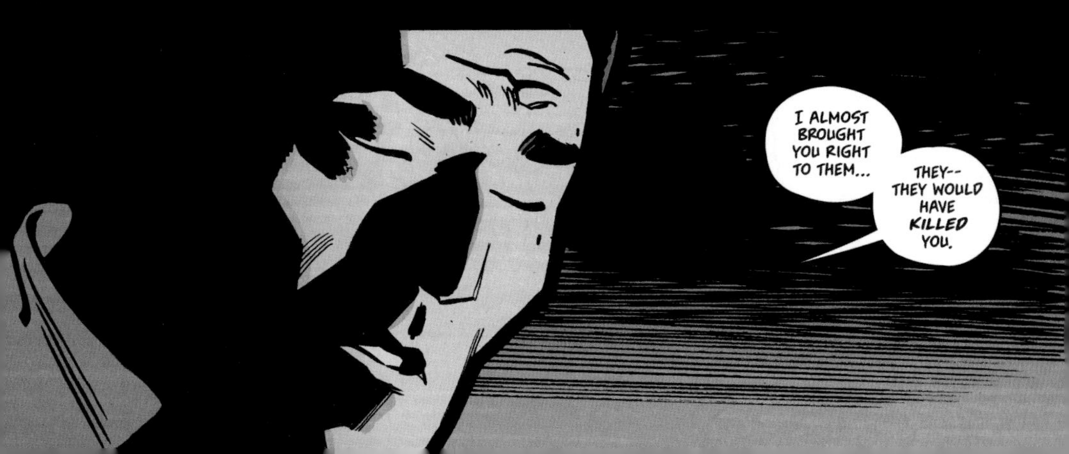
I ALMOST BROUGHT YOU RIGHT TO THEM...
THEY-- THEY WOULD HAVE **KILLED** YOU.

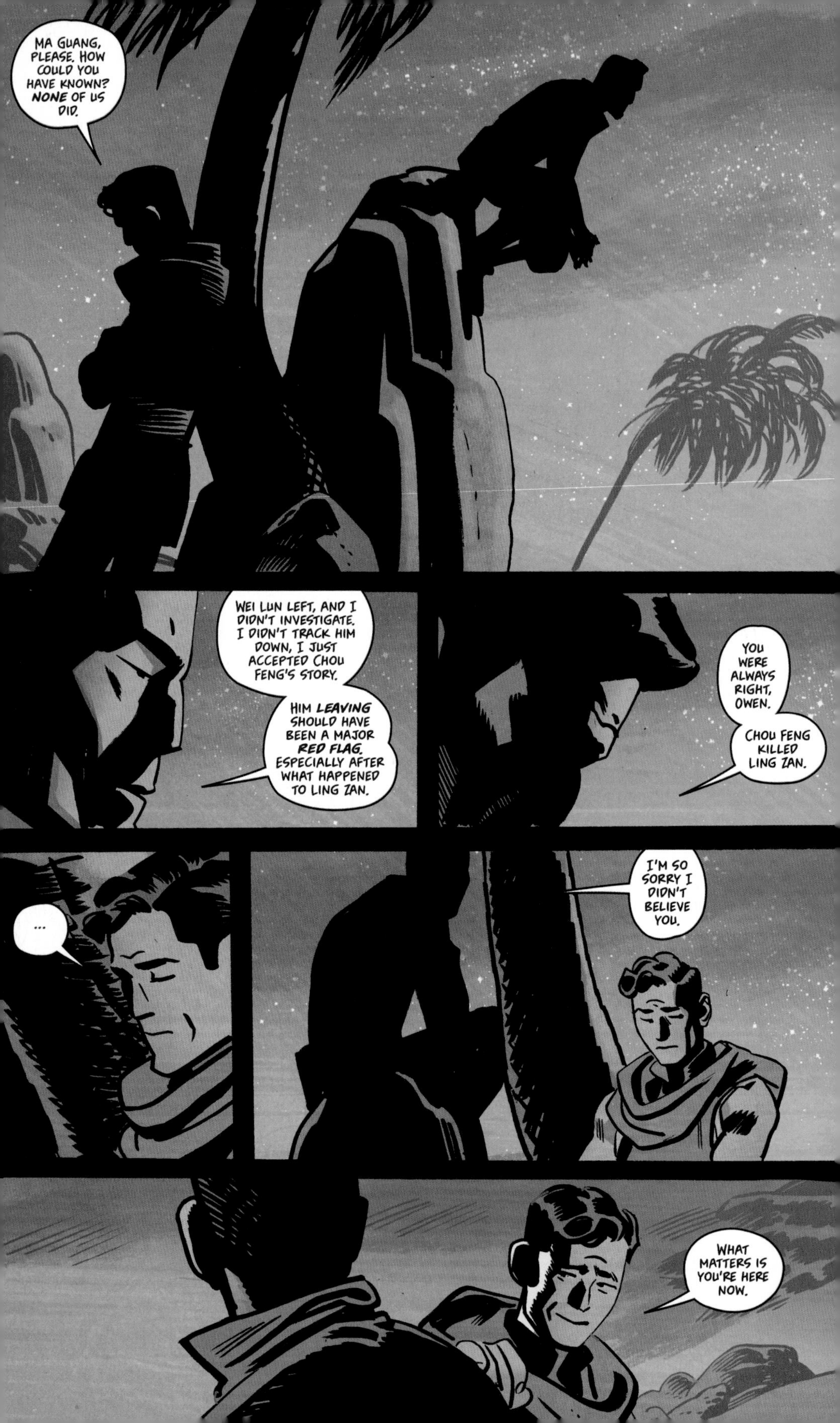
MA GUANG, PLEASE. HOW COULD YOU HAVE KNOWN? NONE OF US DID.
WEI LUN LEFT, AND I DIDN'T INVESTIGATE. I DIDN'T TRACK HIM DOWN, I JUST ACCEPTED CHOU FENG'S STORY.
HIM LEAVING SHOULD HAVE BEEN A MAJOR RED FLAG. ESPECIALLY AFTER WHAT HAPPENED TO LING ZAN.
YOU WERE ALWAYS RIGHT, OWEN.
CHOU FENG KILLED LING ZAN.
...
I'M SO SORRY I DIDN'T BELIEVE YOU.
WHAT MATTERS IS YOU'RE HERE NOW.

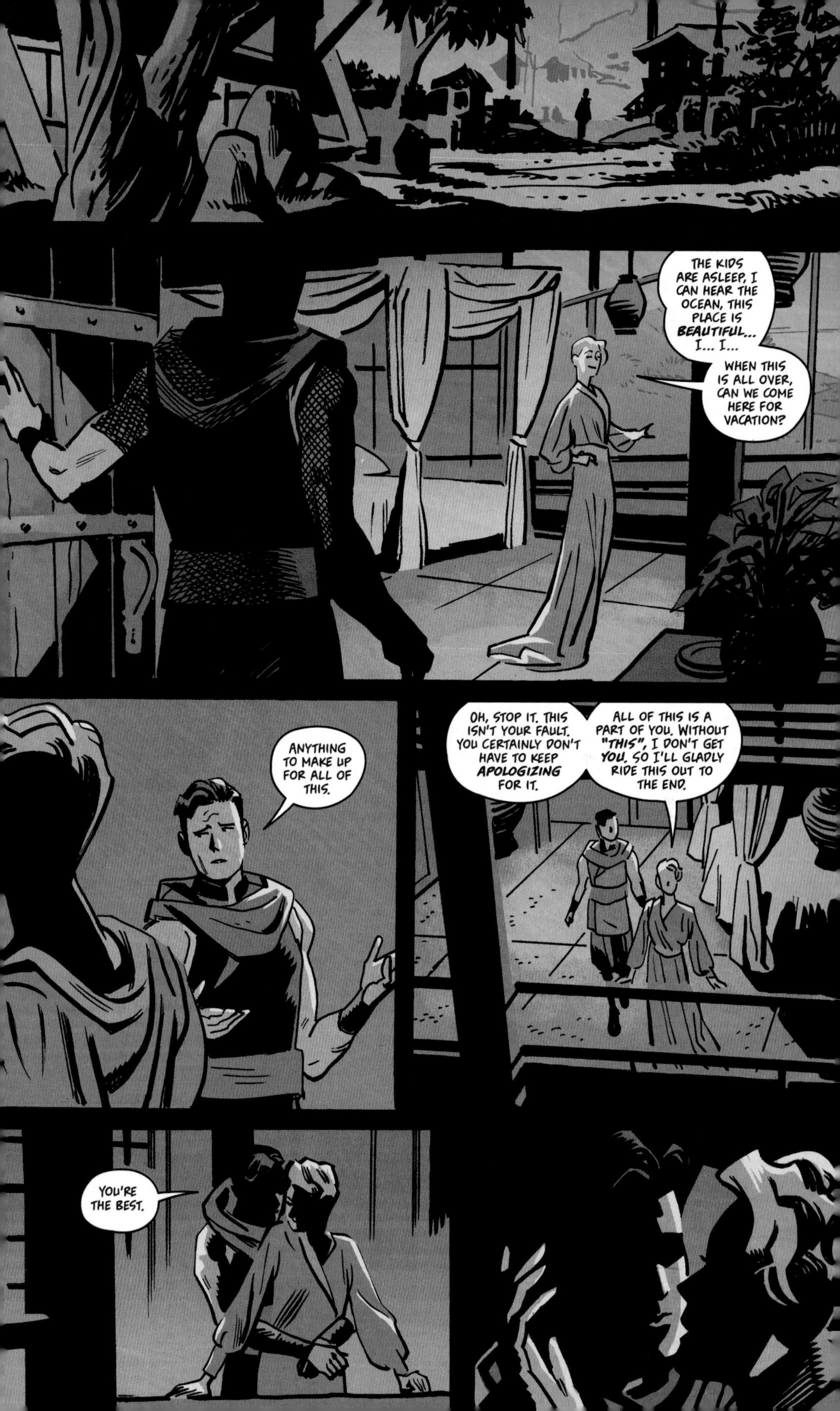
THE KIDS ARE ASLEEP, I CAN HEAR THE OCEAN, THIS PLACE IS BEAUTIFUL... I... I...
WHEN THIS IS ALL OVER, CAN WE COME HERE FOR VACATION?
ANYTHING TO MAKE UP FOR ALL OF THIS.
OH, STOP IT. THIS ISN'T YOUR FAULT. YOU CERTAINLY DON'T HAVE TO KEEP APOLOGIZING FOR IT.
ALL OF THIS IS A PART OF YOU. WITHOUT "THIS", I DON'T GET YOU. SO I'LL GLADLY RIDE THIS OUT TO THE END.
YOU'RE THE BEST.

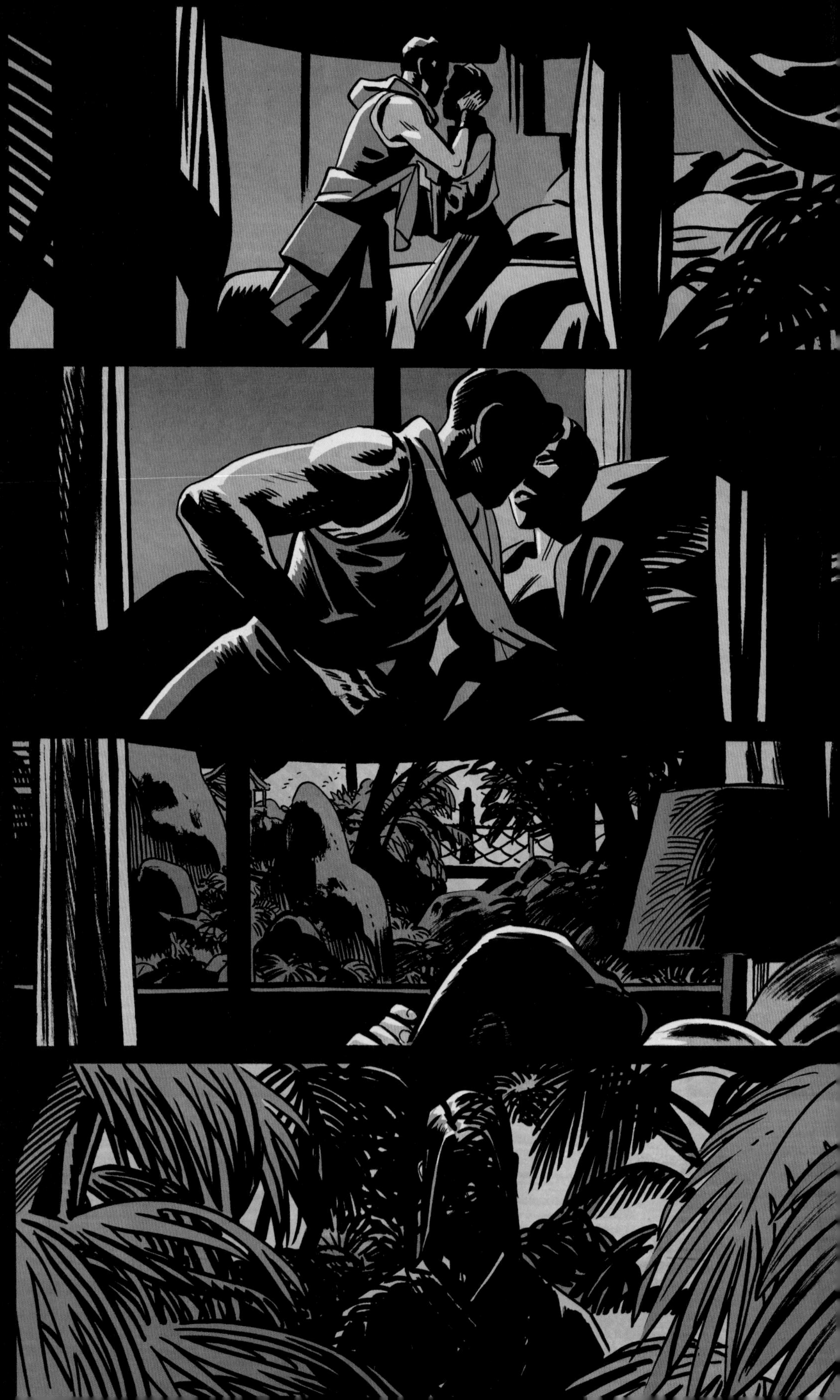

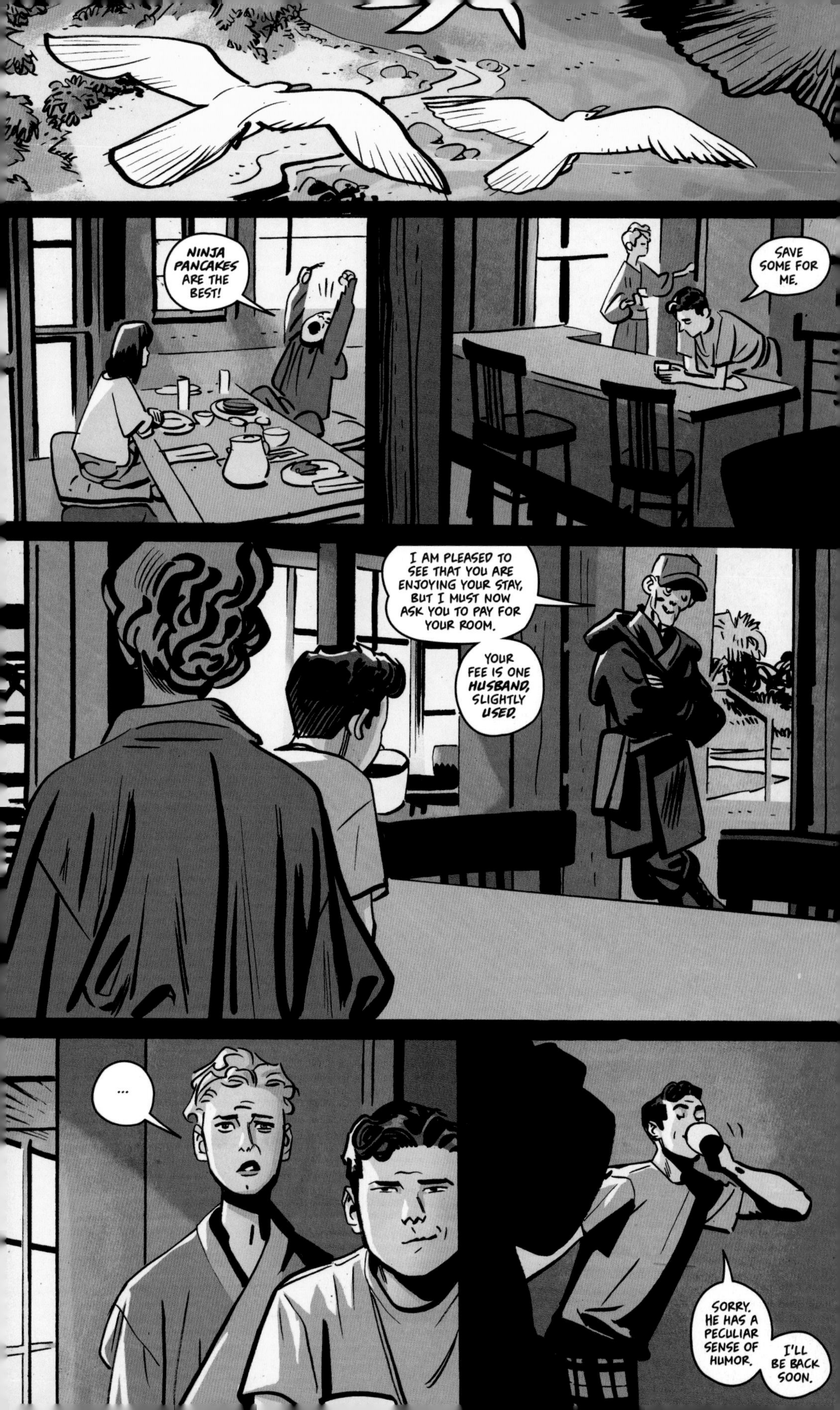
NINJA PANCAKES ARE THE BEST!
SAVE SOME FOR ME.
I AM PLEASED TO SEE THAT YOU ARE ENJOYING YOUR STAY, BUT I MUST NOW ASK YOU TO PAY FOR YOUR ROOM.
YOUR FEE IS ONE HUSBAND, SLIGHTLY USED.
...
SORRY. HE HAS A PECULIAR SENSE OF HUMOR.
I'LL BE BACK SOON.

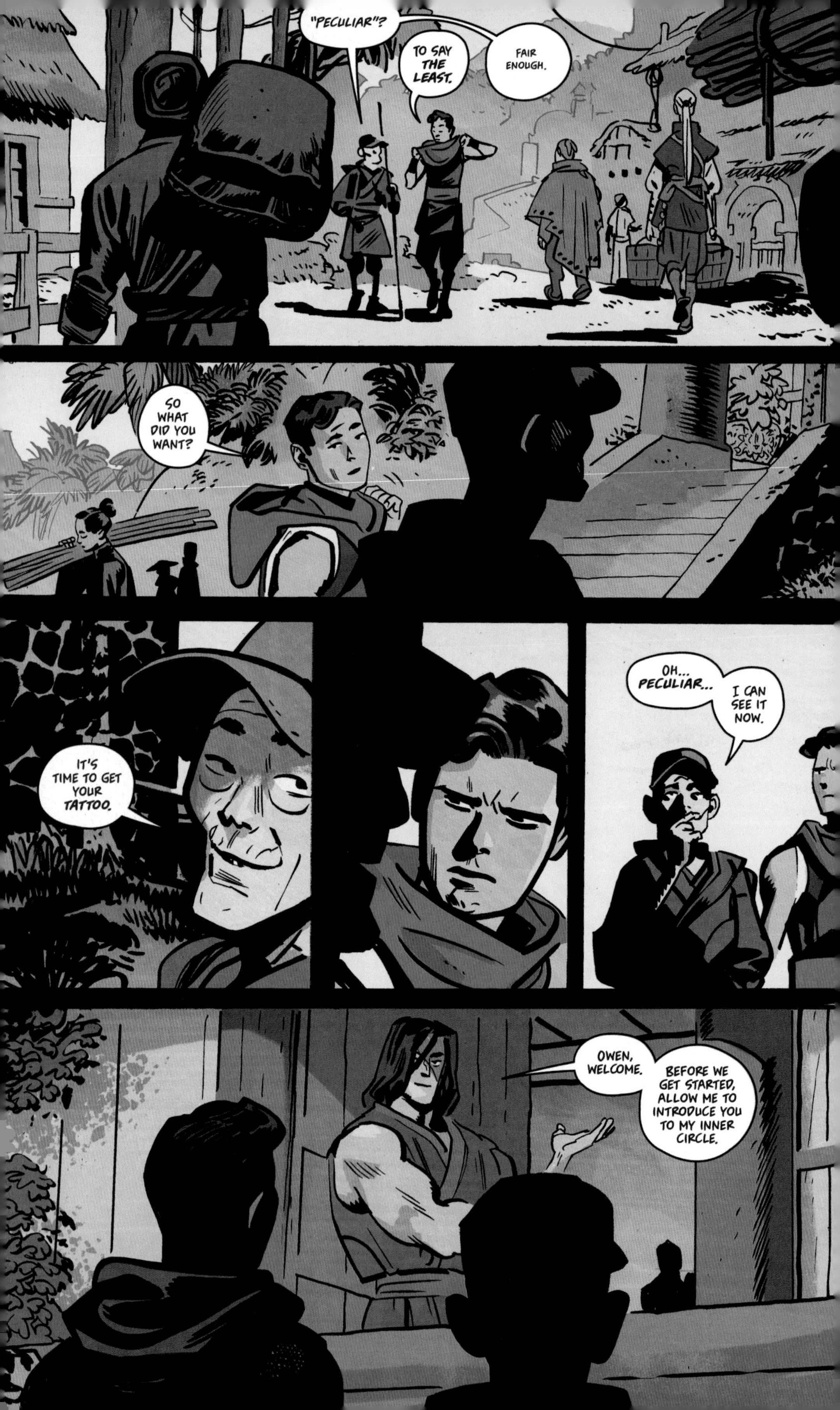

"PECULIAR"?
TO SAY THE LEAST.
FAIR ENOUGH.
SO WHAT DID YOU WANT?
IT'S TIME TO GET YOUR TATTOO.
OH... PECULIAR...
I CAN SEE IT NOW.
OWEN, WELCOME.
BEFORE WE GET STARTED, ALLOW ME TO INTRODUCE YOU TO MY INNER CIRCLE.

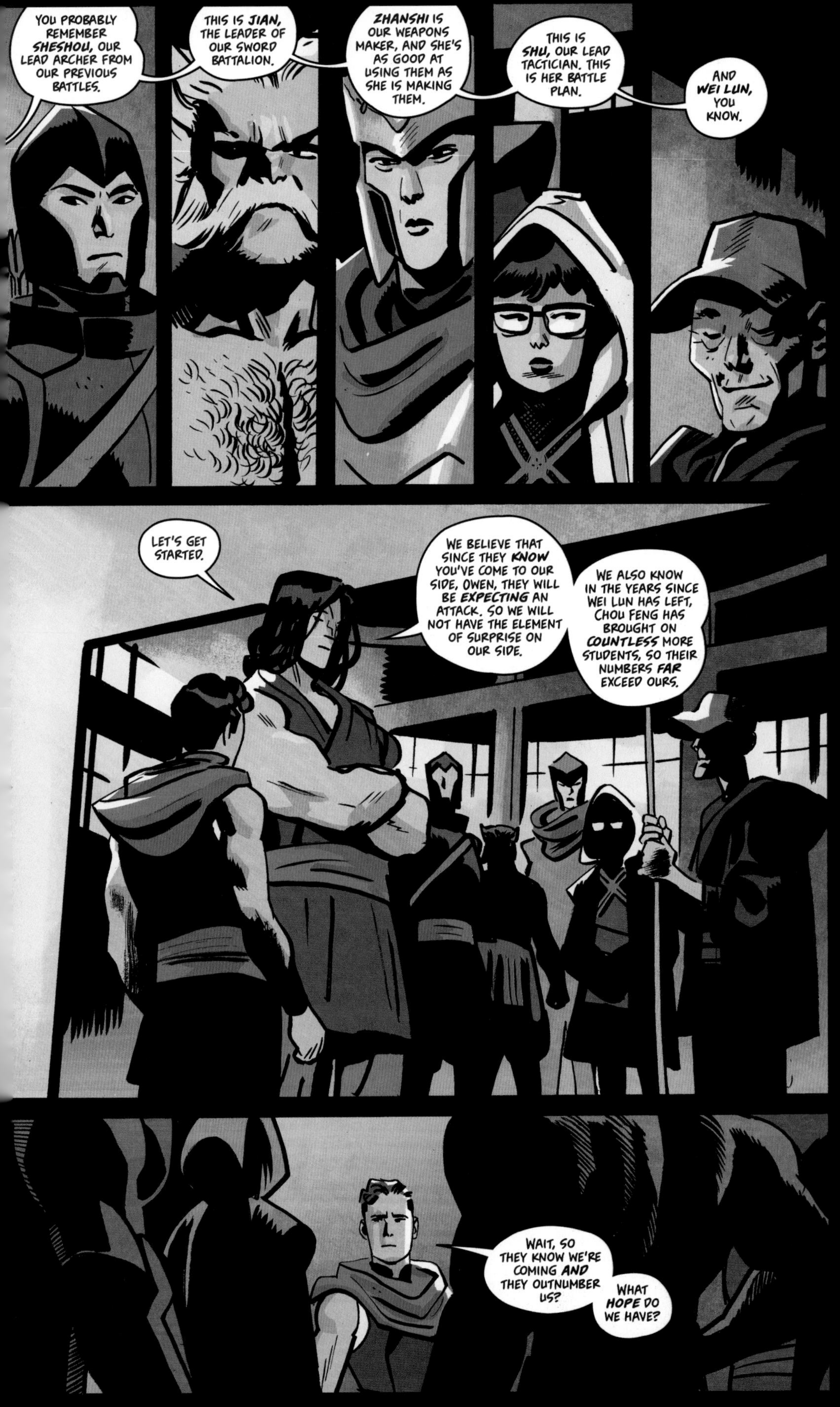
YOU PROBABLY REMEMBER SHESHOU, OUR LEAD ARCHER FROM OUR PREVIOUS BATTLES.
THIS IS JIAN, THE LEADER OF OUR SWORD BATTALION.
ZHANSHI IS OUR WEAPONS MAKER, AND SHE'S AS GOOD AT USING THEM AS SHE IS MAKING THEM.
THIS IS SHU, OUR LEAD TACTICIAN. THIS IS HER BATTLE PLAN.
AND WEI LUN, YOU KNOW.
LET'S GET STARTED.
WE BELIEVE THAT SINCE THEY KNOW YOU'VE COME TO OUR SIDE, OWEN, THEY WILL BE EXPECTING AN ATTACK. SO WE WILL NOT HAVE THE ELEMENT OF SURPRISE ON OUR SIDE.
WE ALSO KNOW IN THE YEARS SINCE WEI LUN HAS LEFT, CHOU FENG HAS BROUGHT ON COUNTLESS MORE STUDENTS, SO THEIR NUMBERS FAR EXCEED OURS.
WAIT, SO THEY KNOW WE'RE COMING AND THEY OUTNUMBER US?
WHAT HOPE DO WE HAVE?

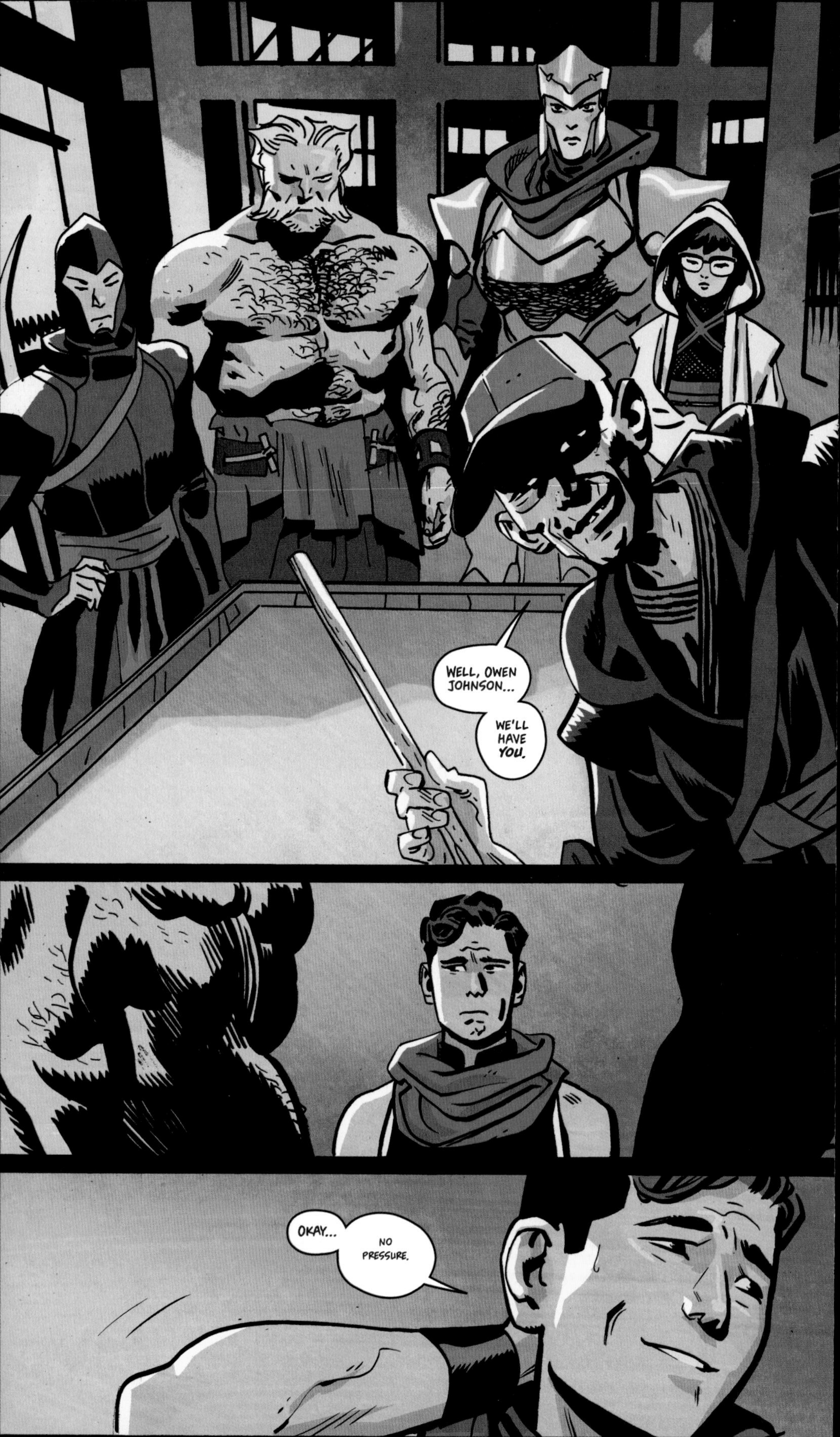
WELL, OWEN JOHNSON...
WE'LL HAVE YOU.
OKAY...
NO PRESSURE.

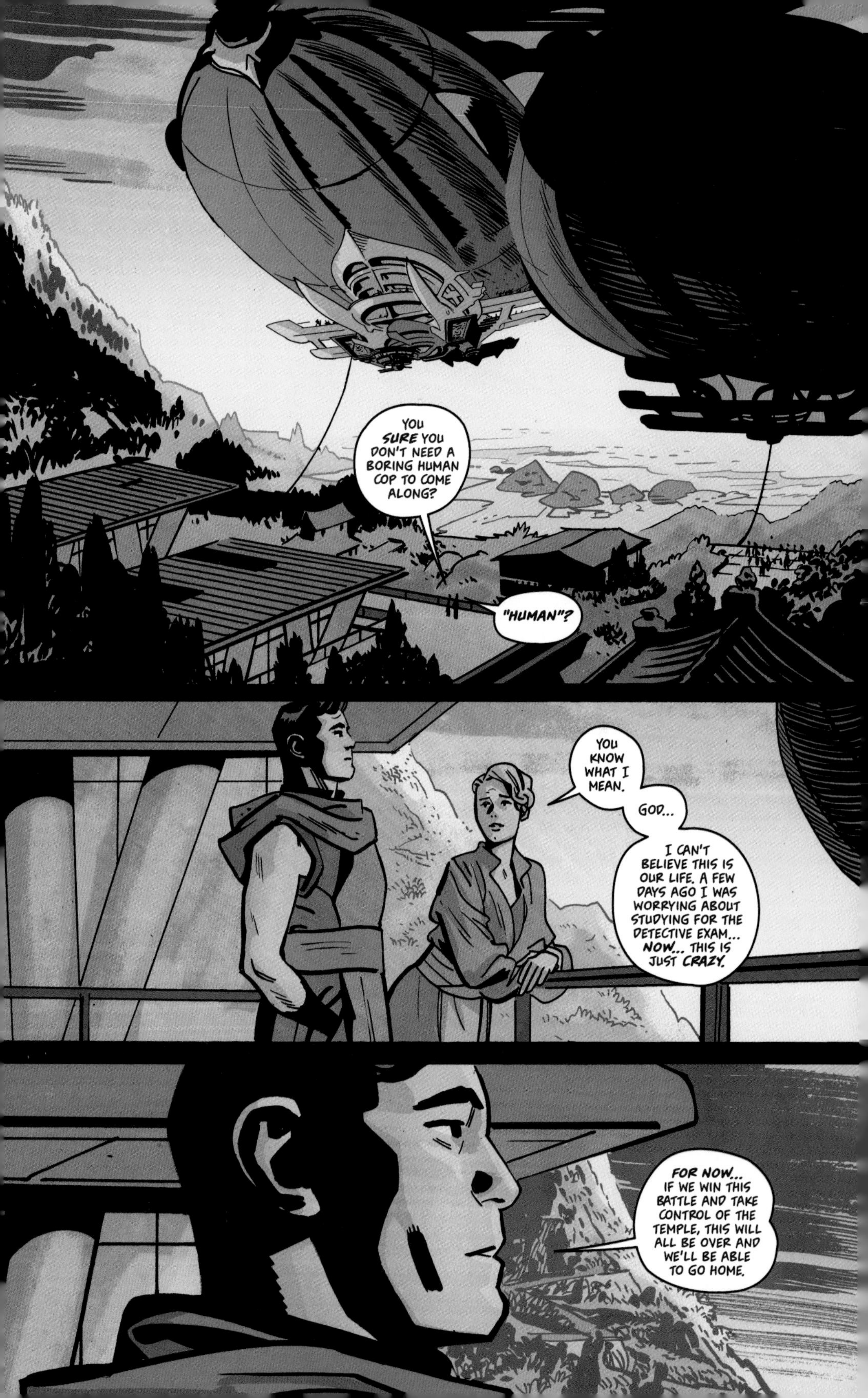
YOU SURE YOU DON'T NEED A BORING HUMAN COP TO COME ALONG?
"HUMAN"?
YOU KNOW WHAT I MEAN.
GOD...
I CAN'T BELIEVE THIS IS OUR LIFE. A FEW DAYS AGO I WAS WORRYING ABOUT STUDYING FOR THE DETECTIVE EXAM... NOW... THIS IS JUST CRAZY.
FOR NOW... IF WE WIN THIS BATTLE AND TAKE CONTROL OF THE TEMPLE, THIS WILL ALL BE OVER AND WE'LL BE ABLE TO GO HOME.

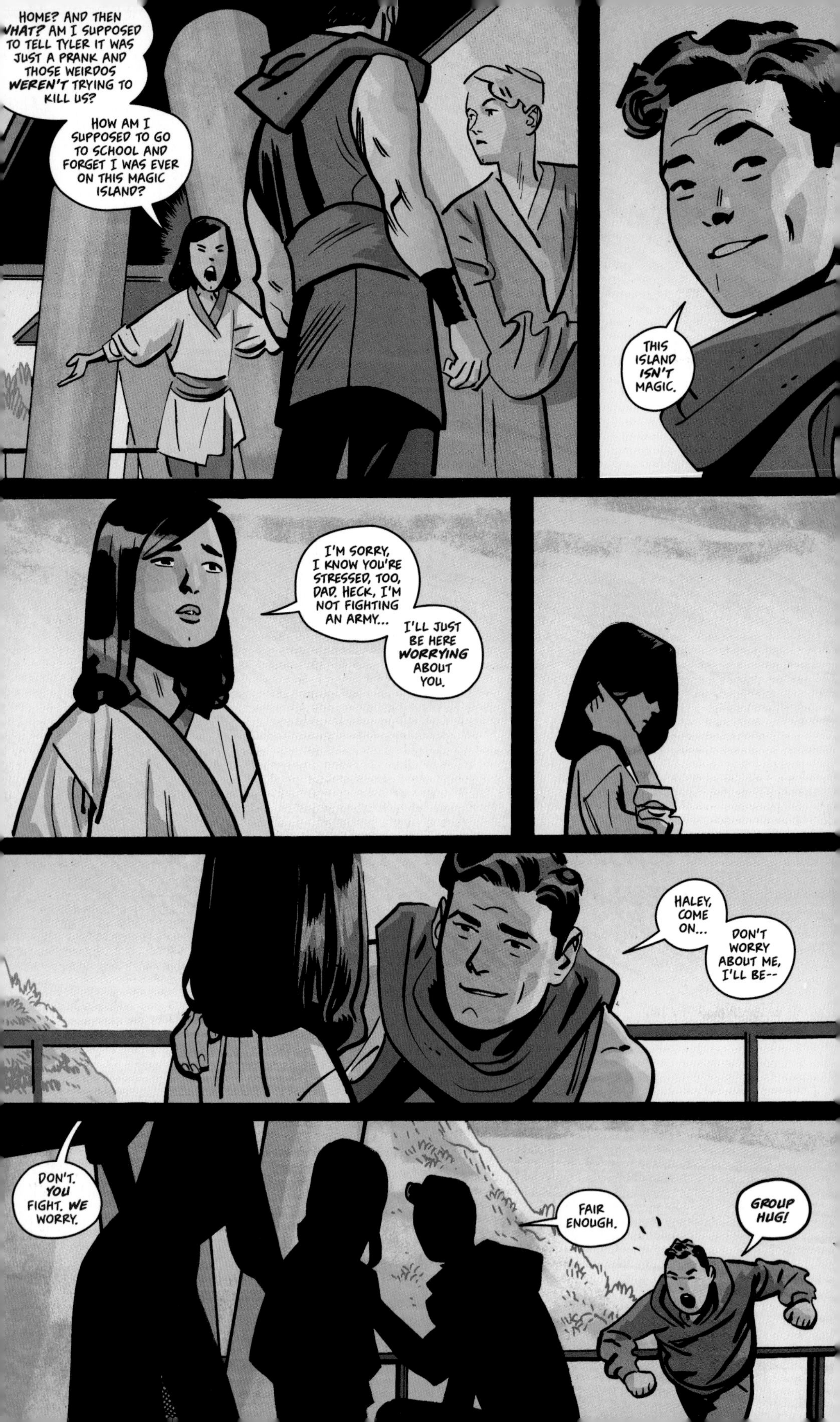
HOME? AND THEN WHAT? AM I SUPPOSED TO TELL TYLER IT WAS JUST A PRANK AND THOSE WEIRDOS WEREN'T TRYING TO KILL US?
HOW AM I SUPPOSED TO GO TO SCHOOL AND FORGET I WAS EVER ON THIS MAGIC ISLAND?
THIS ISLAND ISN'T MAGIC.
I'M SORRY, I KNOW YOU'RE STRESSED, TOO, DAD. HECK, I'M NOT FIGHTING AN ARMY...
I'LL JUST BE HERE WORRYING ABOUT YOU.
HALEY, COME ON...
DON'T WORRY ABOUT ME, I'LL BE--
DON'T. YOU FIGHT. WE WORRY.
FAIR ENOUGH.
GROUP HUG!

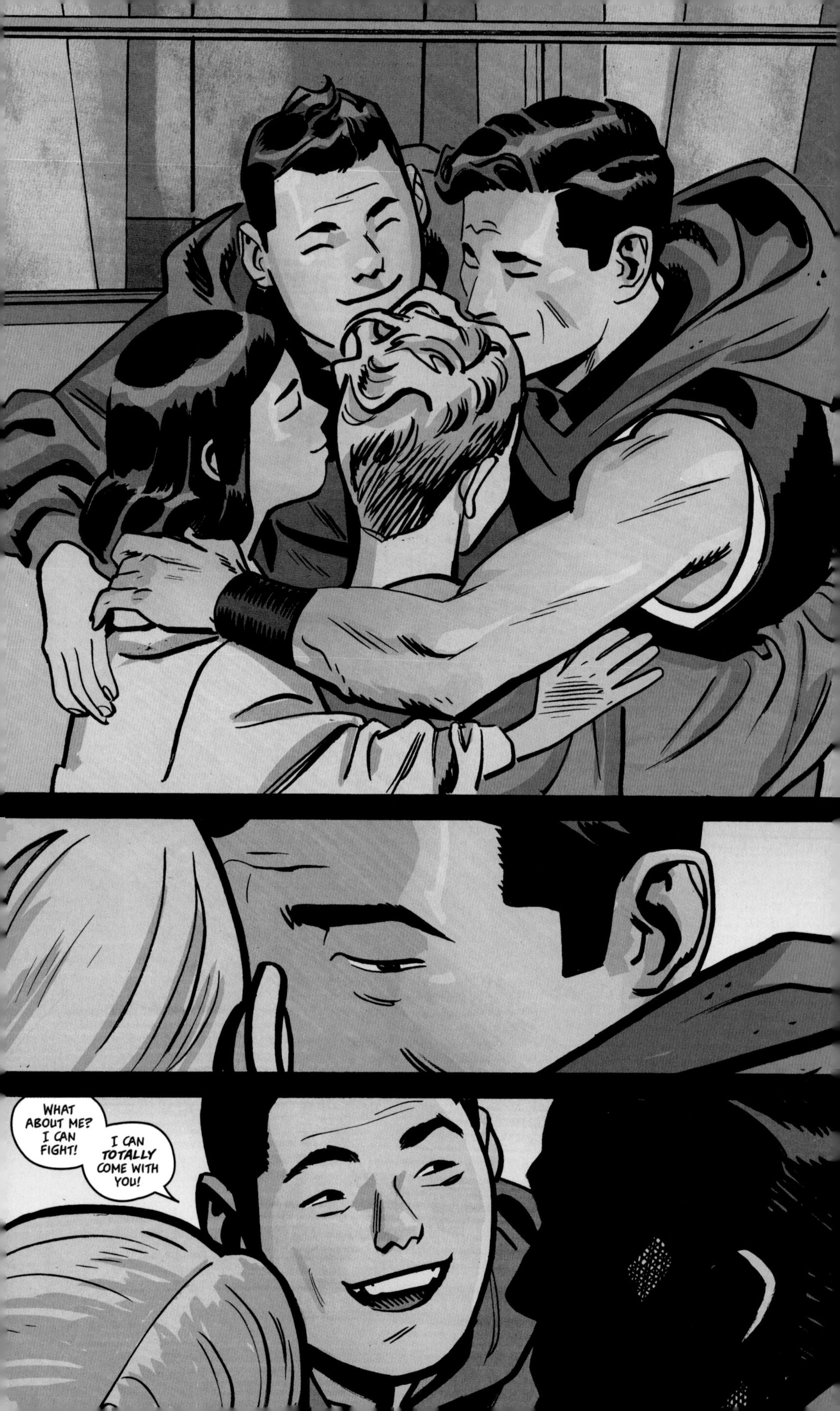
WHAT ABOUT ME? I CAN FIGHT!
I CAN TOTALLY COME WITH YOU!

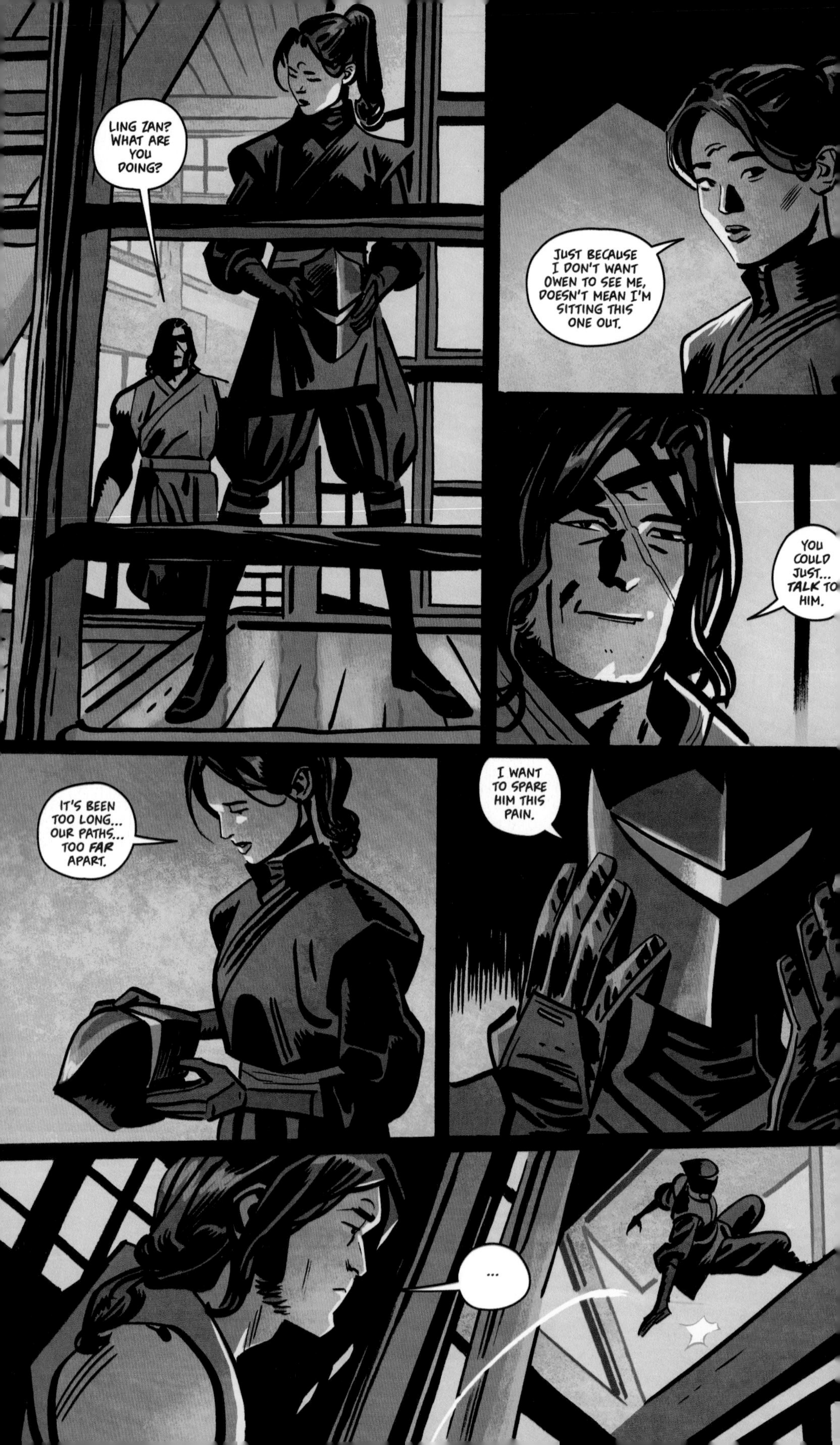
LING ZAN? WHAT ARE YOU DOING?
JUST BECAUSE I DON'T WANT OWEN TO SEE ME, DOESN'T MEAN I'M SITTING THIS ONE OUT.
YOU COULD JUST... TALK TO HIM.
IT'S BEEN TOO LONG... OUR PATHS... TOO FAR APART.
I WANT TO SPARE HIM THIS PAIN.
...

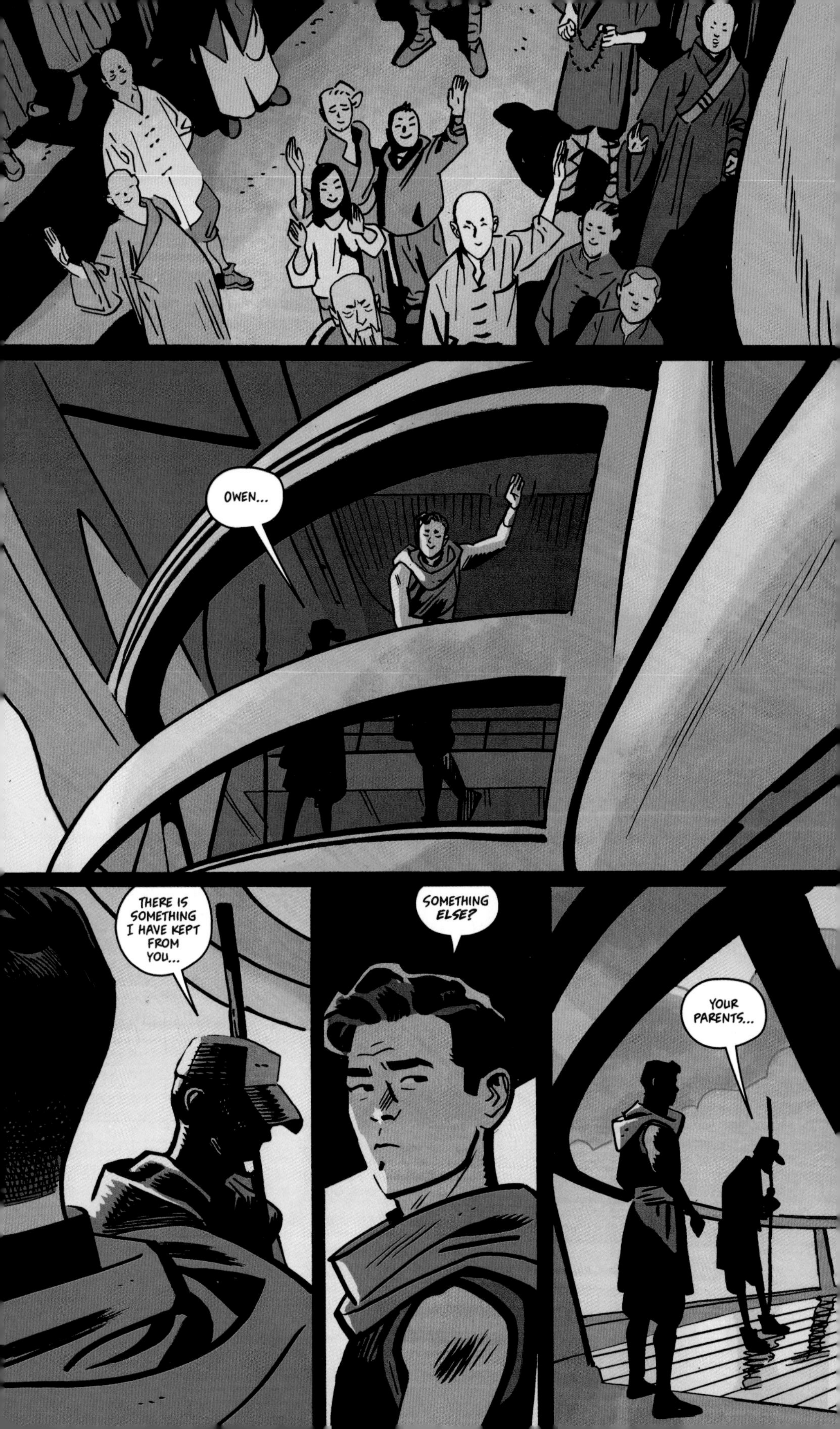
OWEN...
THERE IS SOMETHING I HAVE KEPT FROM YOU...
SOMETHING ELSE?
YOUR PARENTS...

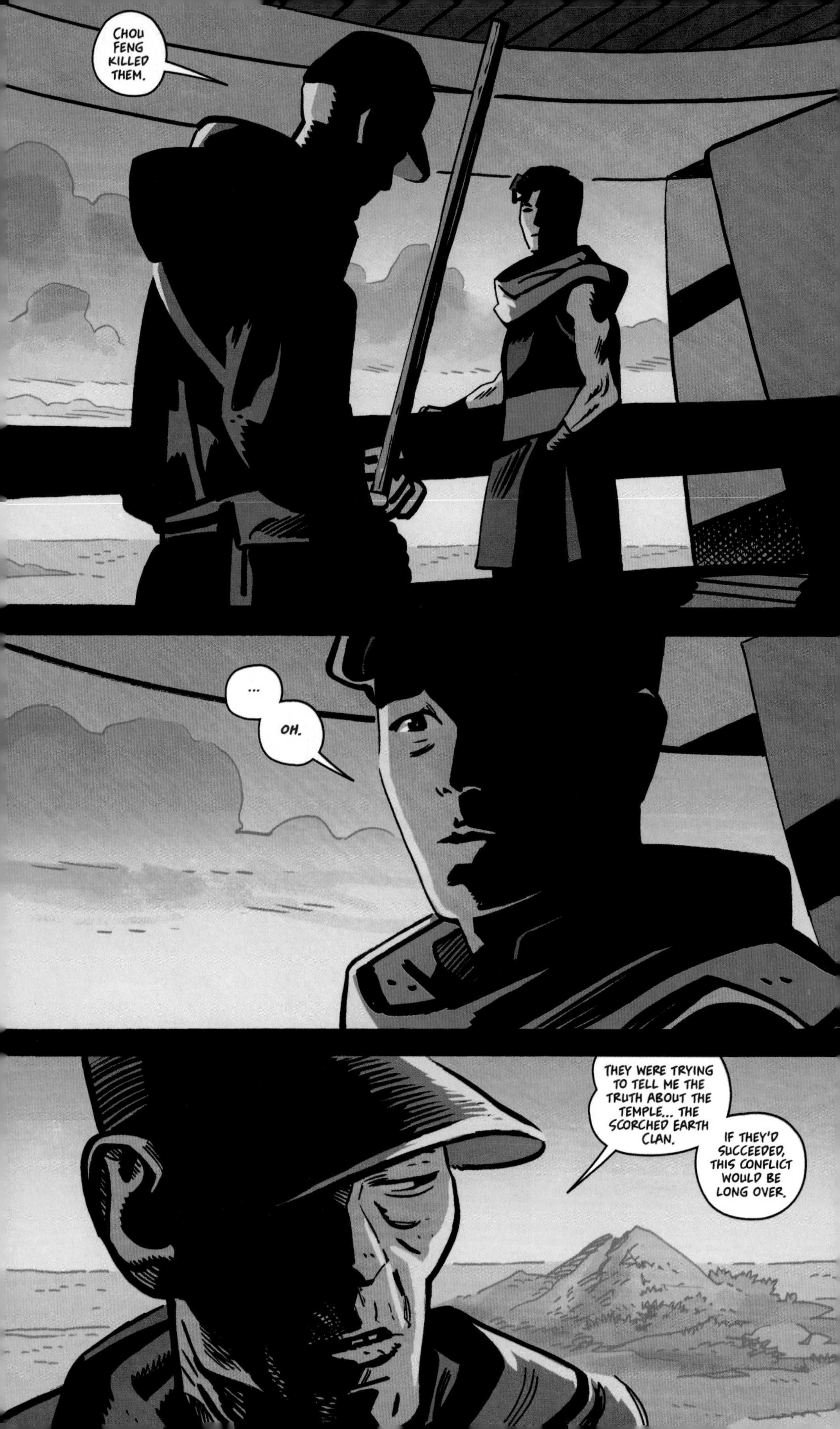

CHOU FENG KILLED THEM.
...
OH.
THEY WERE TRYING TO TELL ME THE TRUTH ABOUT THE TEMPLE... THE SCORCHED EARTH CLAN.
IF THEY'D SUCCEEDED, THIS CONFLICT WOULD BE LONG OVER.

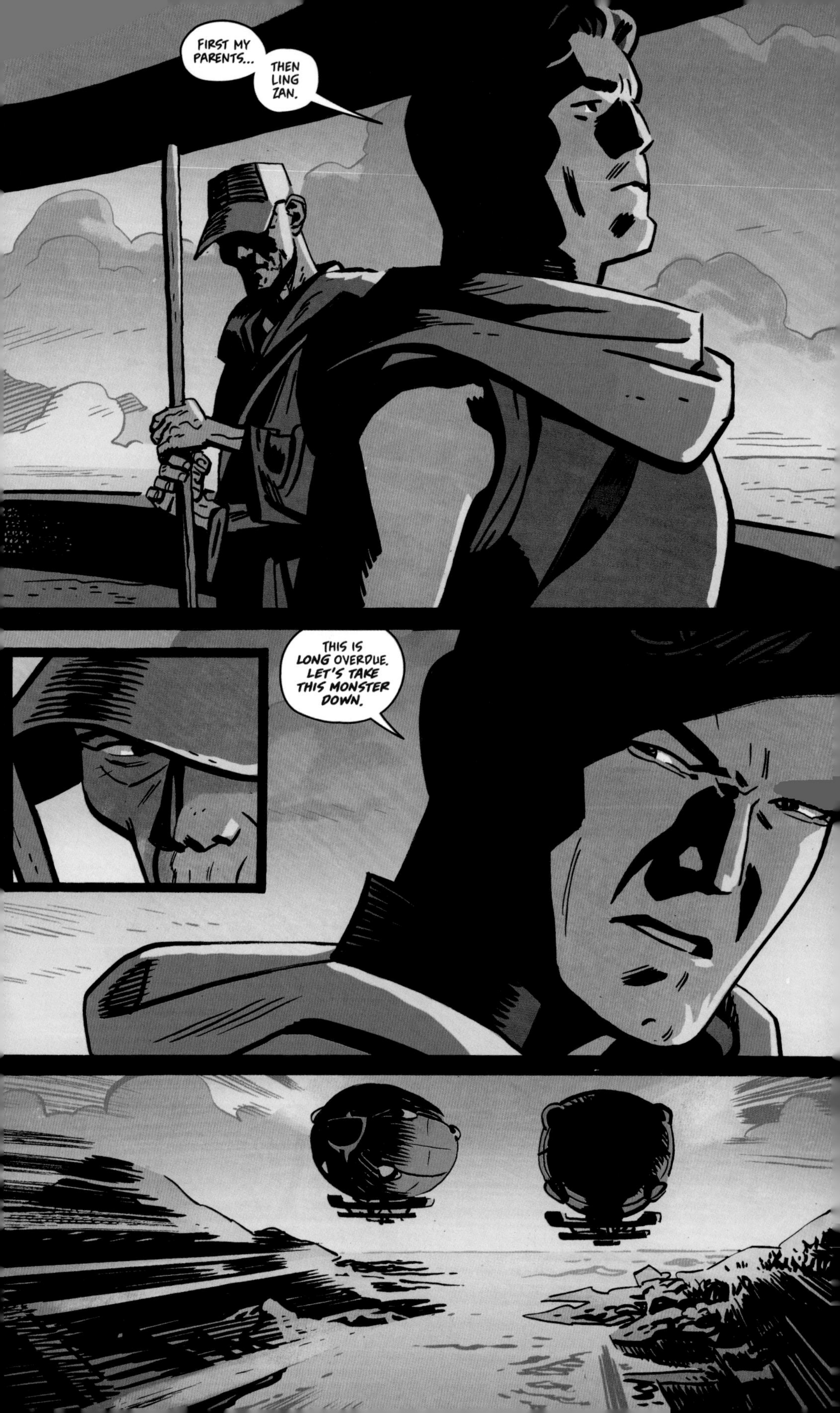
FIRST MY PARENTS...
THEN LING ZAN.
THIS IS LONG OVERDUE. LET'S TAKE THIS MONSTER DOWN.

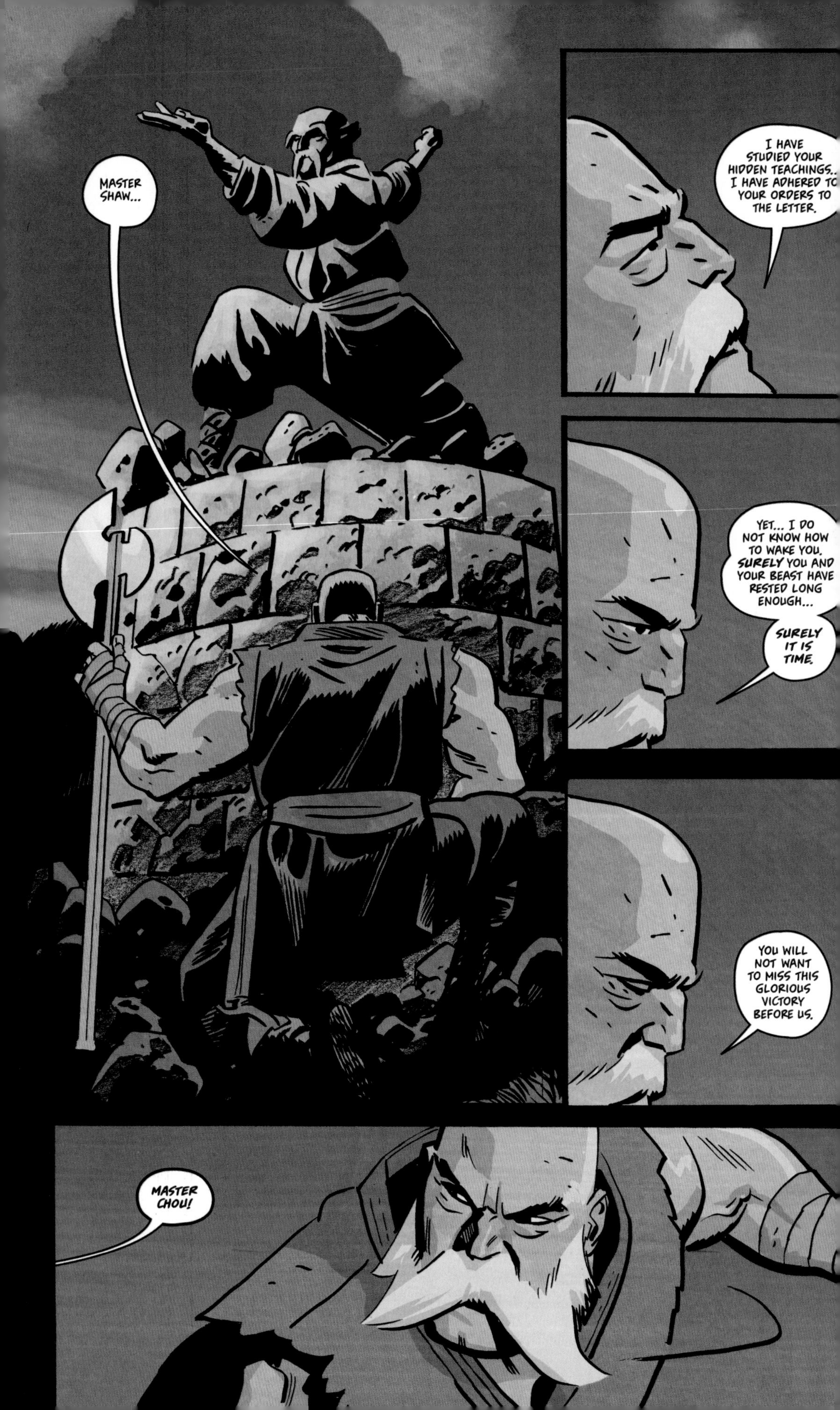
MASTER SHAW...
I HAVE STUDIED YOUR HIDDEN TEACHINGS... I HAVE ADHERED TO YOUR ORDERS TO THE LETTER.
YET... I DO NOT KNOW HOW TO WAKE YOU. SURELY YOU AND YOUR BEAST HAVE RESTED LONG ENOUGH...
SURELY IT IS TIME.
YOU WILL NOT WANT TO MISS THIS GLORIOUS VICTORY BEFORE US.
MASTER CHOU!

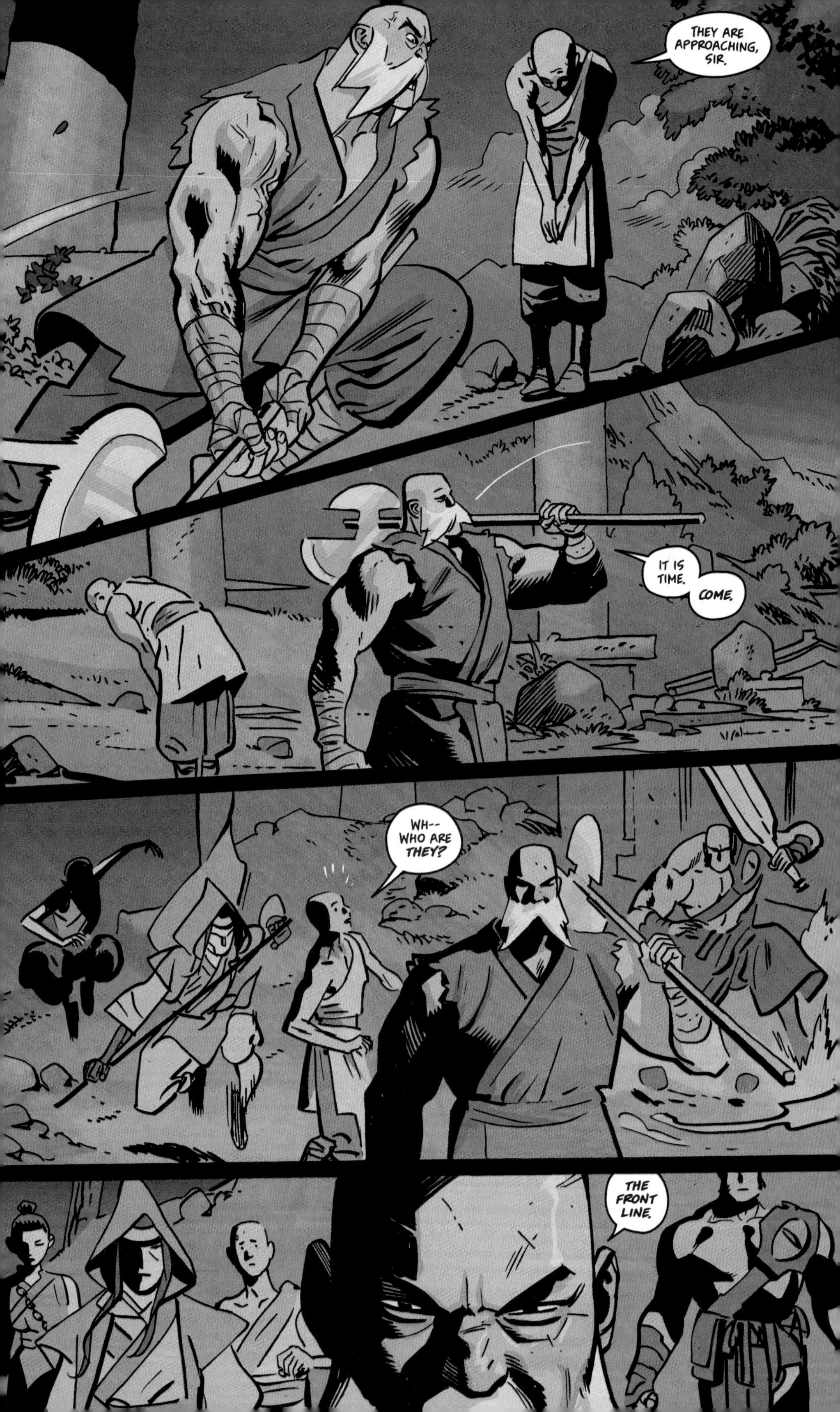
THEY ARE APPROACHING, SIR.
IT IS TIME.
COME.
WH-- WHO ARE THEY?
THE FRONT LINE.

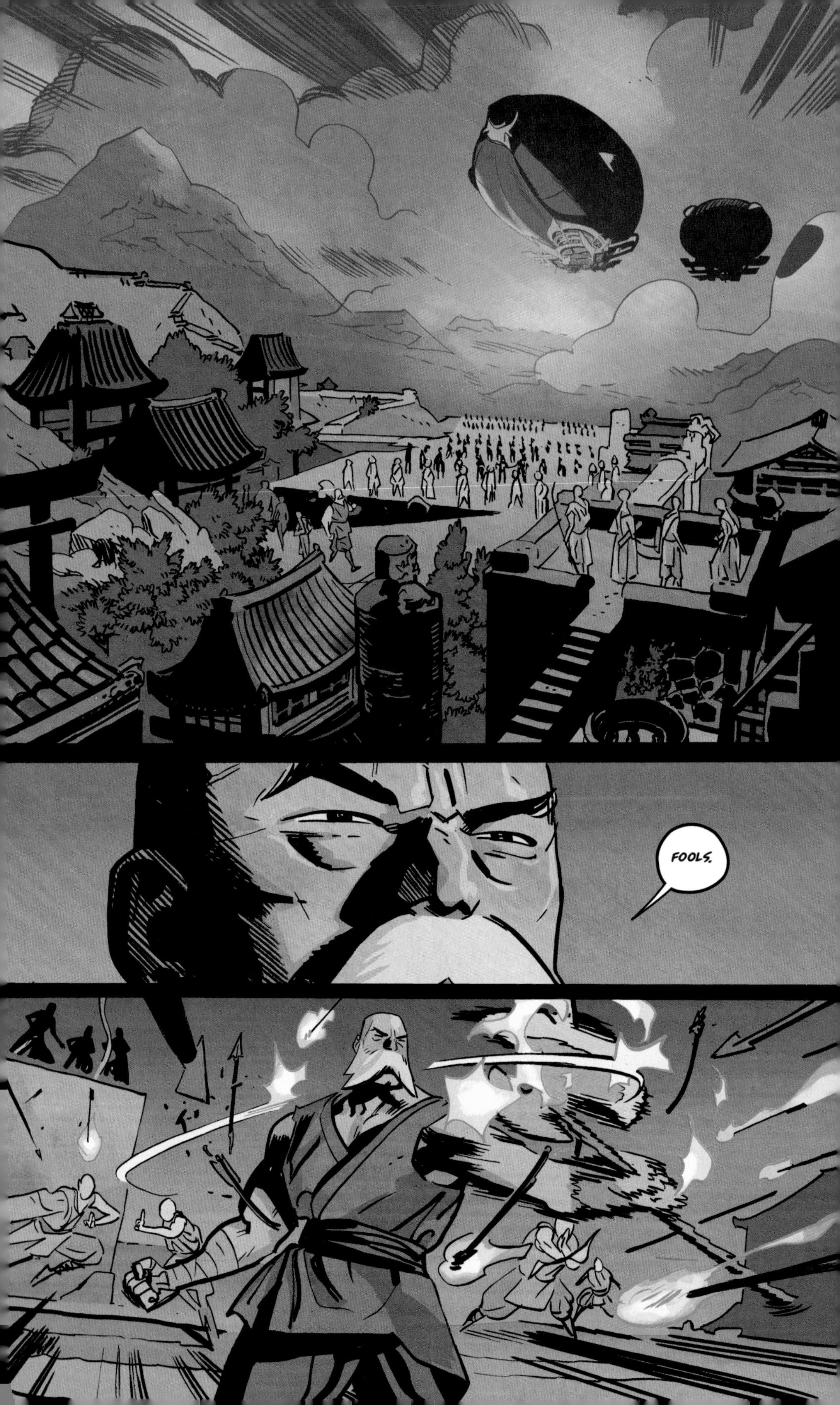
FOOLS.

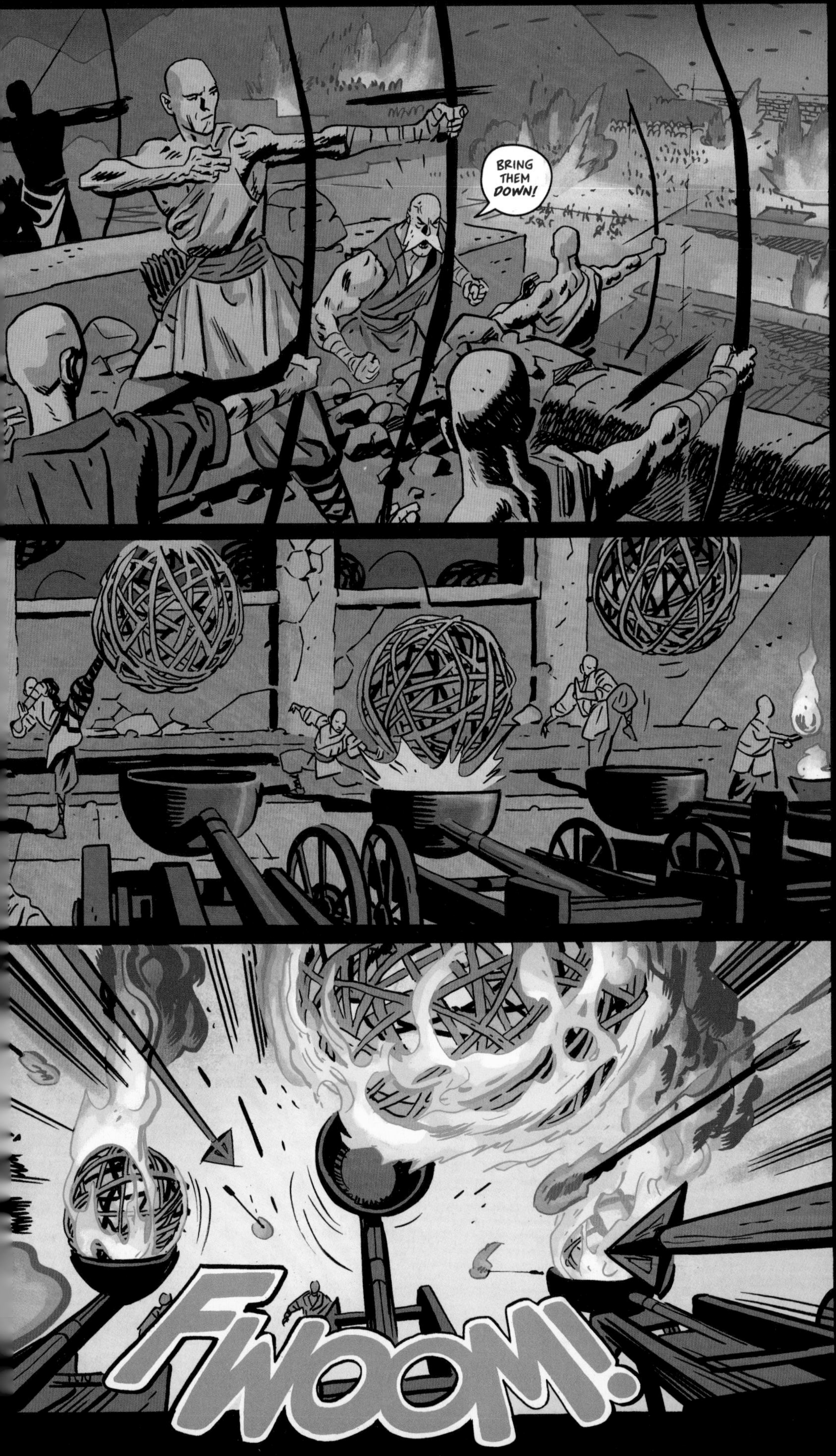
BRING THEM DOWN!
FWOOM!

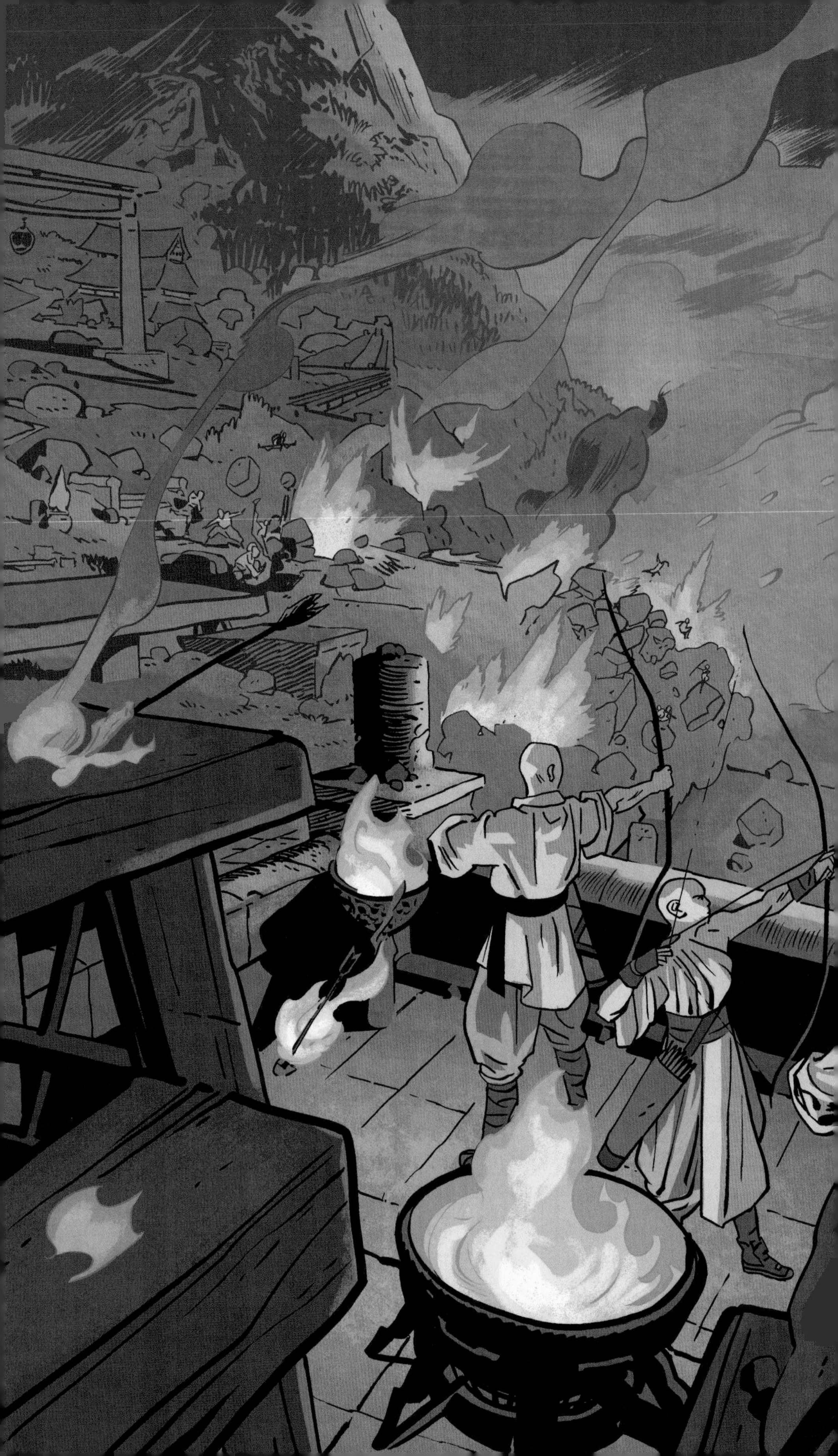

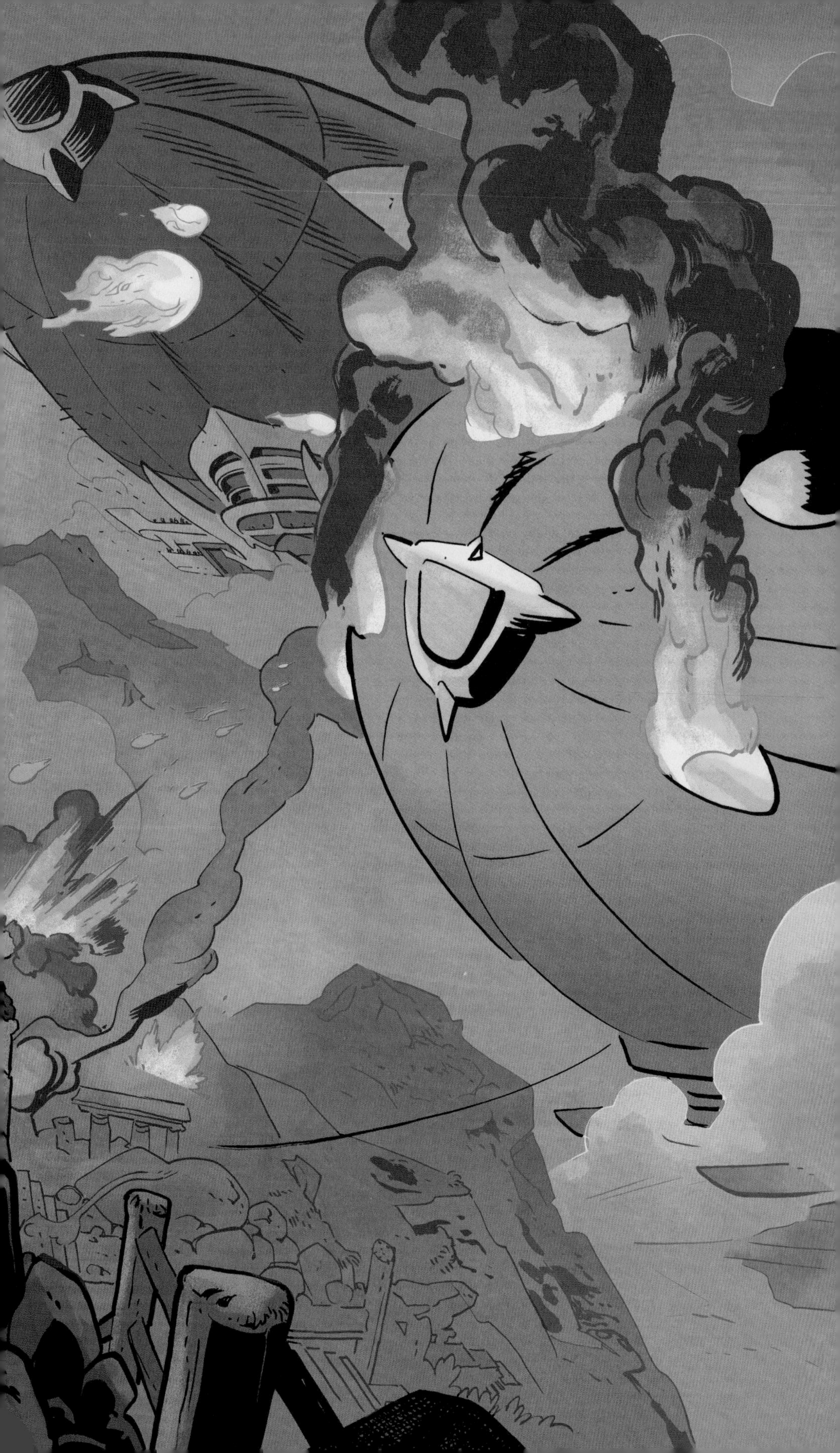

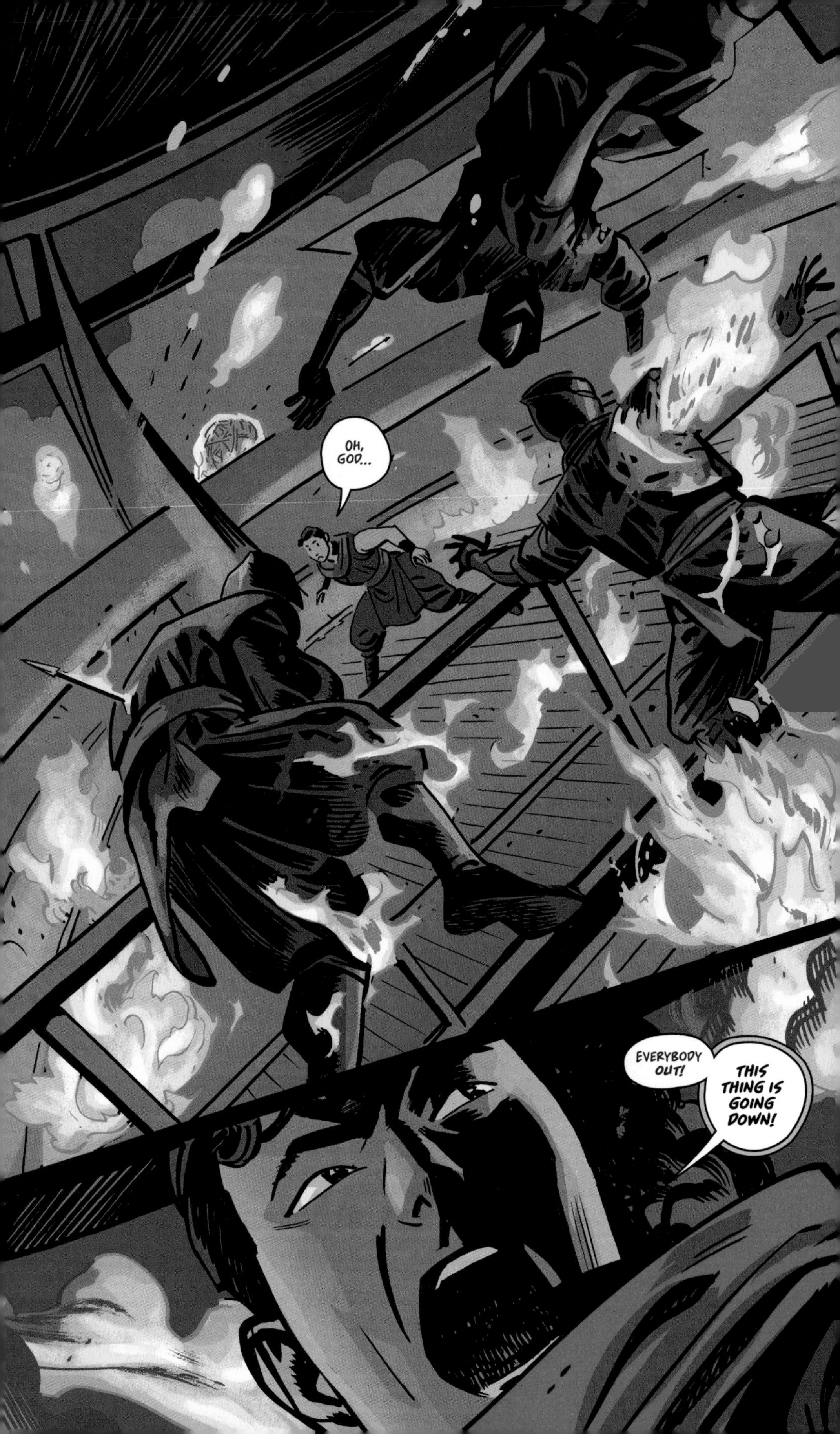
OH, GOD...
EVERYBODY OUT!
THIS THING IS GOING DOWN!

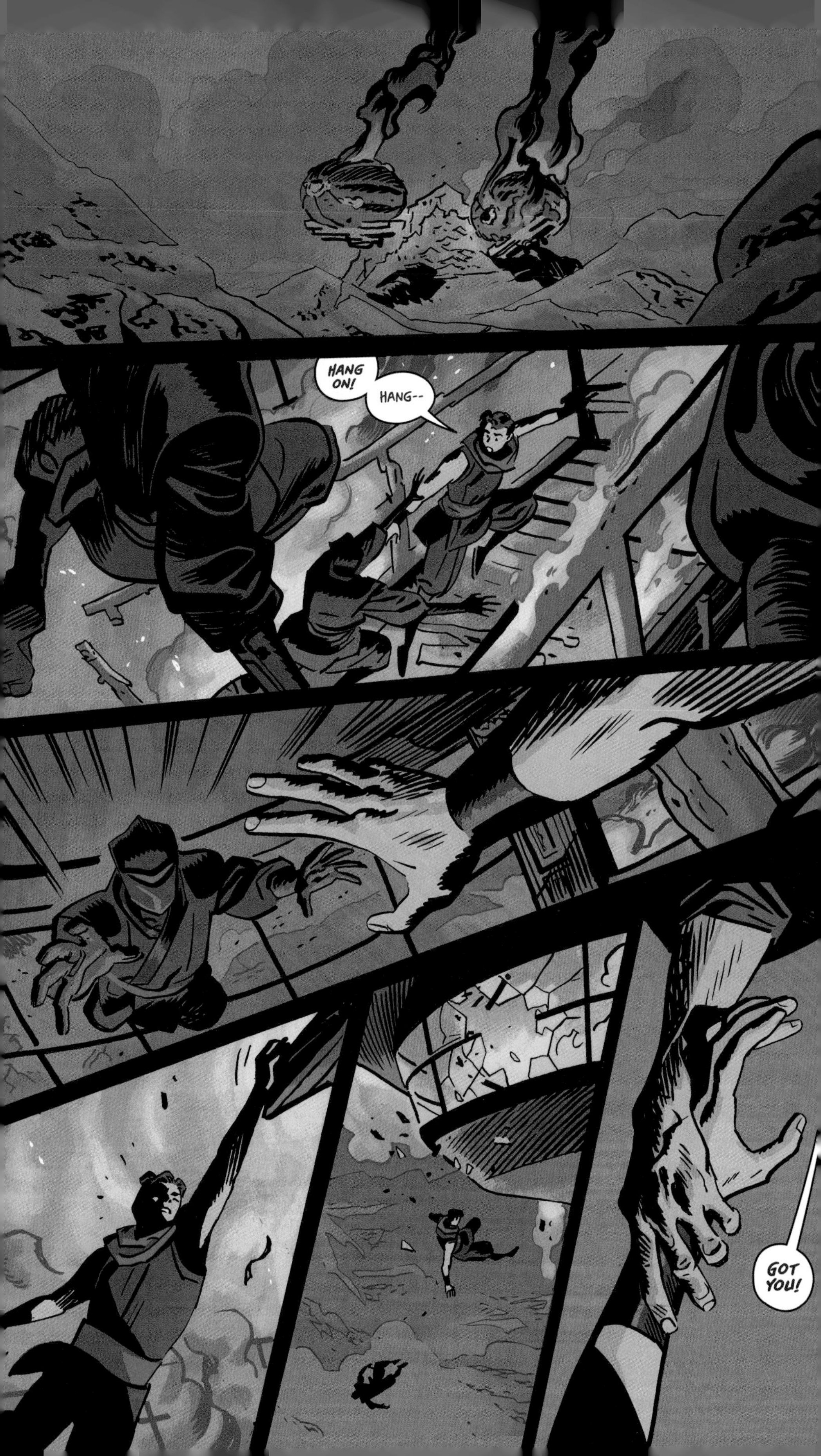
HANG ON!
HANG--
GOT YOU!

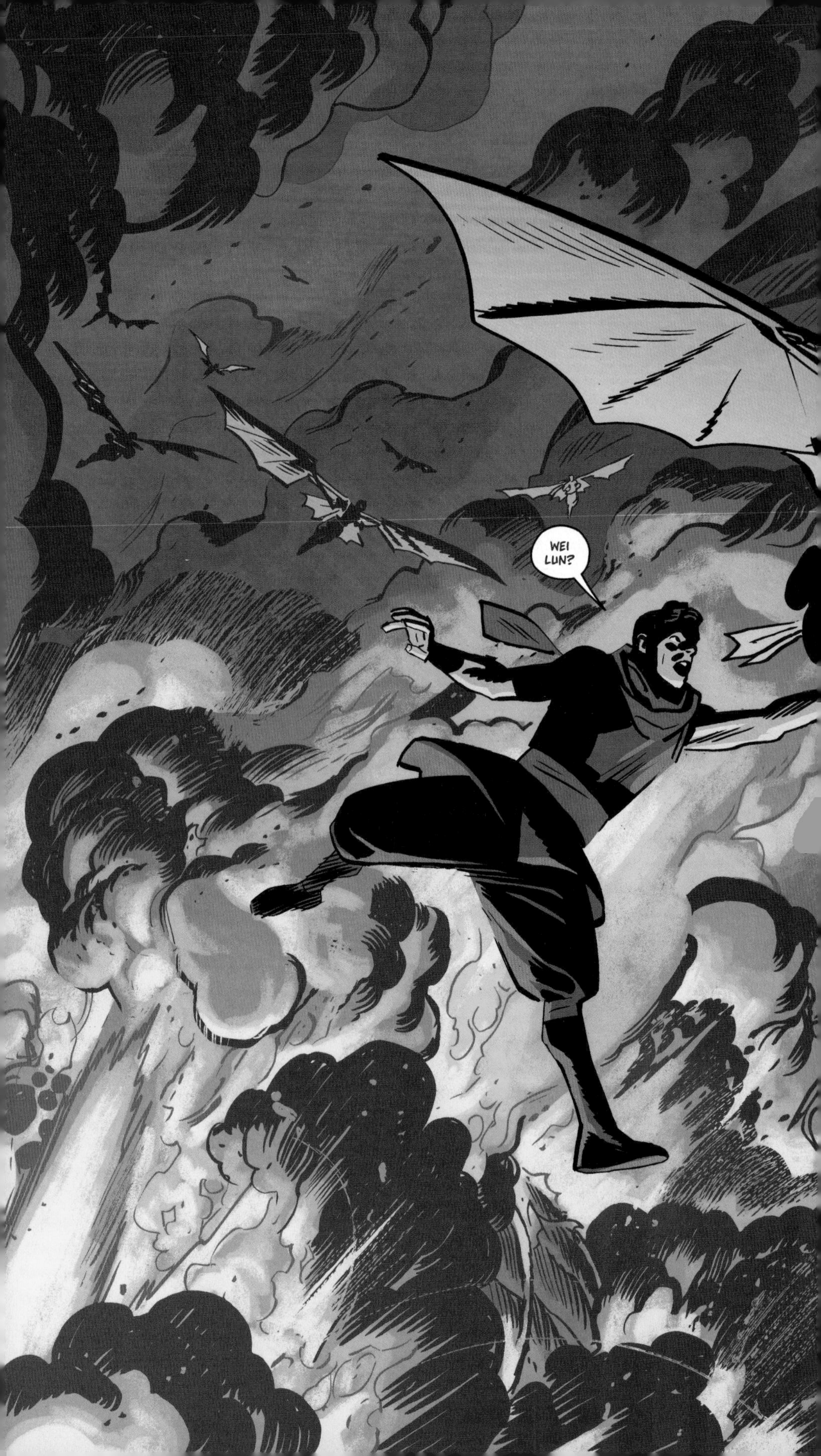
WEI LUN?

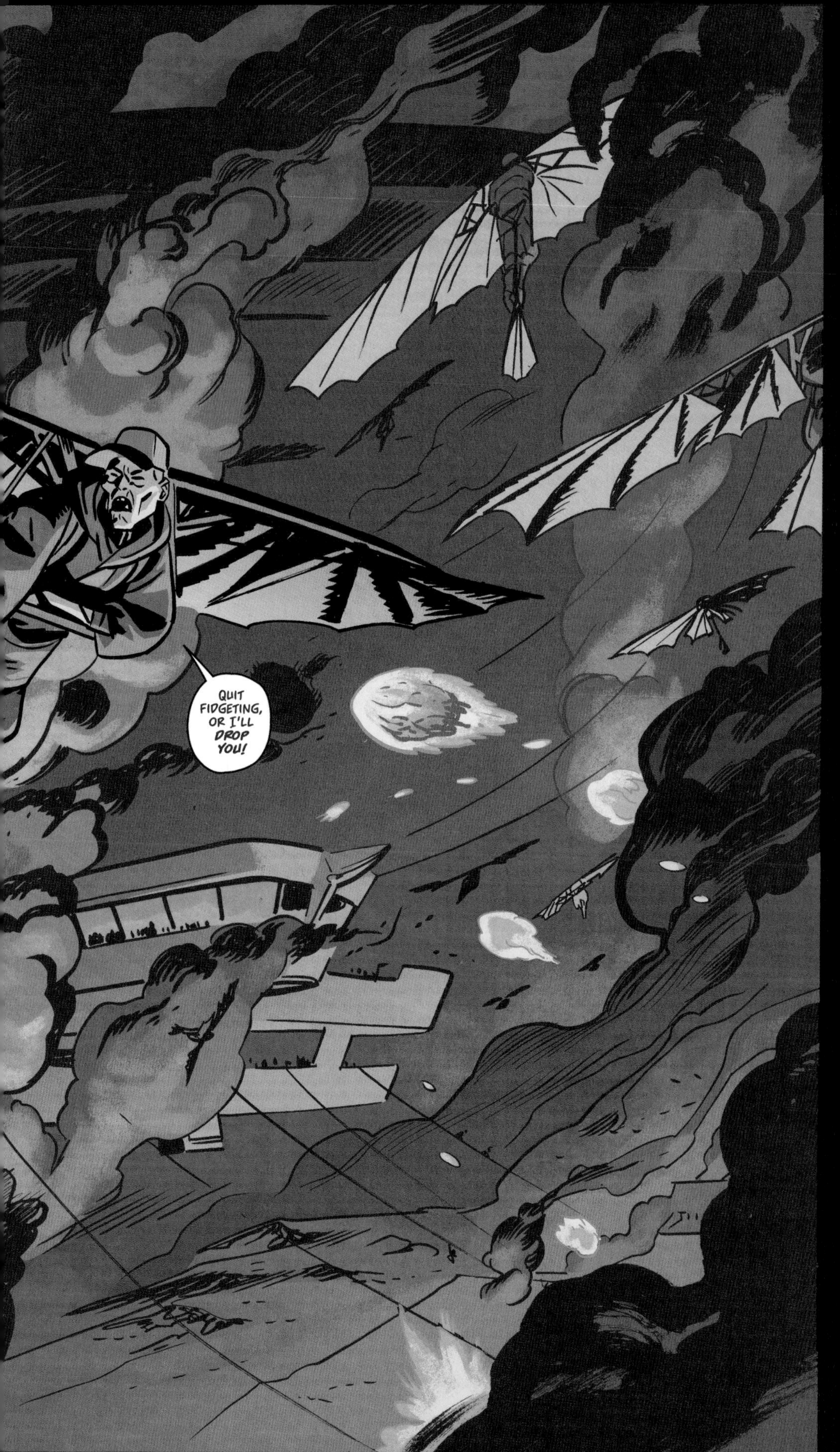
QUIT FIDGETING, OR I'LL DROP YOU!

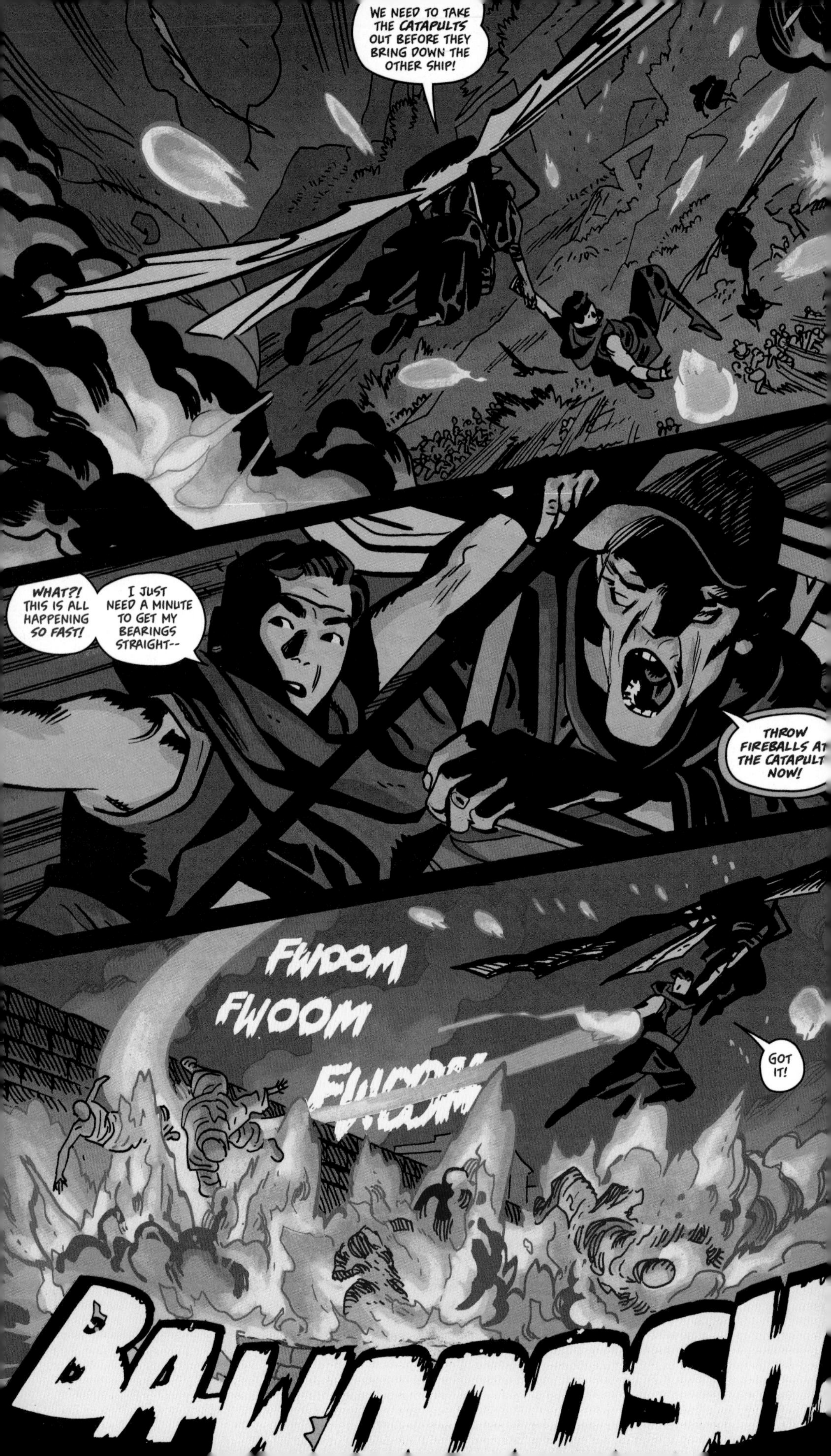
WE NEED TO TAKE THE CATAPULTS OUT BEFORE THEY BRING DOWN THE OTHER SHIP!
WHAT?! THIS IS ALL HAPPENING SO FAST!
I JUST NEED A MINUTE TO GET MY BEARINGS STRAIGHT--
THROW FIREBALLS AT THE CATAPULT NOW!
FWOOM
FWOOM
GOT IT!

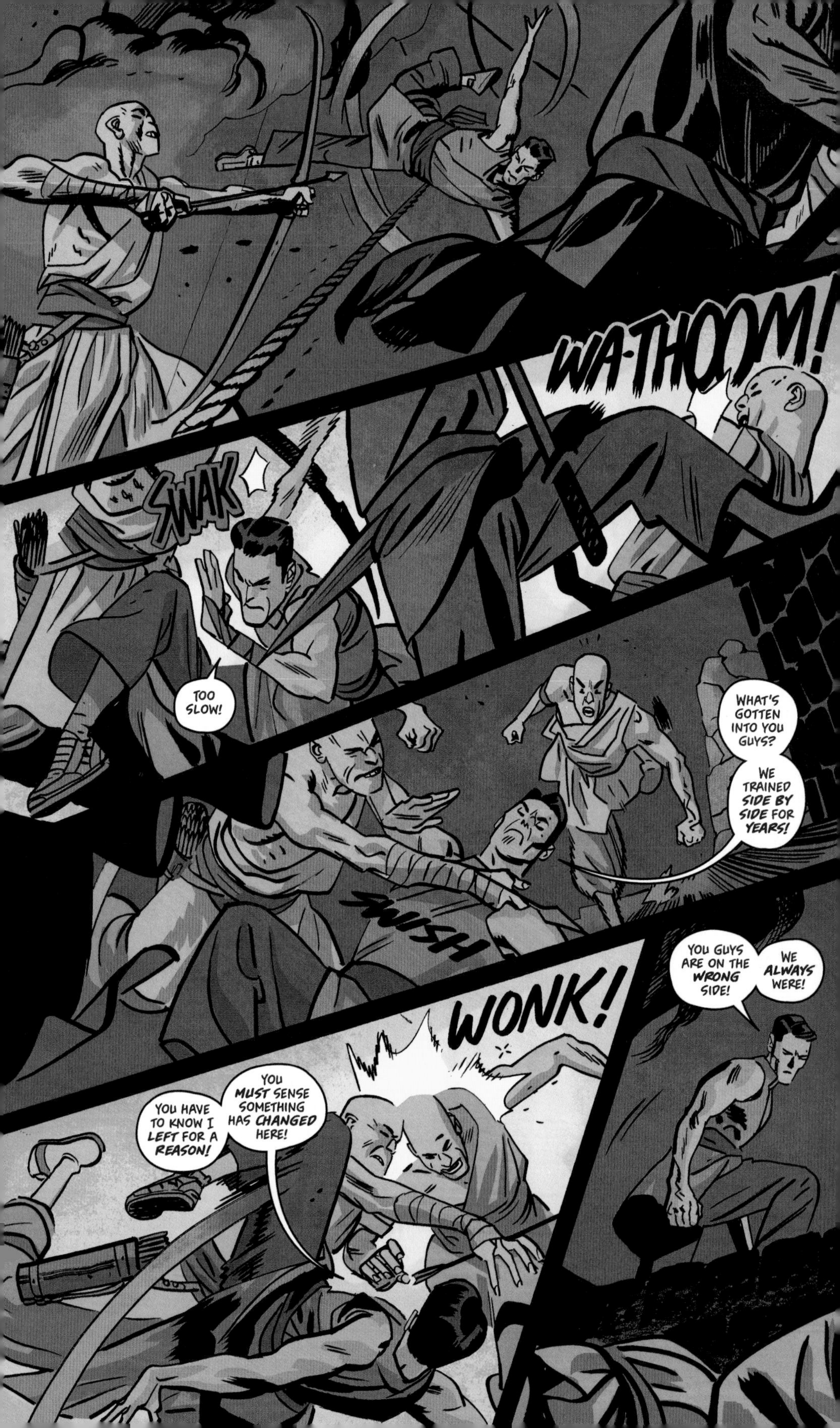
WA-THOOM!
SWAK
TOO SLOW!
WHAT'S GOTTEN INTO YOU GUYS?
WE TRAINED SIDE BY SIDE FOR YEARS!
SWISH
YOU GUYS ARE ON THE WRONG SIDE!
WE ALWAYS WERE!
WONK!
YOU HAVE TO KNOW I LEFT FOR A REASON!
YOU MUST SENSE SOMETHING HAS CHANGED HERE!

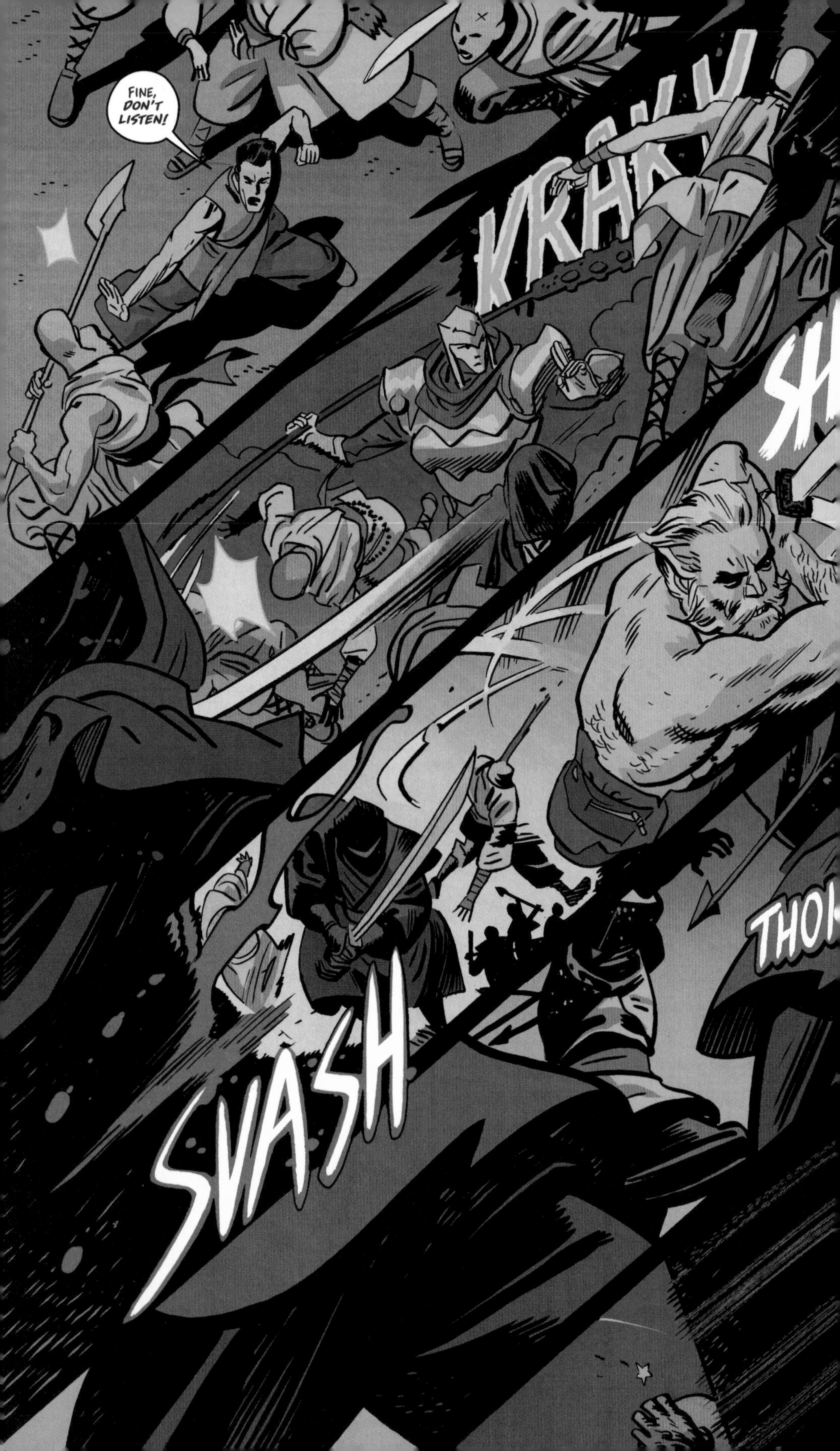
FINE, DON'T LISTEN!
KRAKK
SVASH
THOI

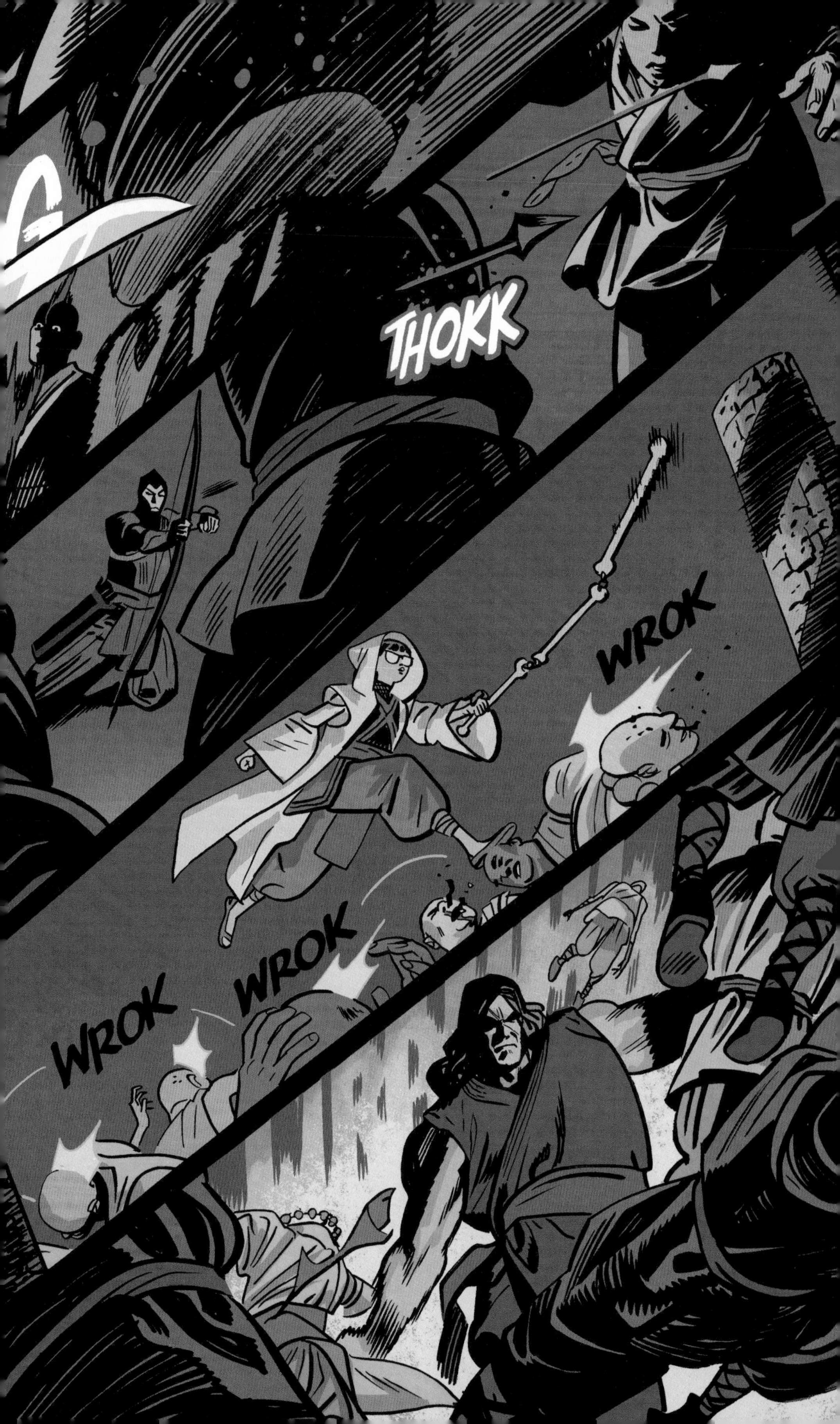
THOKK
WROK
WROK
WROK

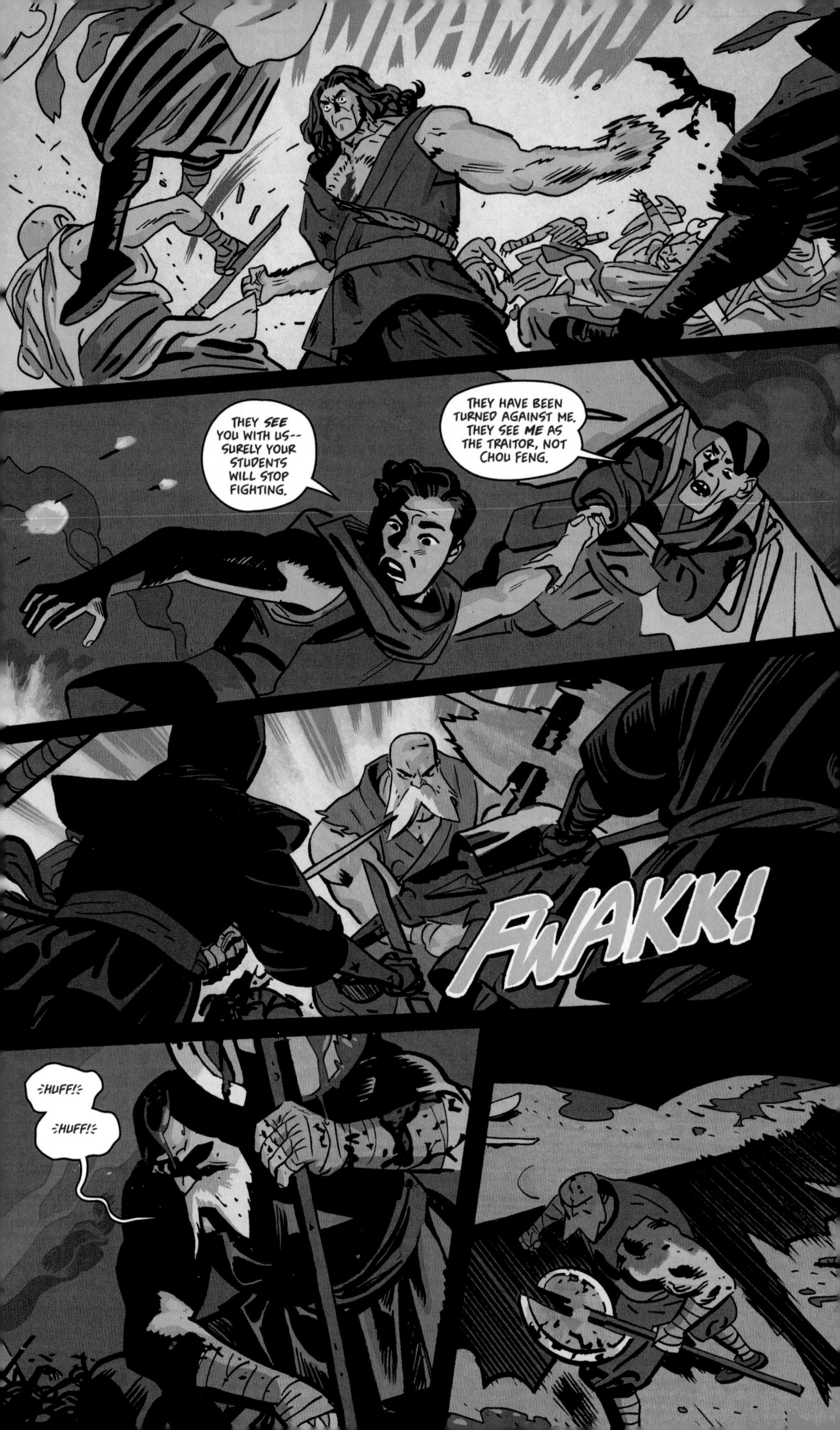

THEY SEE YOU WITH US-- SURELY YOUR STUDENTS WILL STOP FIGHTING.
THEY HAVE BEEN TURNED AGAINST ME. THEY SEE ME AS THE TRAITOR, NOT CHOU FENG.
FWAKK!
HUFF!
HUFF!

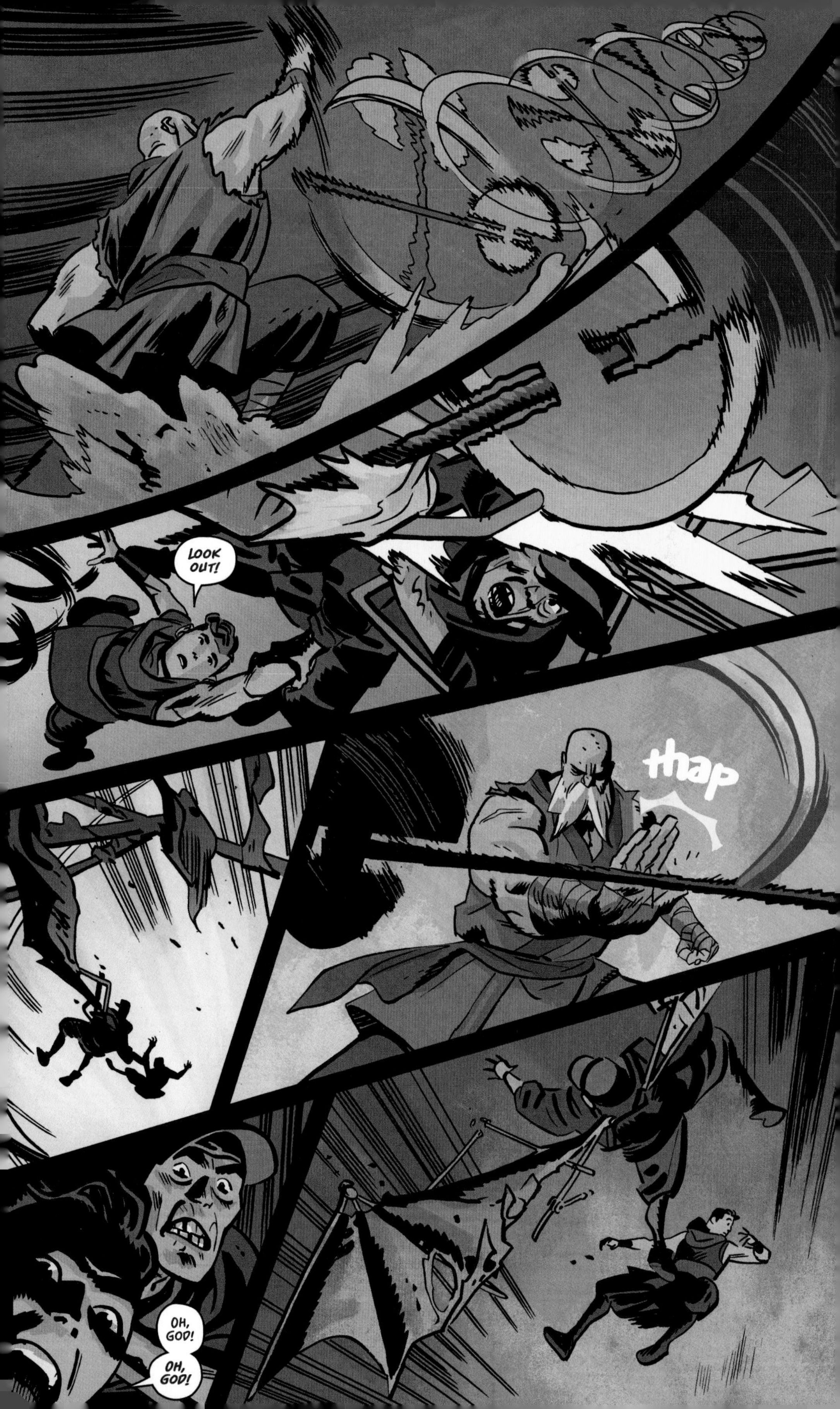
LOOK OUT!
thap
OH, GOD!
OH, GOD!

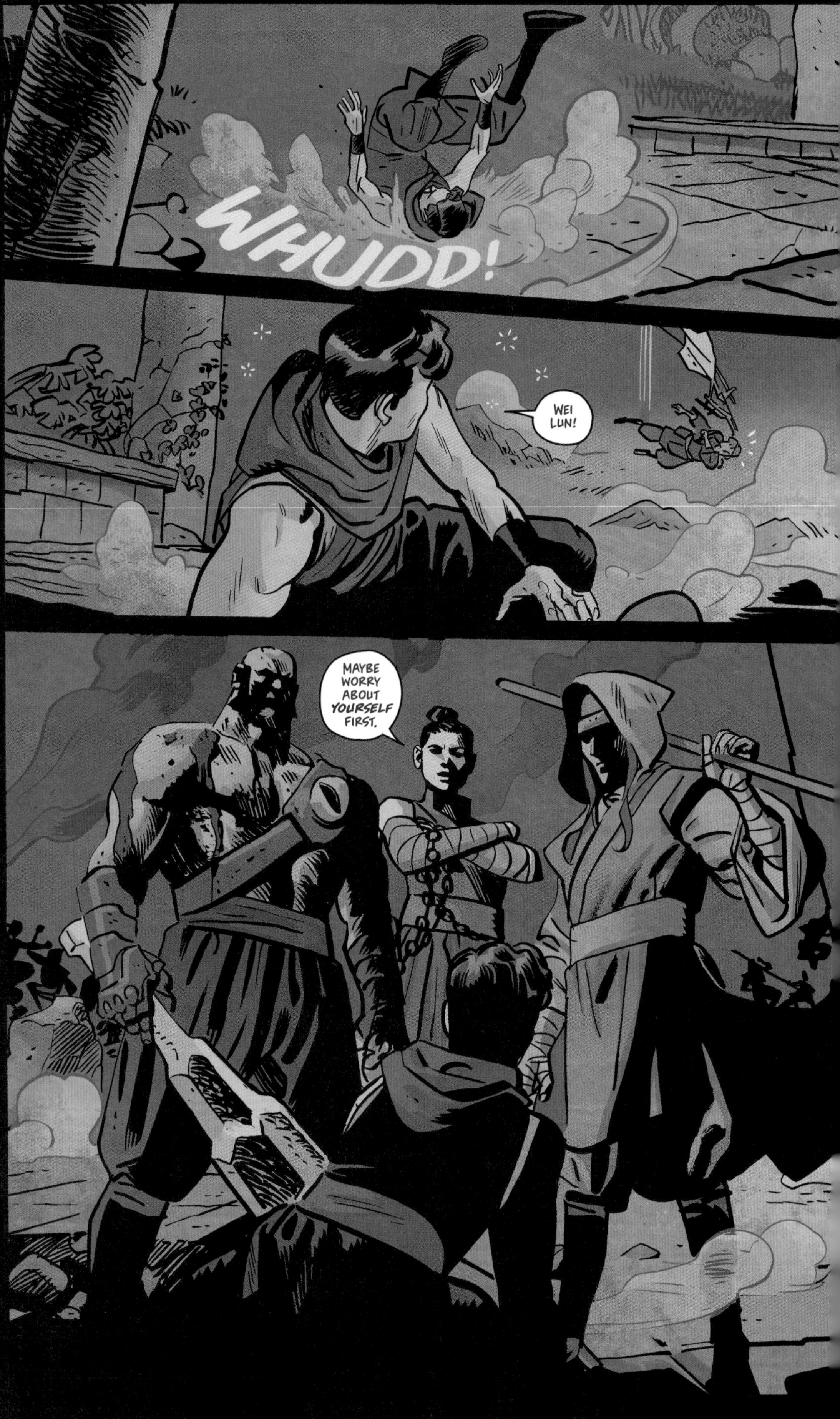
WHUDD!
WEI LUN!
MAYBE WORRY ABOUT YOURSELF FIRST.

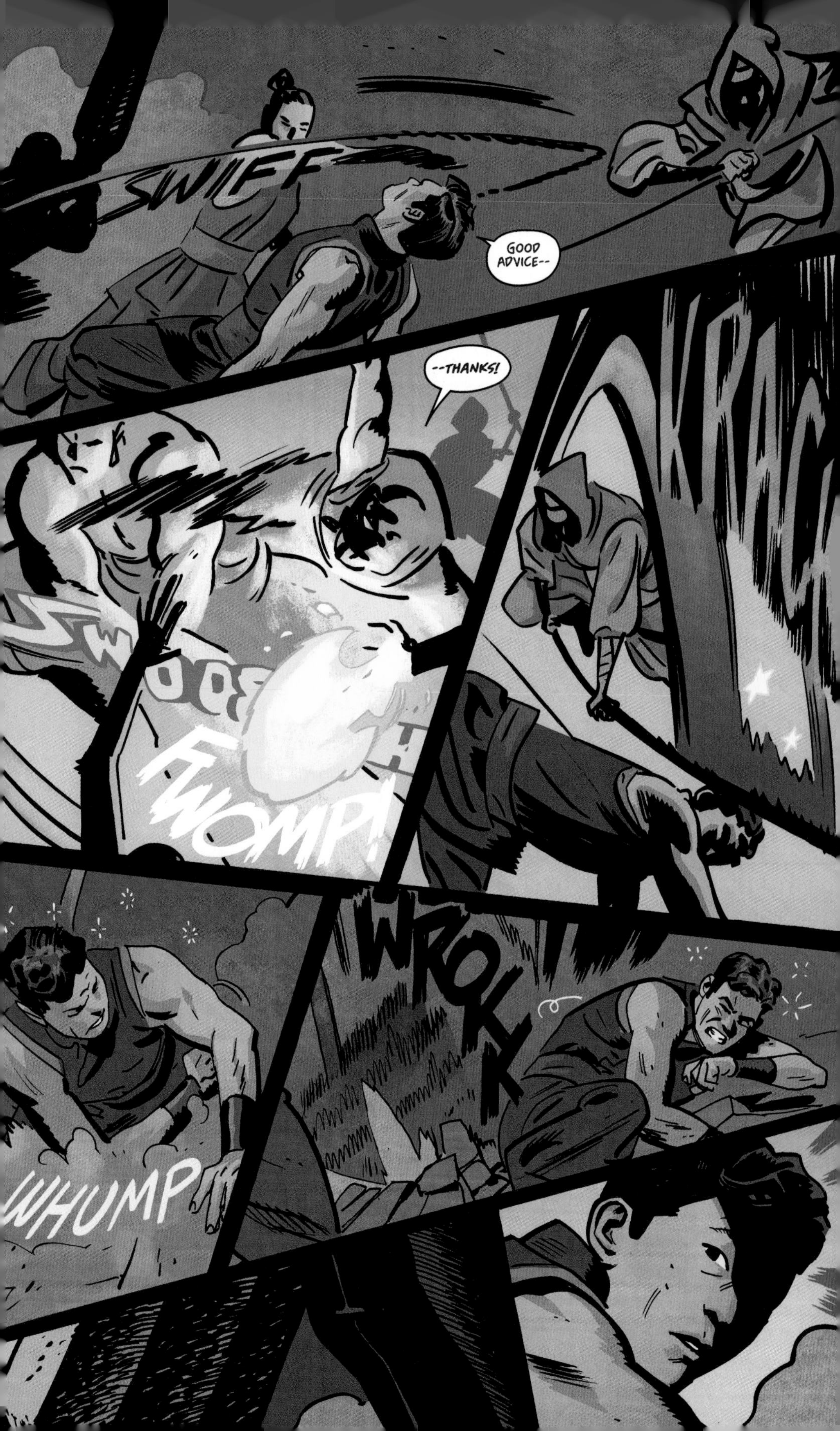
SWIFF
GOOD ADVICE--
--THANKS!
KRACK
SWOOSH
FWOMP!
WHUMP
WROKK

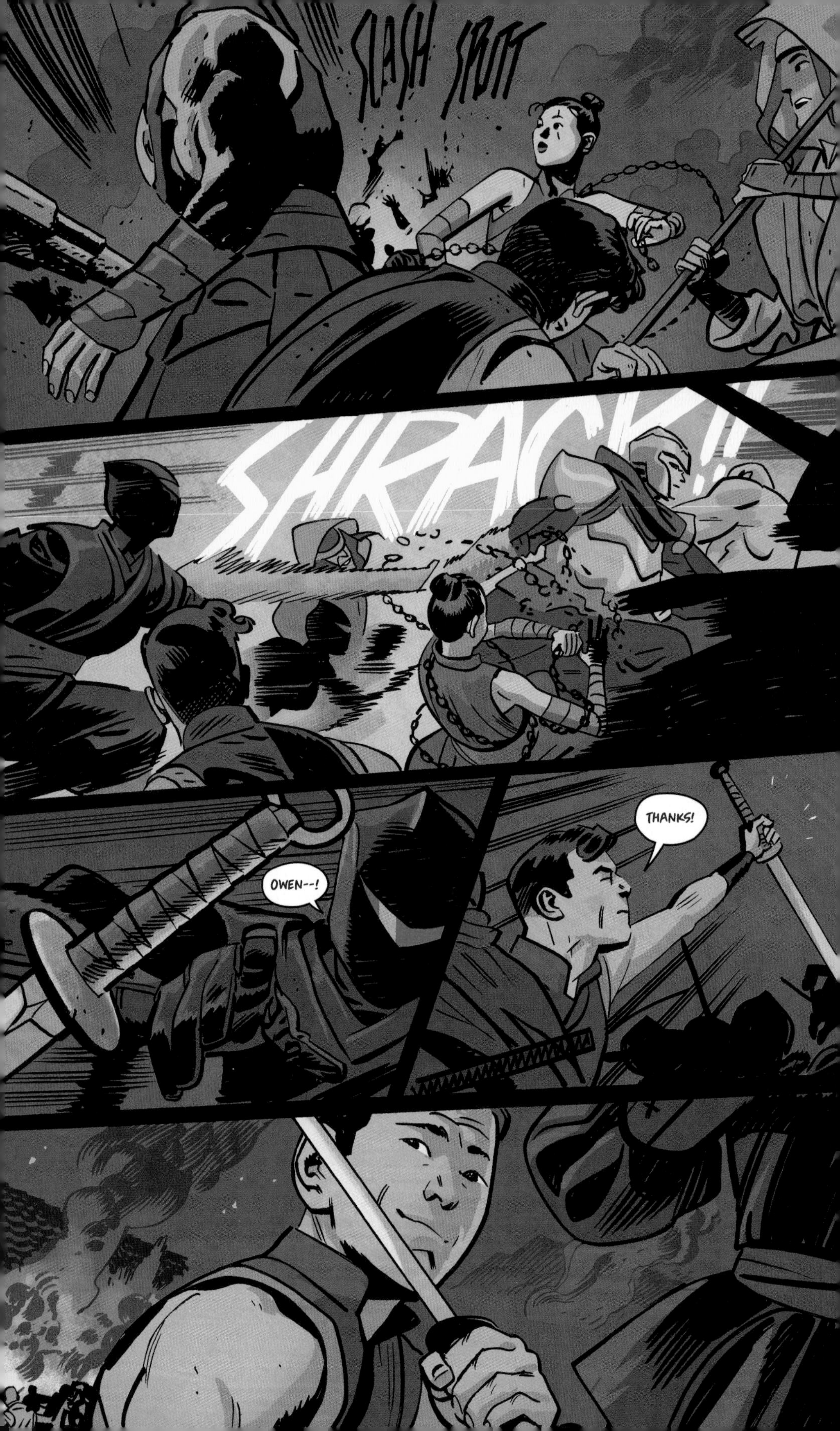
SLASH
SPLUTT
SHRACK!!
OWEN--!
THANKS!

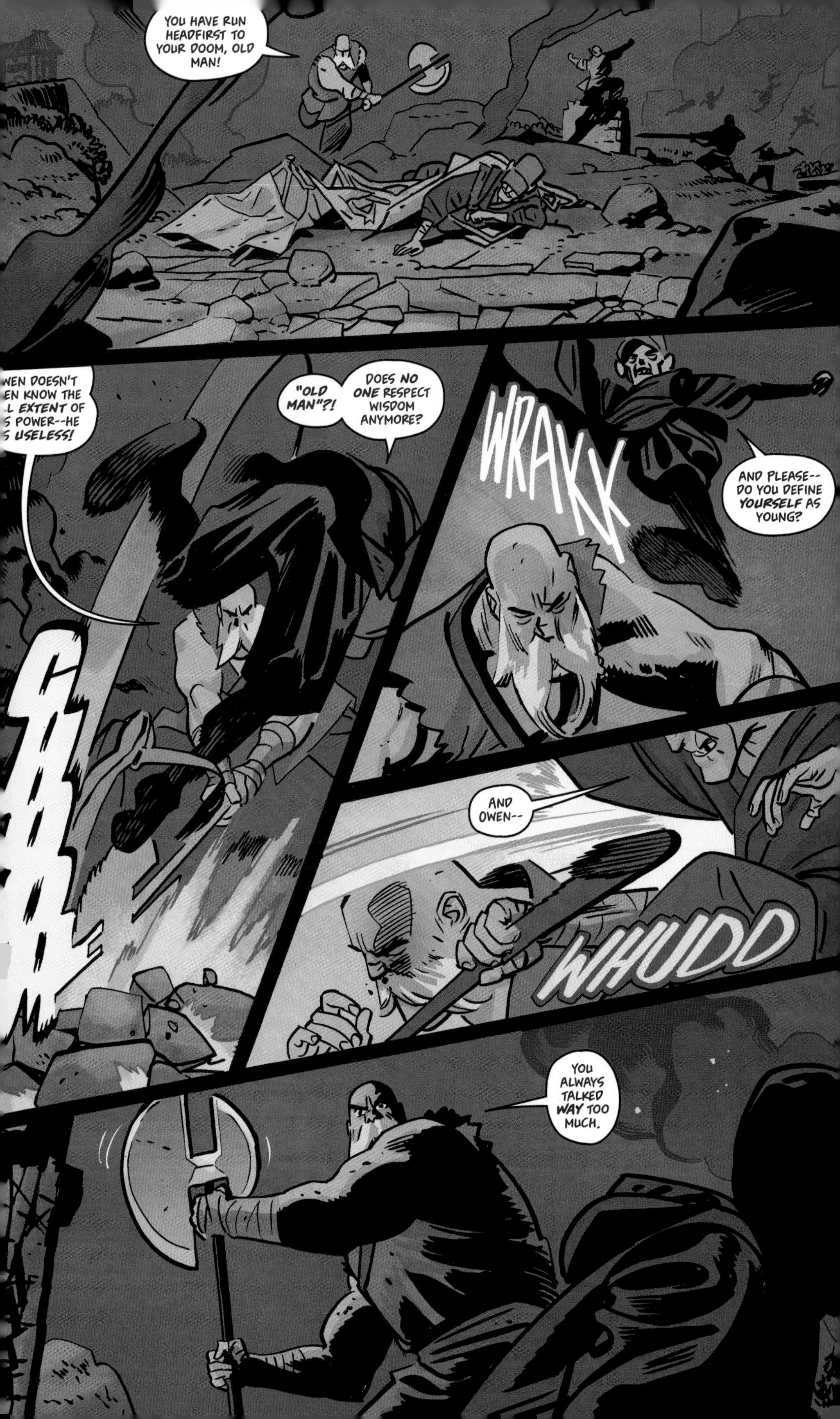
YOU HAVE RUN HEADFIRST TO YOUR DOOM, OLD MAN!
WEN DOESN'T EN KNOW THE L EXTENT OF S POWER--HE S USELESS!
"OLD MAN"?!
DOES NO ONE RESPECT WISDOM ANYMORE?
WRAKK
AND PLEASE-- DO YOU DEFINE YOURSELF AS YOUNG?
AND OWEN--
WHUDD
YOU ALWAYS TALKED WAY TOO MUCH.

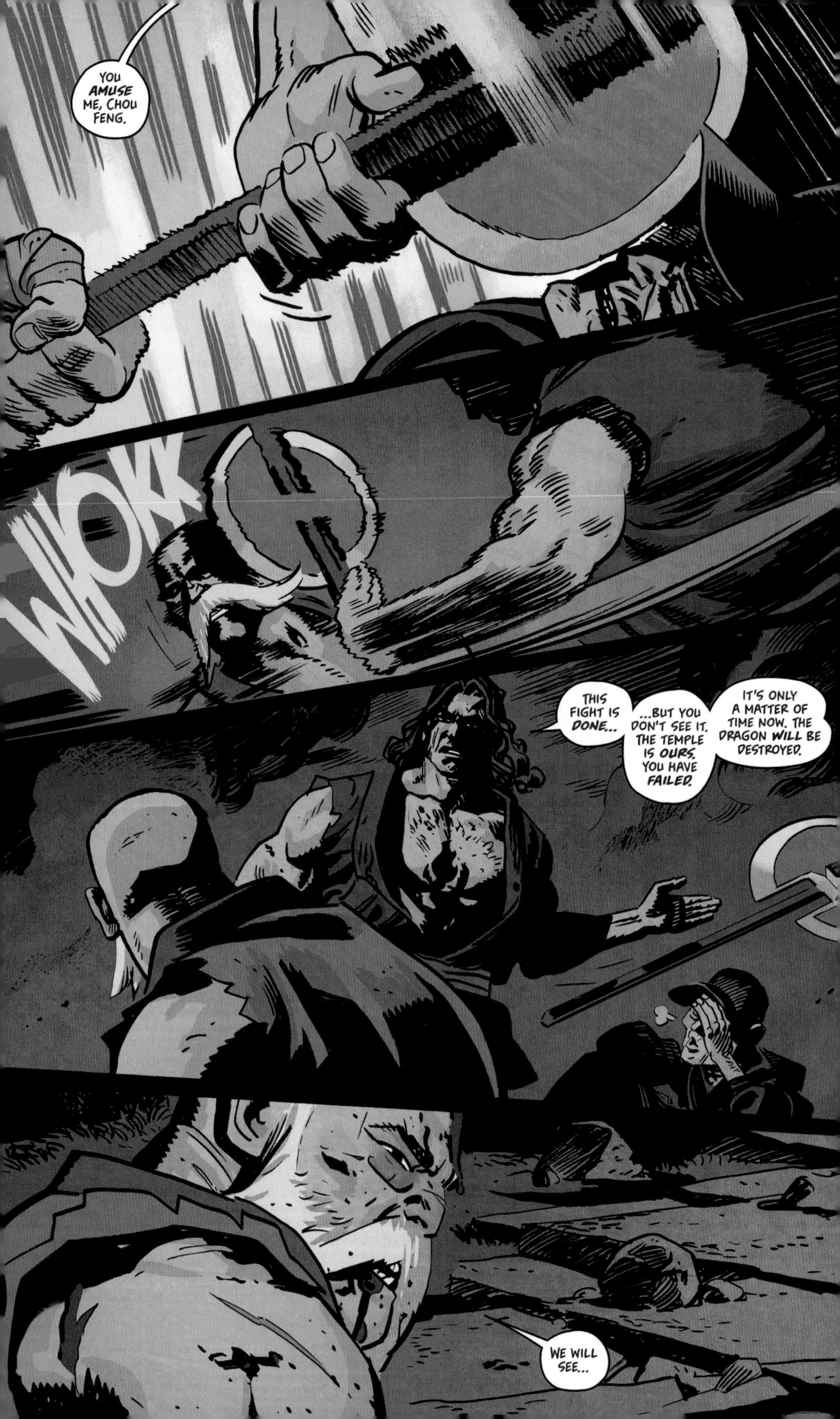
YOU AMUSE ME, CHOU FENG.
WOK
THIS FIGHT IS DONE...
...BUT YOU DON'T SEE IT. THE TEMPLE IS OURS. YOU HAVE FAILED.
IT'S ONLY A MATTER OF TIME NOW. THE DRAGON WILL BE DESTROYED.
WE WILL SEE...

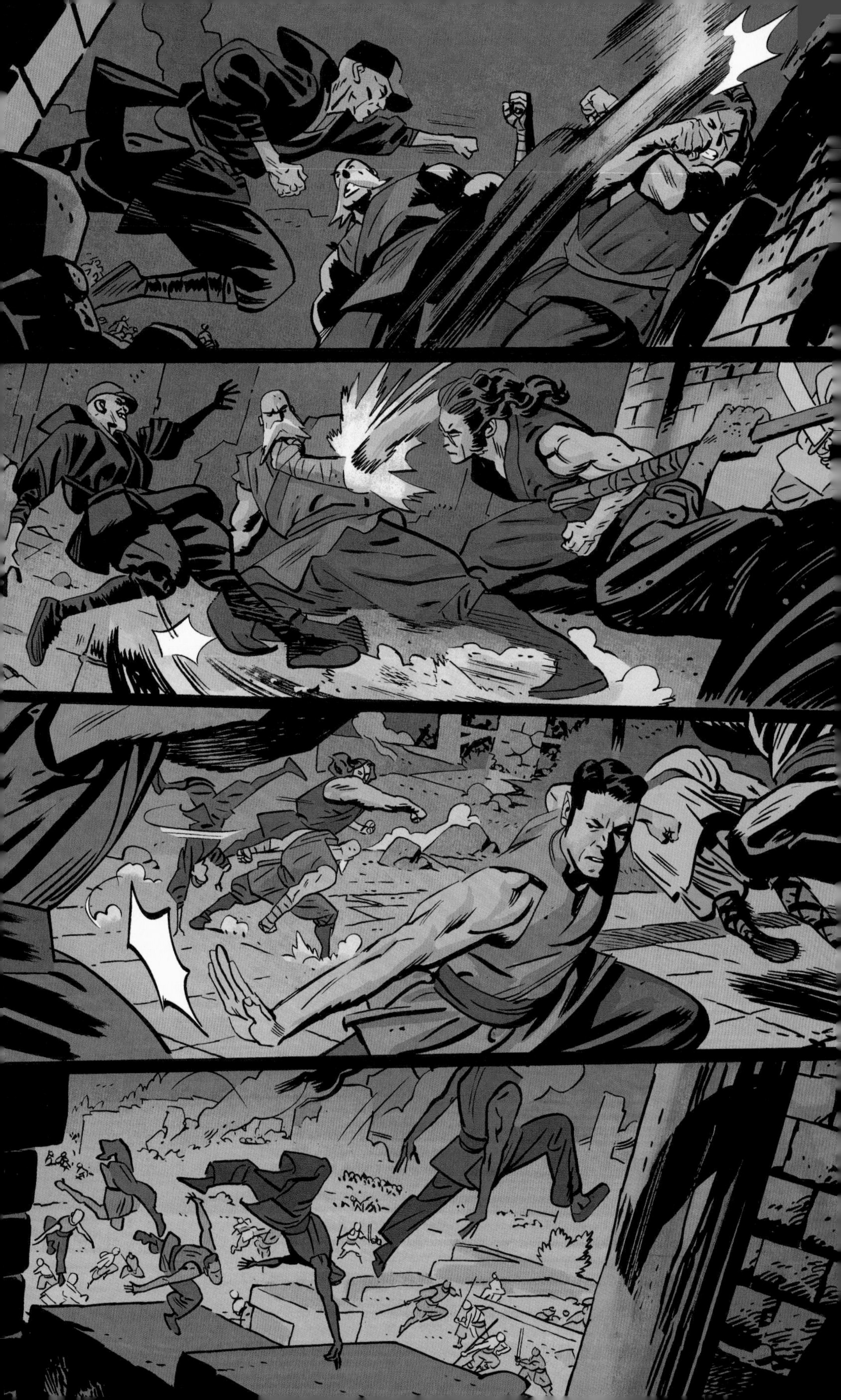

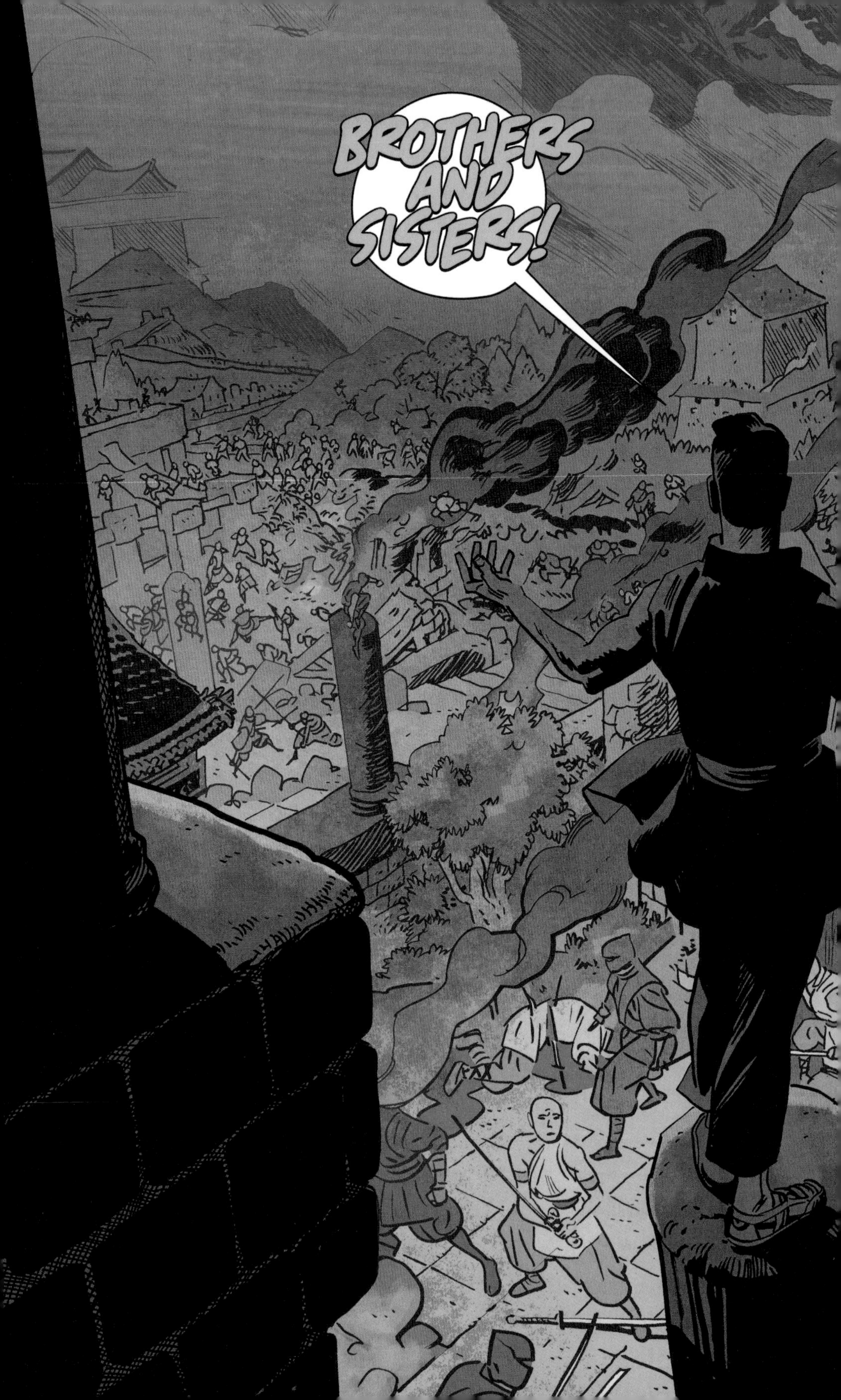
BROTHERS AND SISTERS!

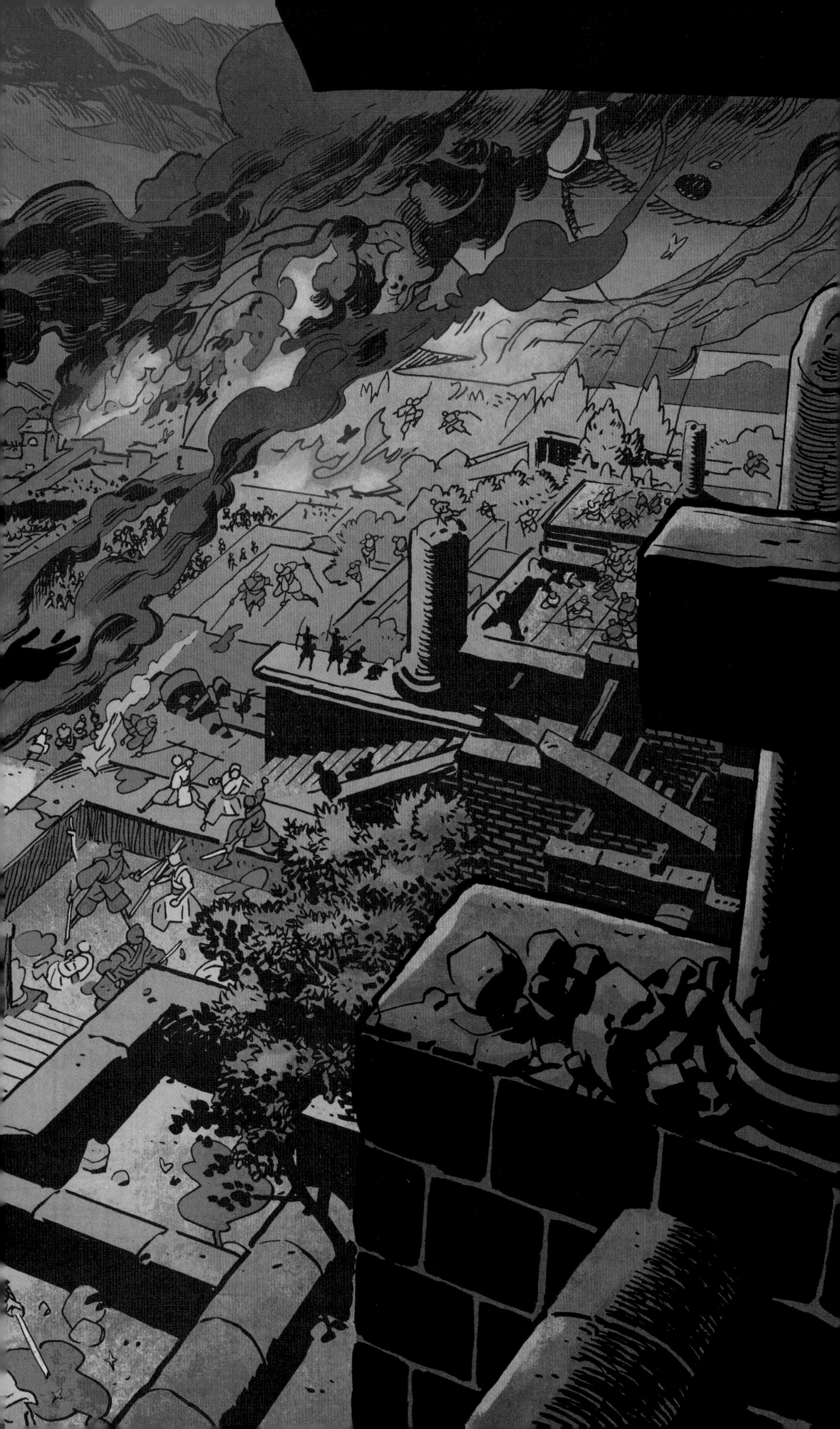

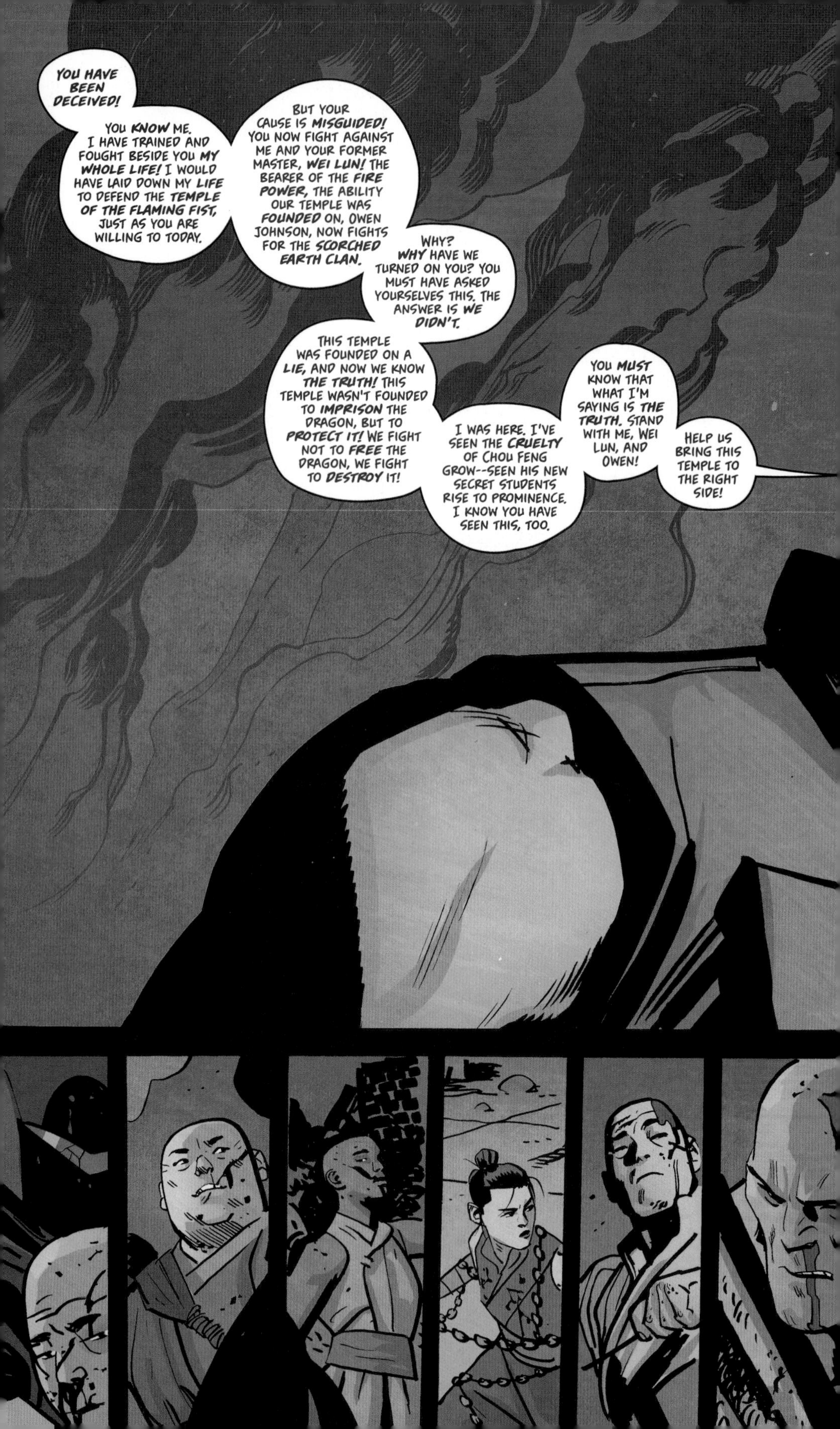
YOU HAVE BEEN DECEIVED!
YOU KNOW ME. I HAVE TRAINED AND FOUGHT BESIDE YOU MY WHOLE LIFE! I WOULD HAVE LAID DOWN MY LIFE TO DEFEND THE TEMPLE OF THE FLAMING FIST, JUST AS YOU ARE WILLING TO TODAY.
BUT YOUR CAUSE IS MISGUIDED! YOU NOW FIGHT AGAINST ME AND YOUR FORMER MASTER, WEI LUN! THE BEARER OF THE FIRE POWER, THE ABILITY OUR TEMPLE WAS FOUNDED ON, OWEN JOHNSON, NOW FIGHTS FOR THE SCORCHED EARTH CLAN.
WHY? WHY HAVE WE TURNED ON YOU? YOU MUST HAVE ASKED YOURSELVES THIS. THE ANSWER IS WE DIDN'T.
THIS TEMPLE WAS FOUNDED ON A LIE, AND NOW WE KNOW THE TRUTH! THIS TEMPLE WASN'T FOUNDED TO IMPRISON THE DRAGON, BUT TO PROTECT IT! WE FIGHT NOT TO FREE THE DRAGON, WE FIGHT TO DESTROY IT!
I WAS HERE. I'VE SEEN THE CRUELTY OF CHOU FENG GROW--SEEN HIS NEW SECRET STUDENTS RISE TO PROMINENCE. I KNOW YOU HAVE SEEN THIS, TOO.
YOU MUST KNOW THAT WHAT I'M SAYING IS THE TRUTH. STAND WITH ME, WEI LUN, AND OWEN!
HELP US BRING THIS TEMPLE TO THE RIGHT SIDE!

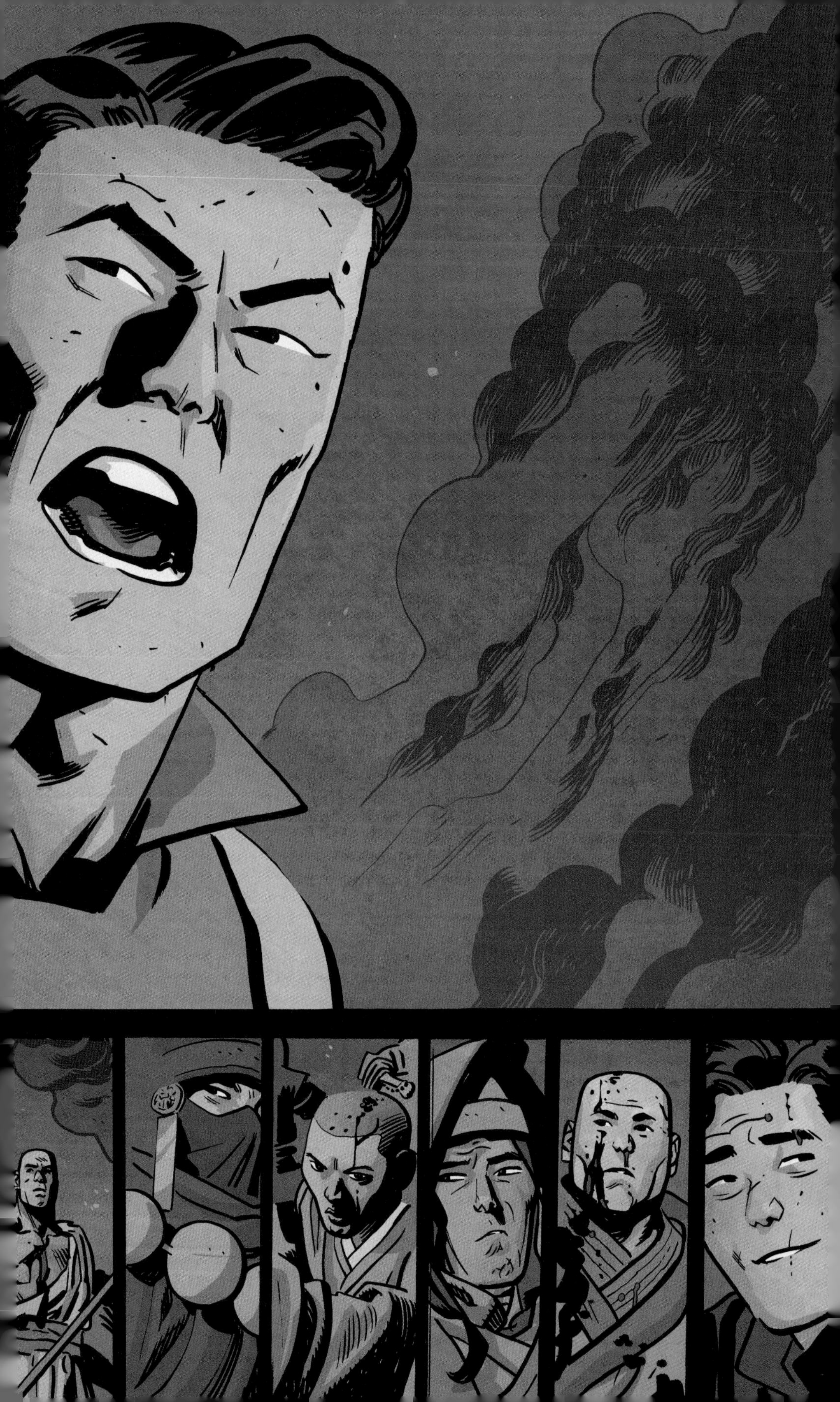

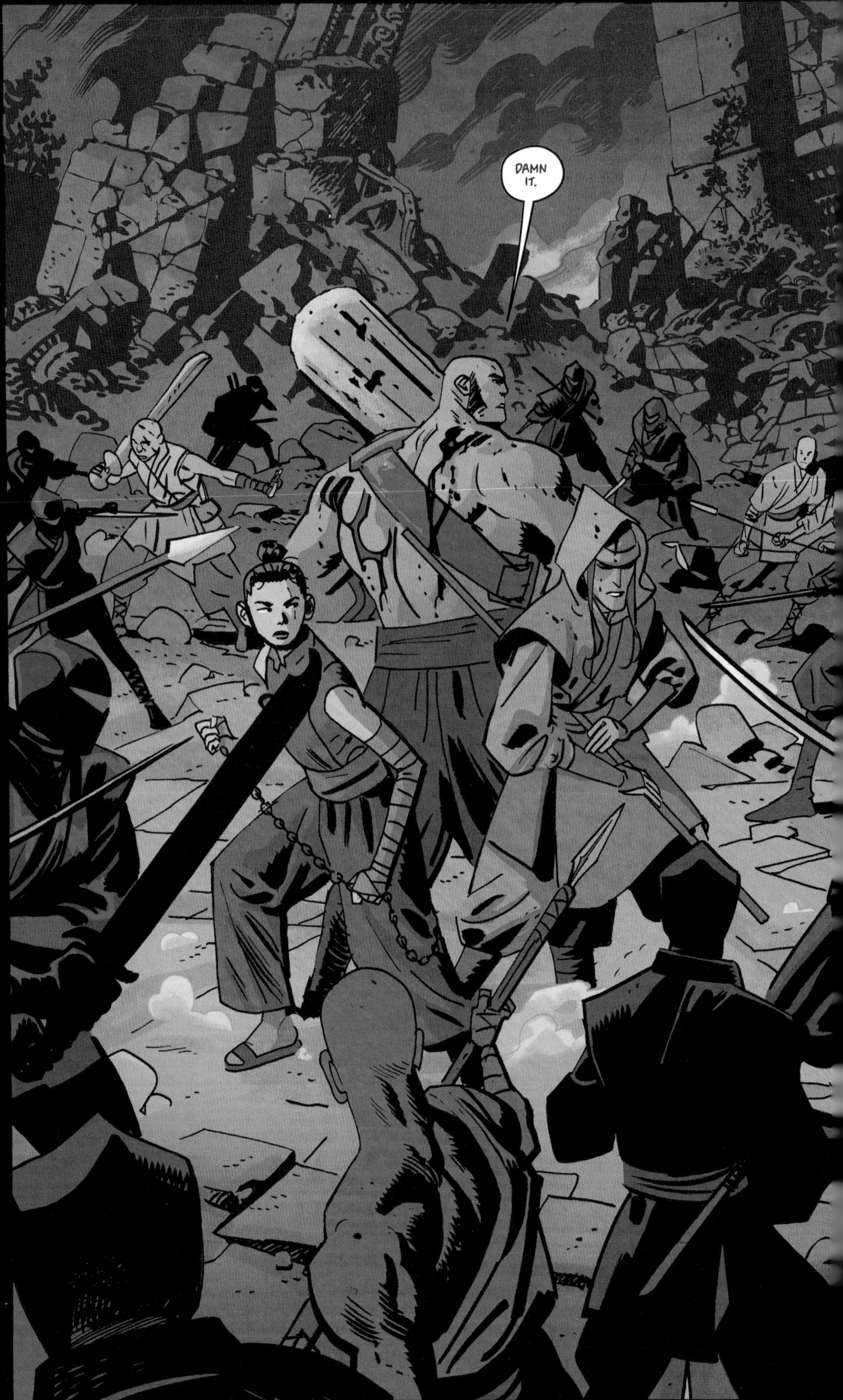
DAMN IT.

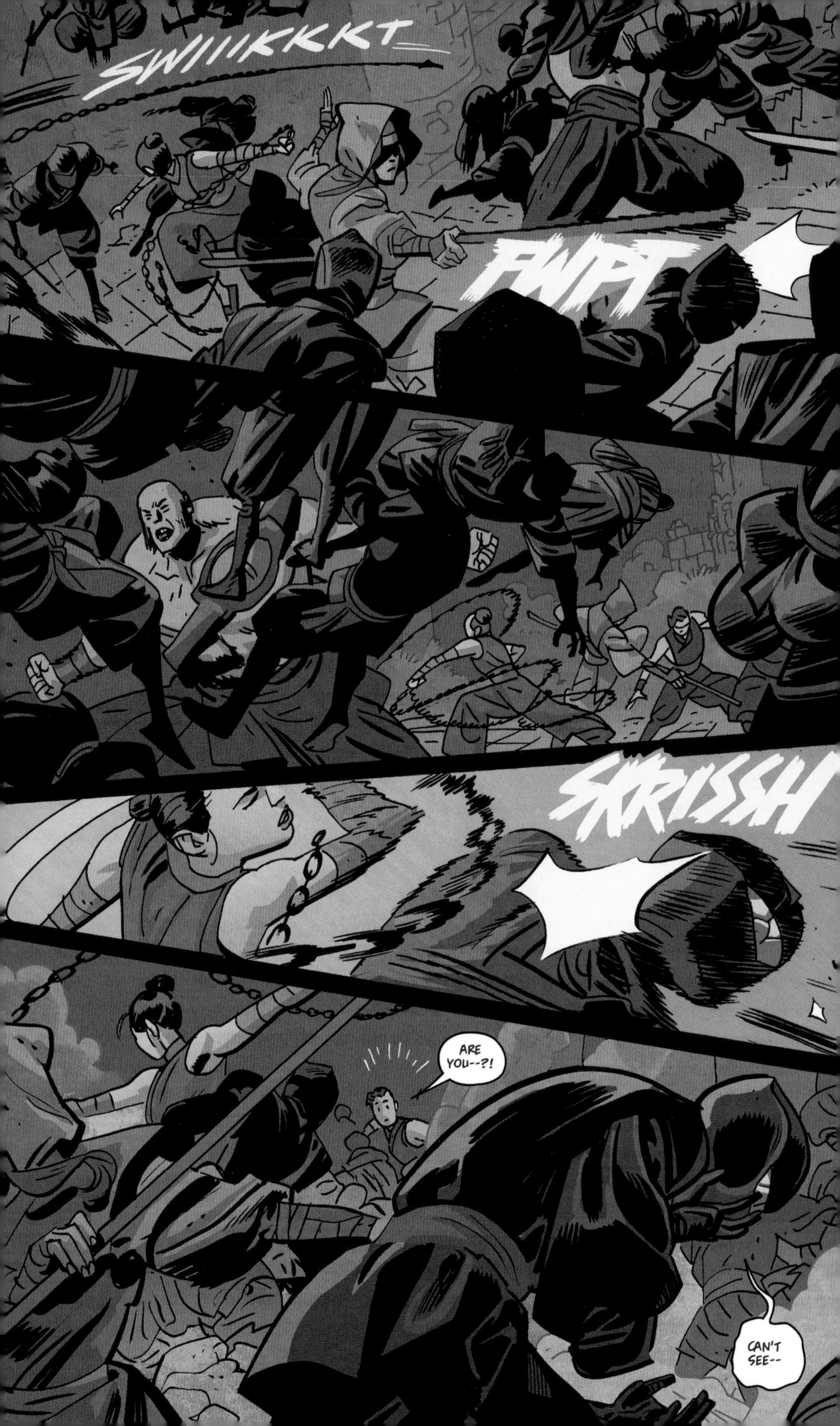
SWIIIKKKT
FWPT
SKRISSH
ARE YOU--?!
CAN'T SEE--

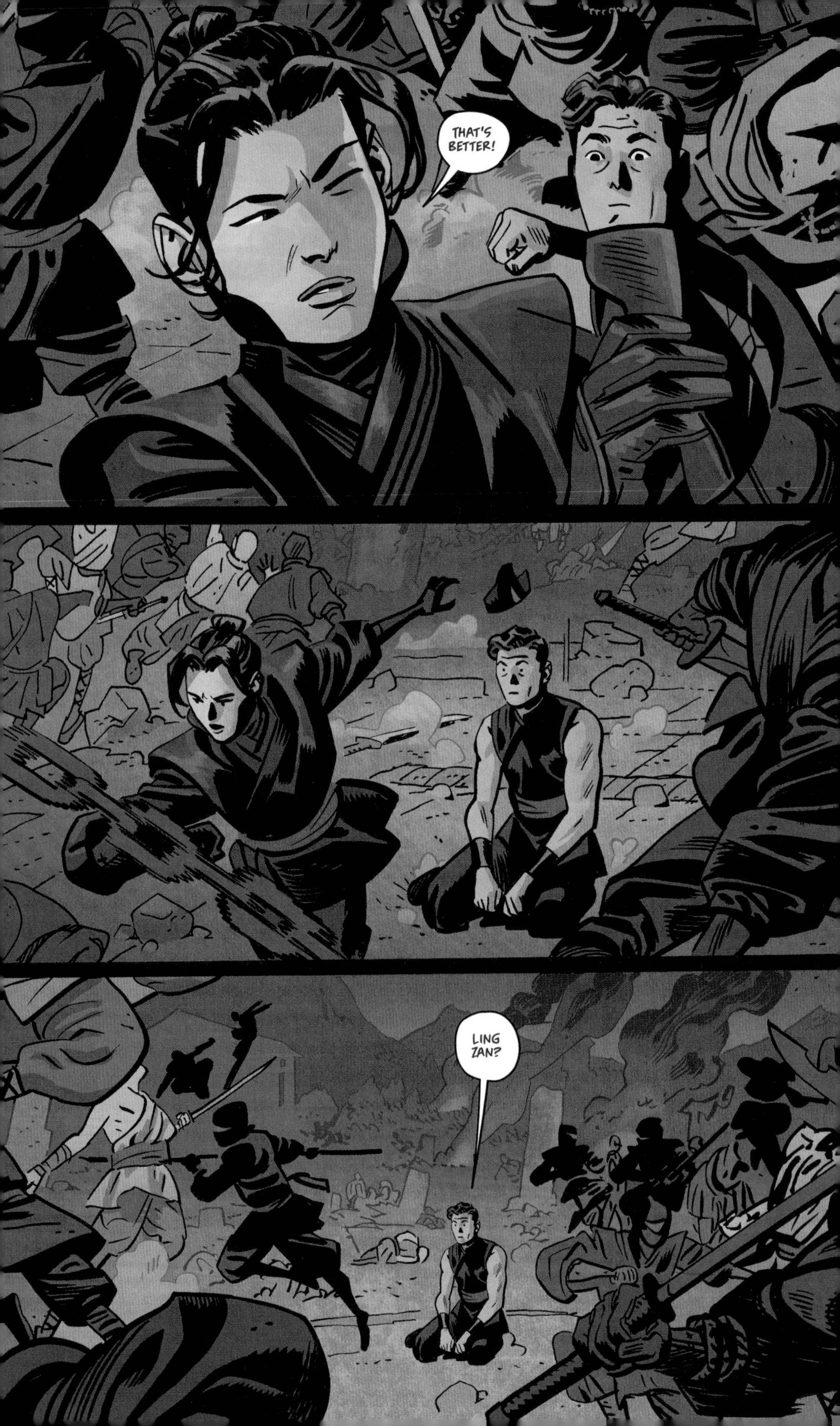
THAT'S BETTER!
LING ZAN?

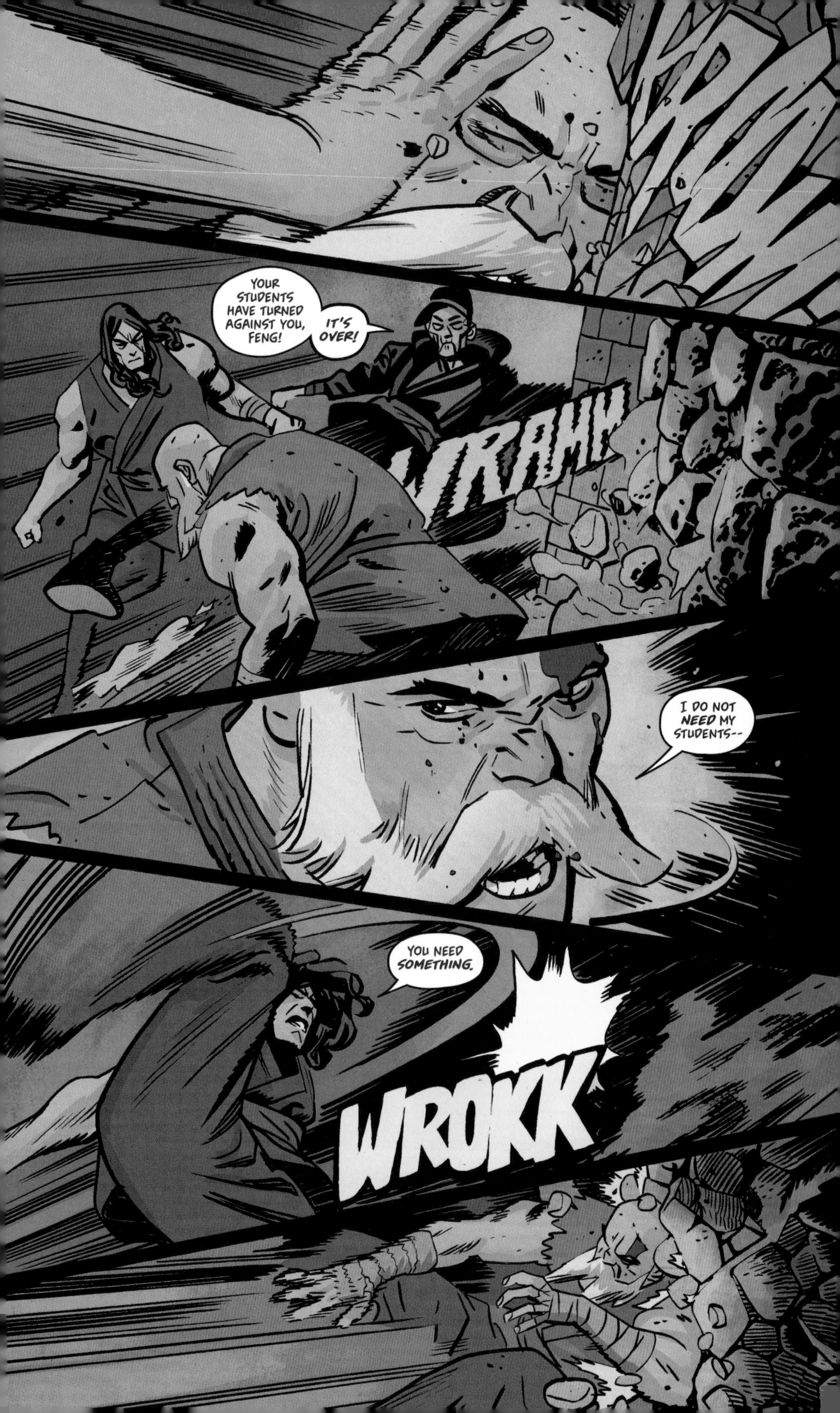
YOUR STUDENTS HAVE TURNED AGAINST YOU, FENG!
IT'S OVER!
WRAMM
I DO NOT NEED MY STUDENTS--
YOU NEED SOMETHING.
WROKK

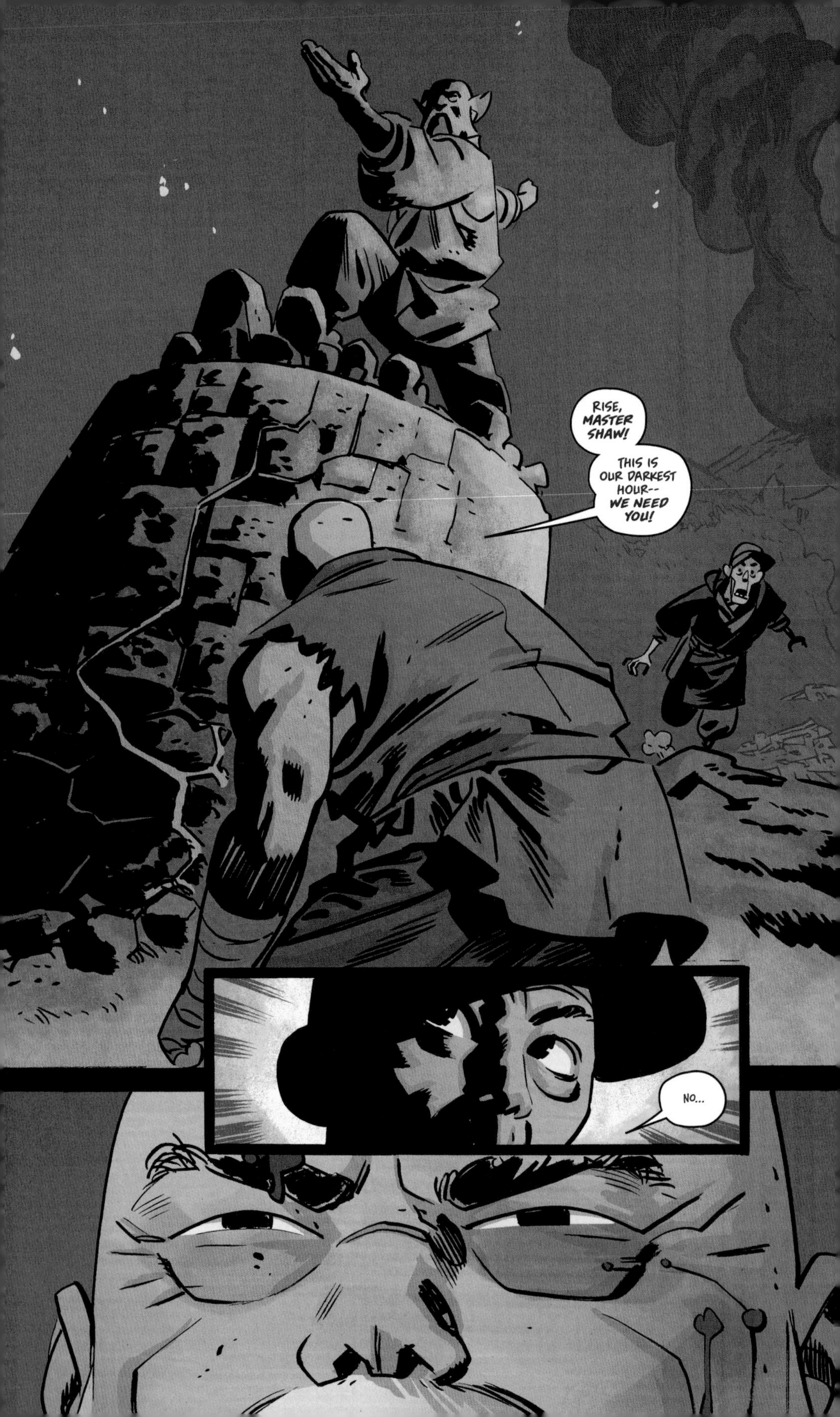
RISE, MASTER SHAW!
THIS IS OUR DARKEST HOUR-- WE NEED YOU!
NO...

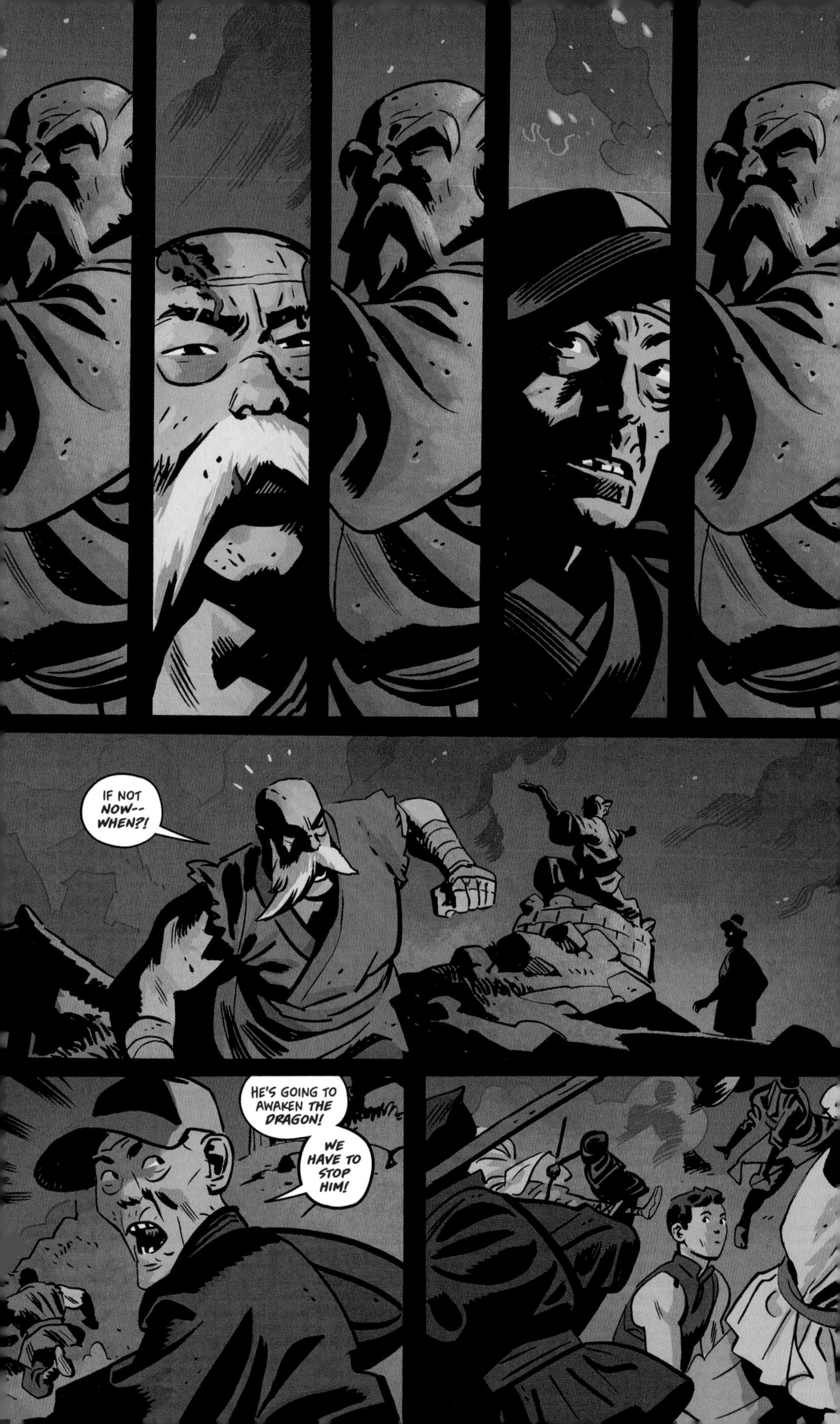
IF NOT NOW-- WHEN?!
HE'S GOING TO AWAKEN THE DRAGON!
WE HAVE TO STOP HIM!

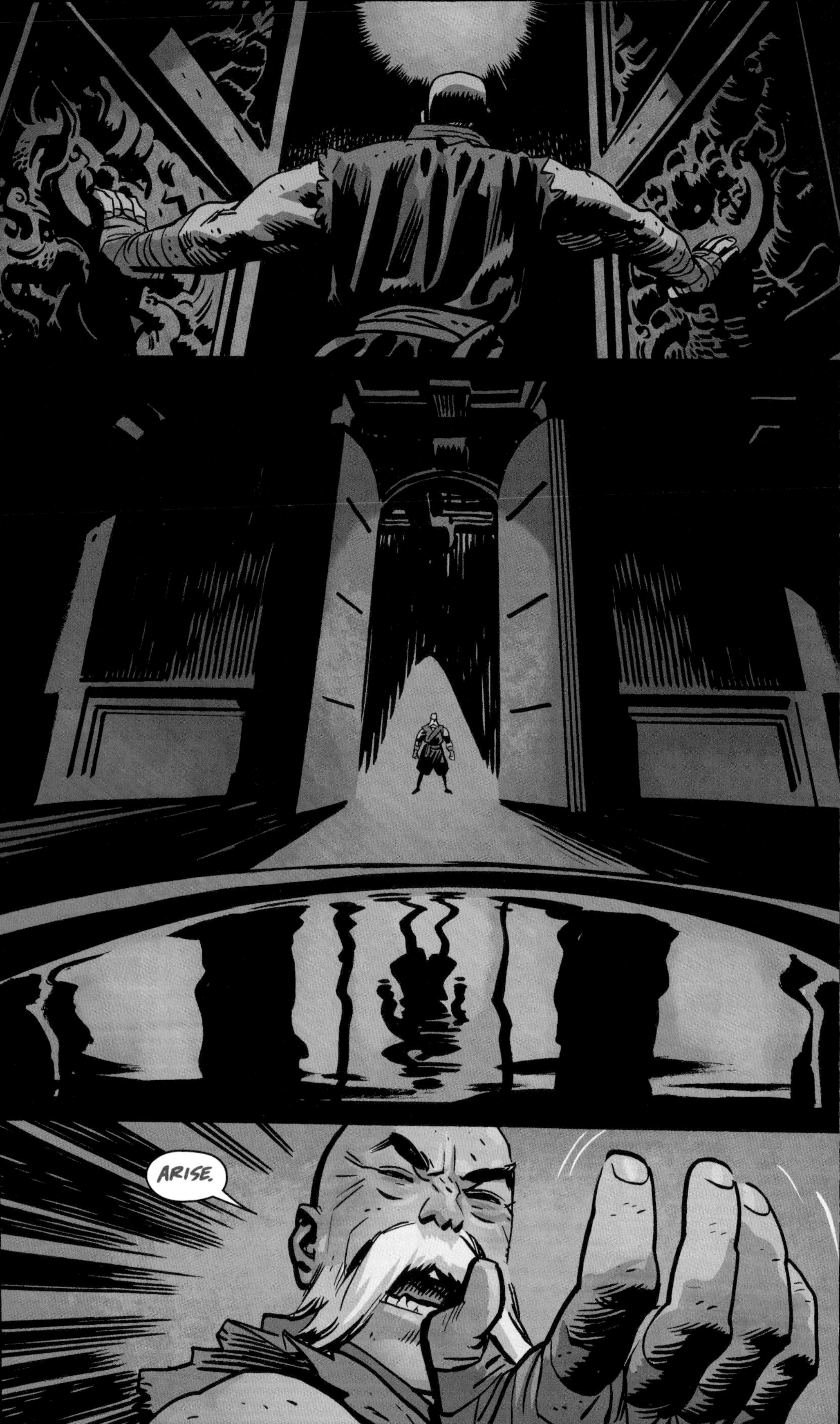
ARISE.

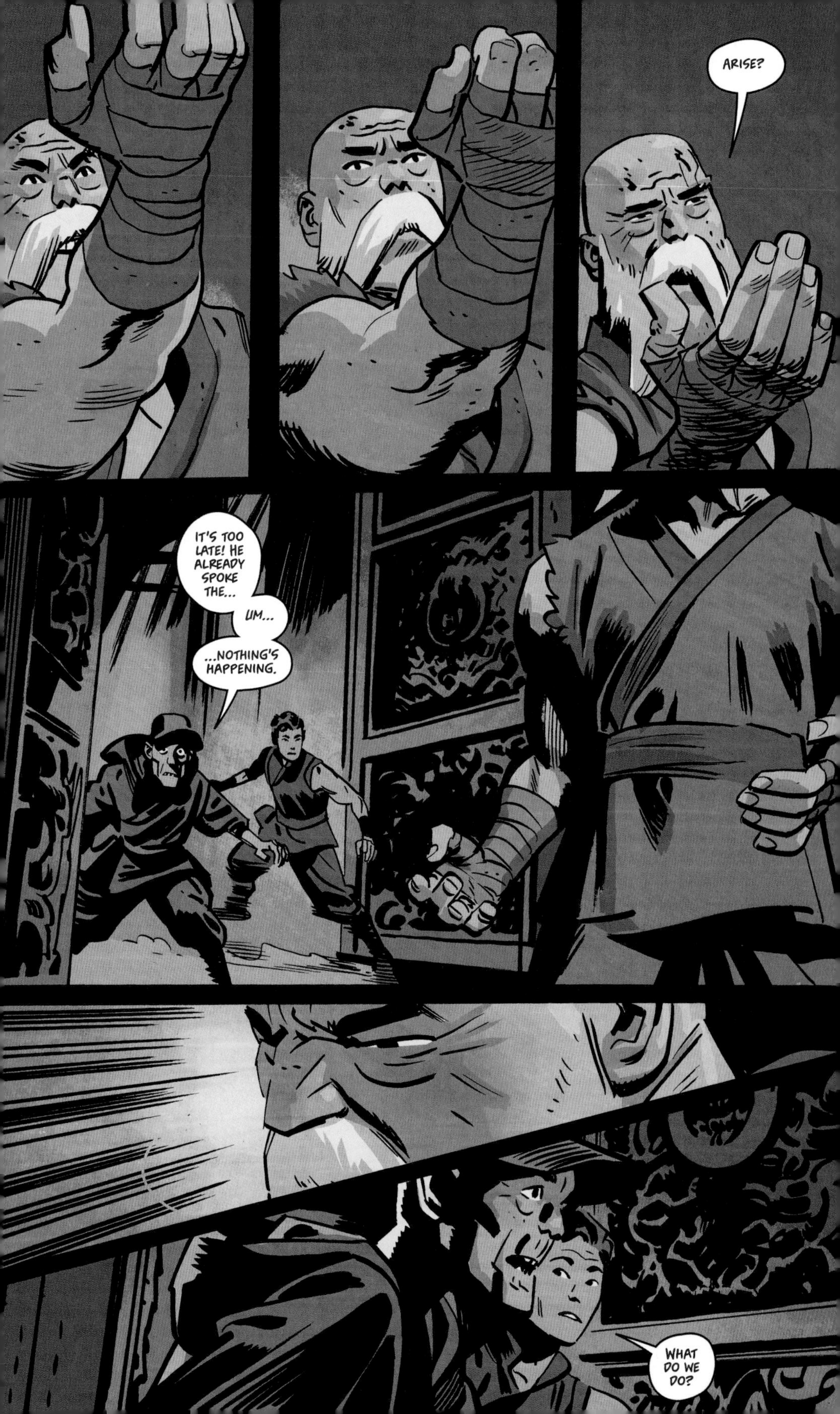
ARISE?
IT'S TOO LATE! HE ALREADY SPOKE THE...
UM...
...NOTHING'S HAPPENING.
WHAT DO WE DO?

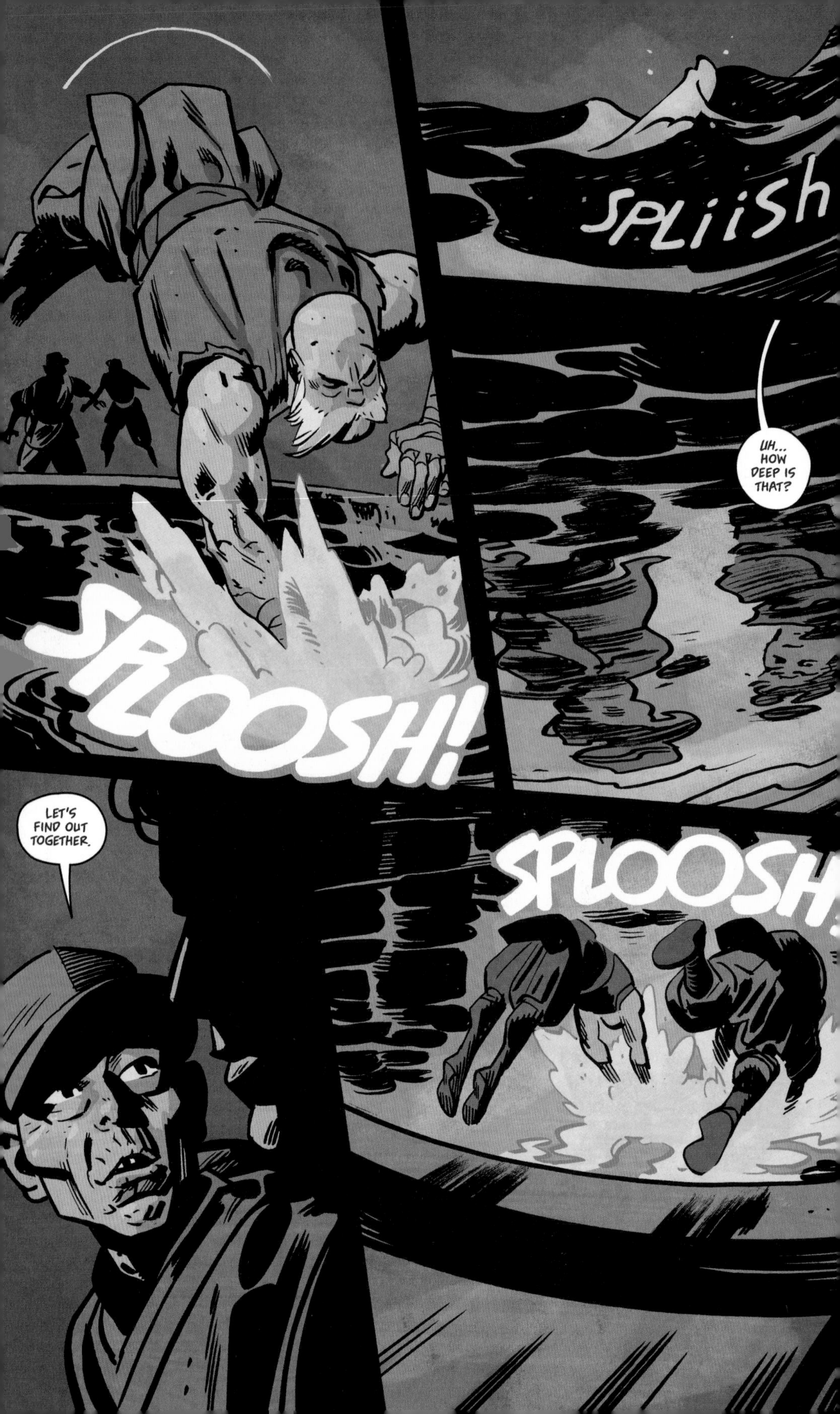
SPLOOSH!
SPLiiSh
UH... HOW DEEP IS THAT?
LET'S FIND OUT TOGETHER.
SPLOOSH!

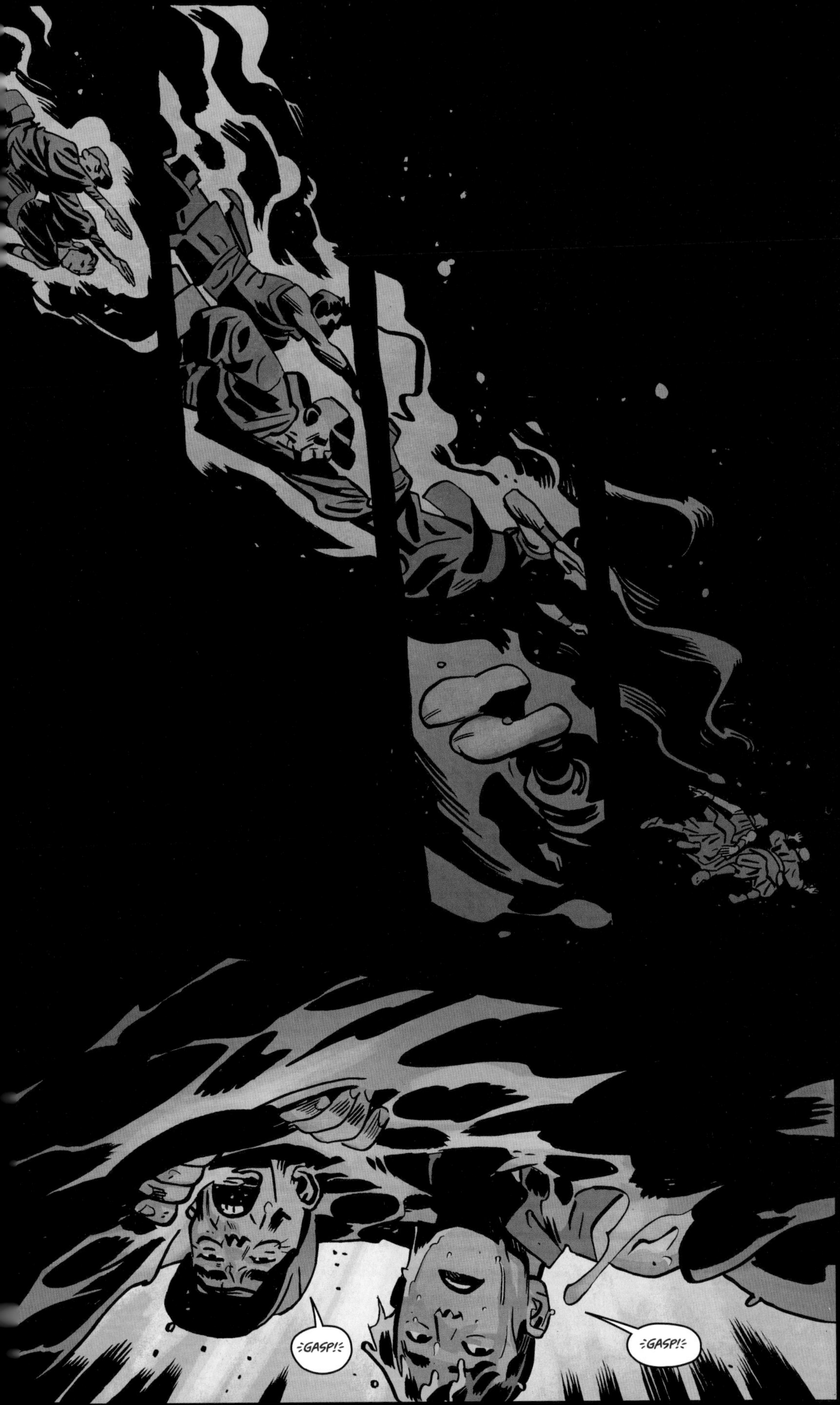
GASP!
GASP!

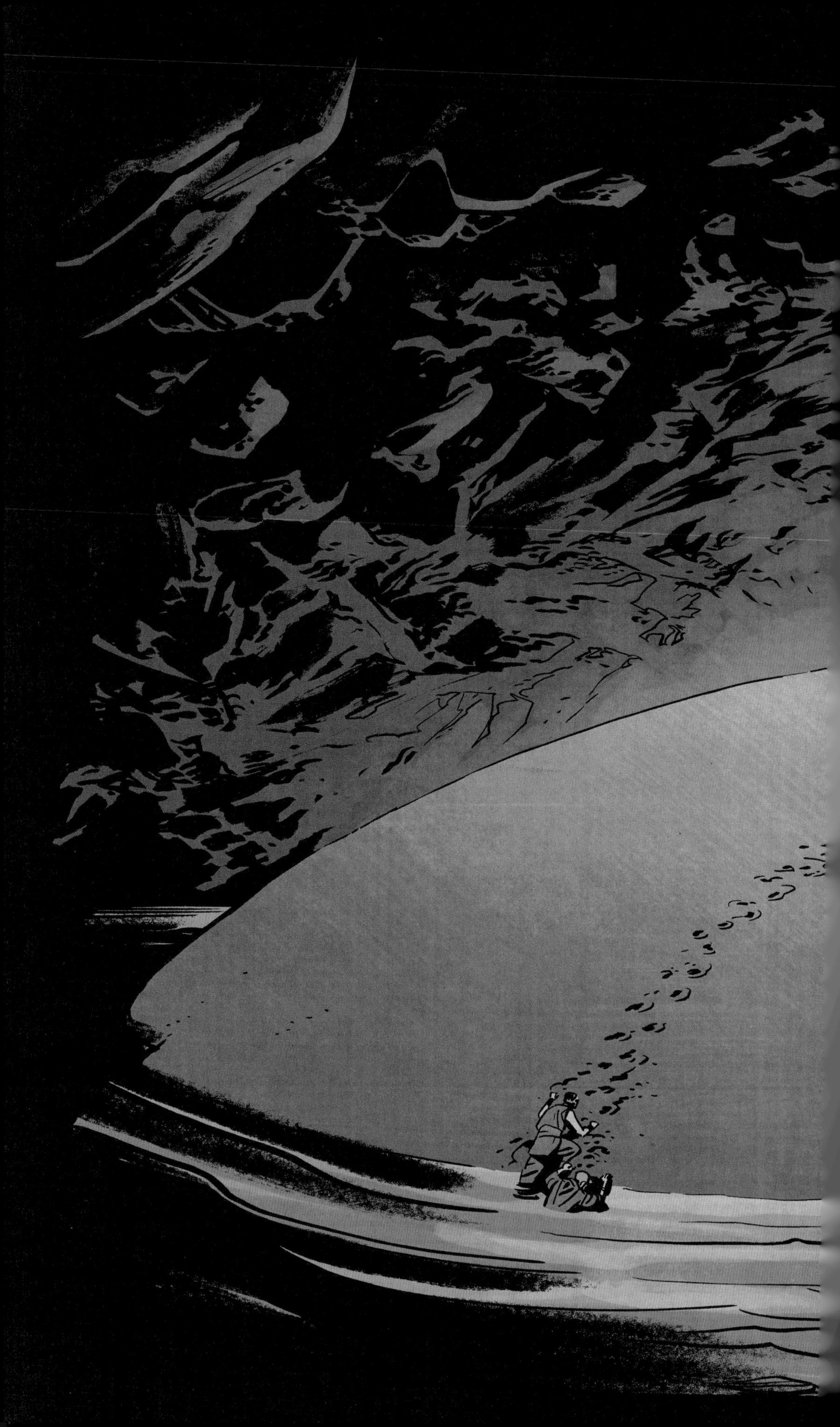

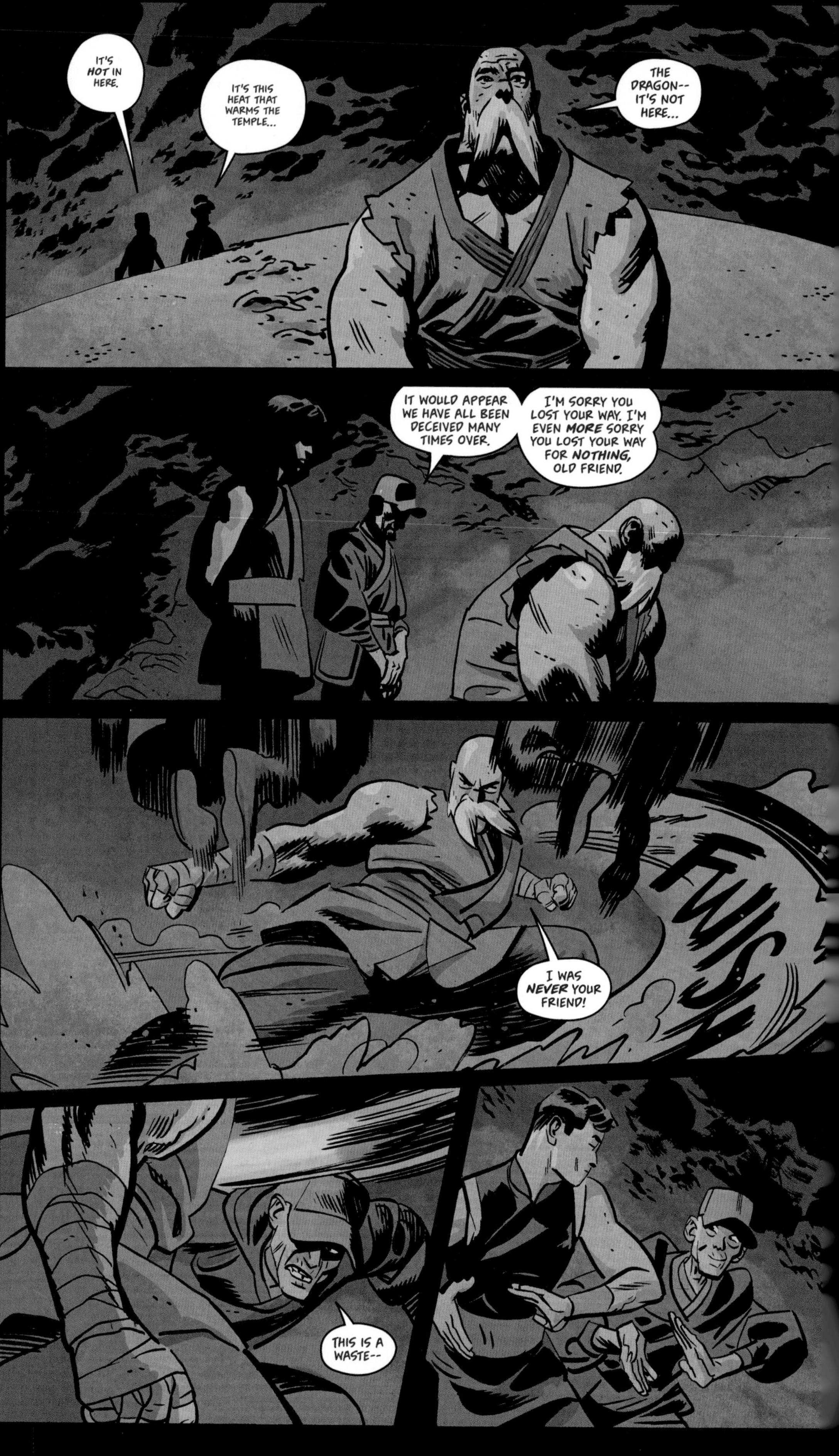
IT'S HOT IN HERE.
IT'S THIS HEAT THAT WARMS THE TEMPLE...
THE DRAGON-- IT'S NOT HERE...
IT WOULD APPEAR WE HAVE ALL BEEN DECEIVED MANY TIMES OVER.
I'M SORRY YOU LOST YOUR WAY. I'M EVEN MORE SORRY YOU LOST YOUR WAY FOR NOTHING, OLD FRIEND.
FWISH
I WAS NEVER YOUR FRIEND!
THIS IS A WASTE--

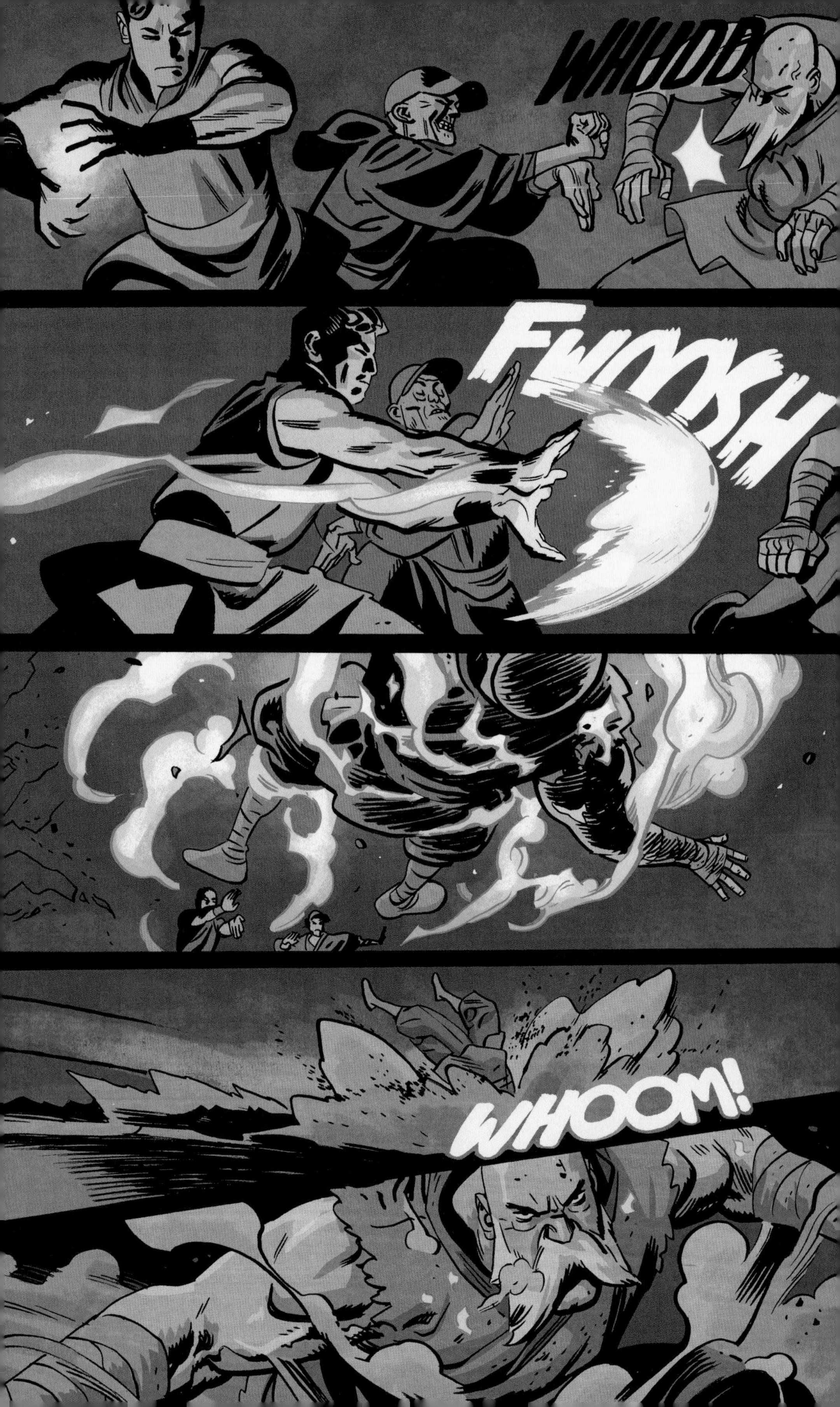
WHUDD
FWOOSH
WHOOM!

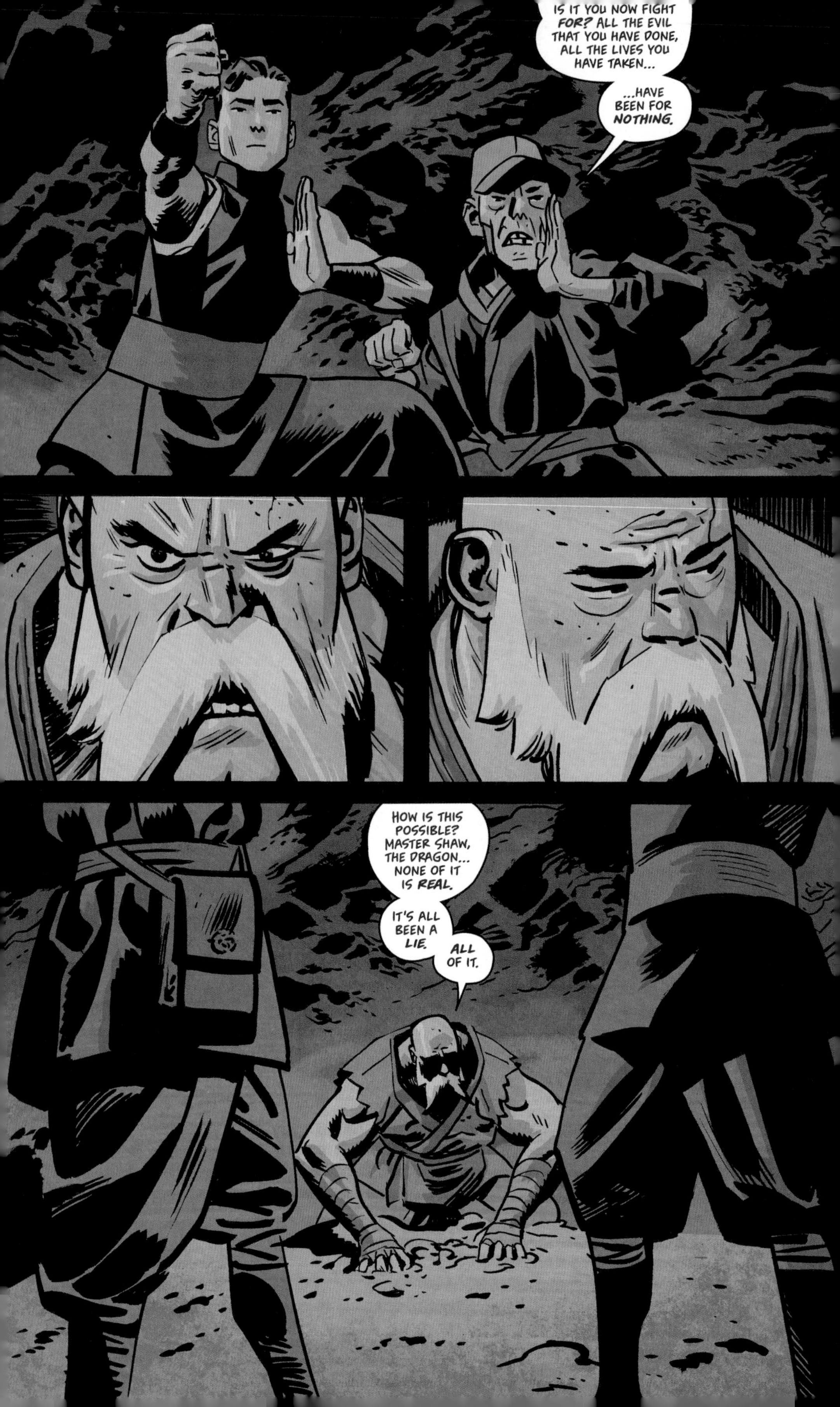
IS IT YOU NOW FIGHT FOR? ALL THE EVIL THAT YOU HAVE DONE, ALL THE LIVES YOU HAVE TAKEN...
...HAVE BEEN FOR NOTHING.
HOW IS THIS POSSIBLE? MASTER SHAW, THE DRAGON... NONE OF IT IS REAL.
IT'S ALL BEEN A LIE.
ALL OF IT.

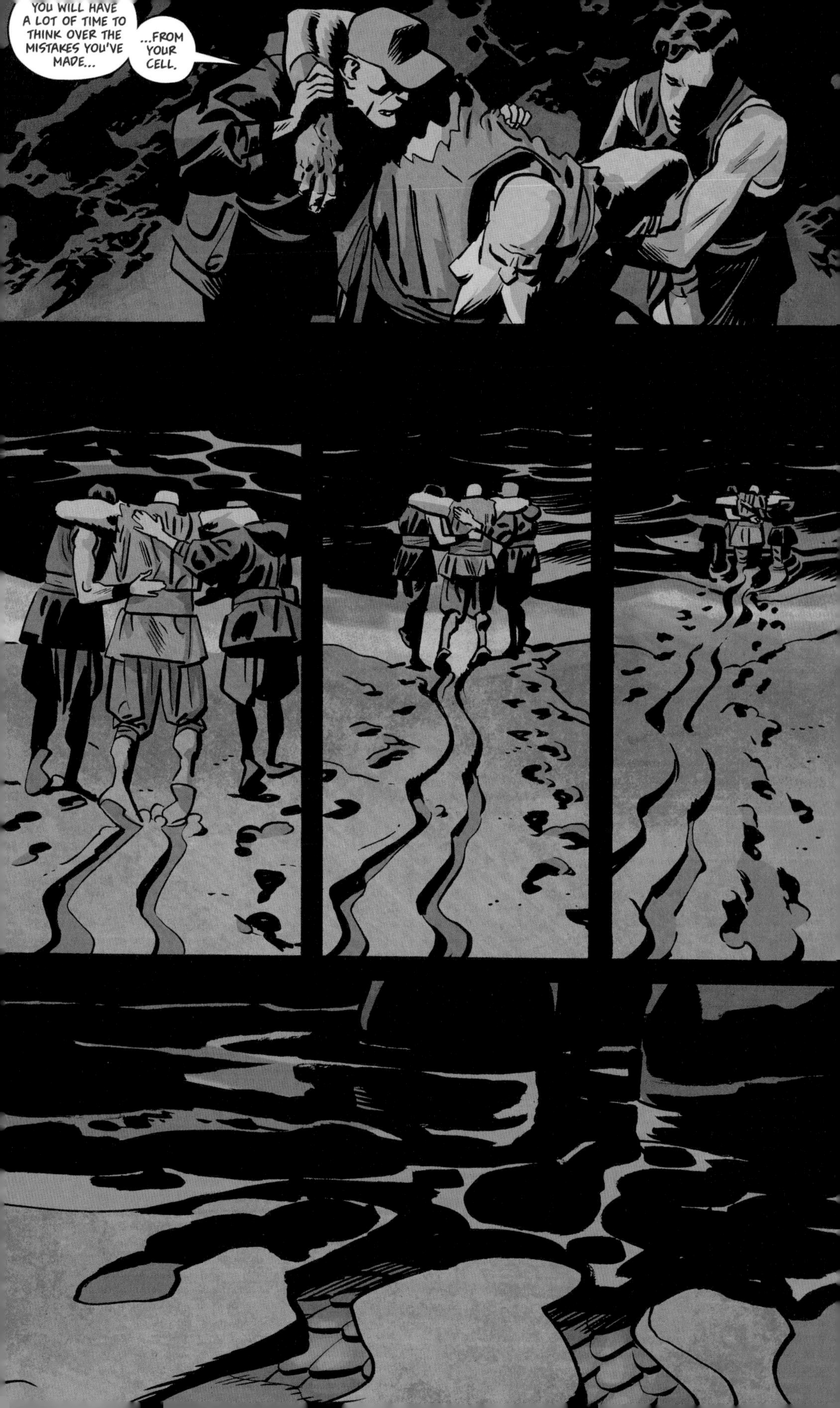

YOU WILL HAVE A LOT OF TIME TO THINK OVER THE MISTAKES YOU'VE MADE...
...FROM YOUR CELL.

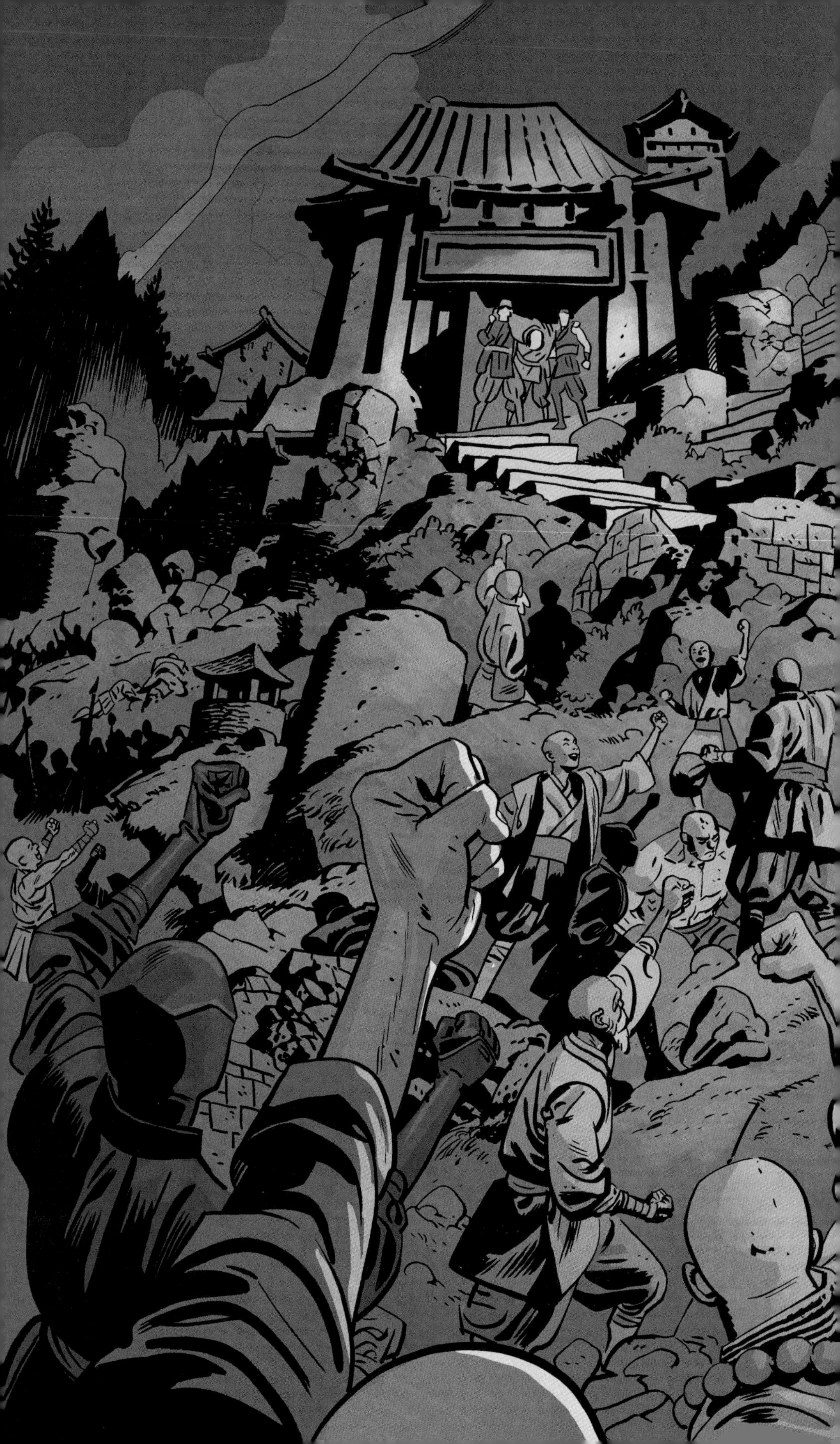

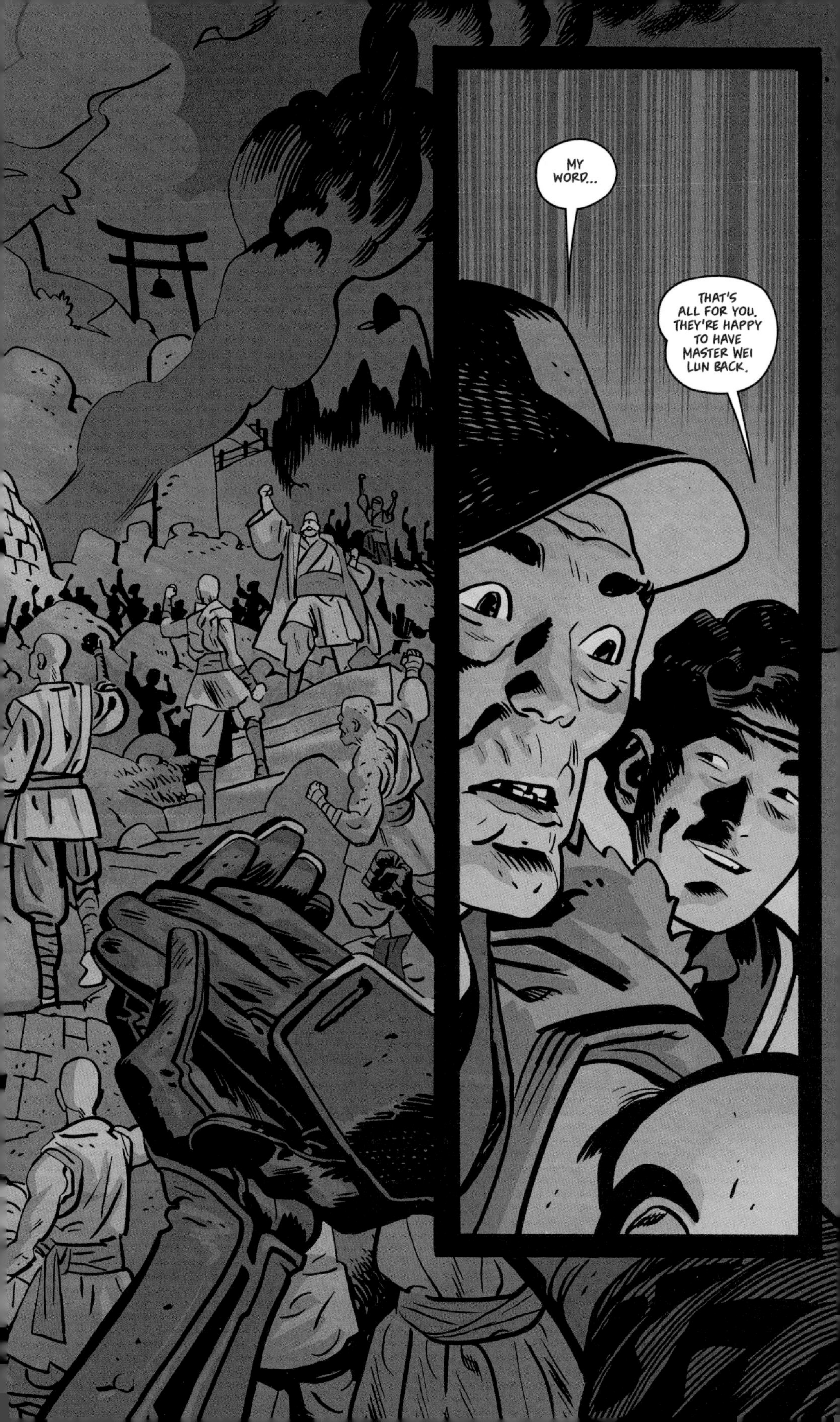
MY WORD...
THAT'S ALL FOR YOU. THEY'RE HAPPY TO HAVE MASTER WEI LUN BACK.

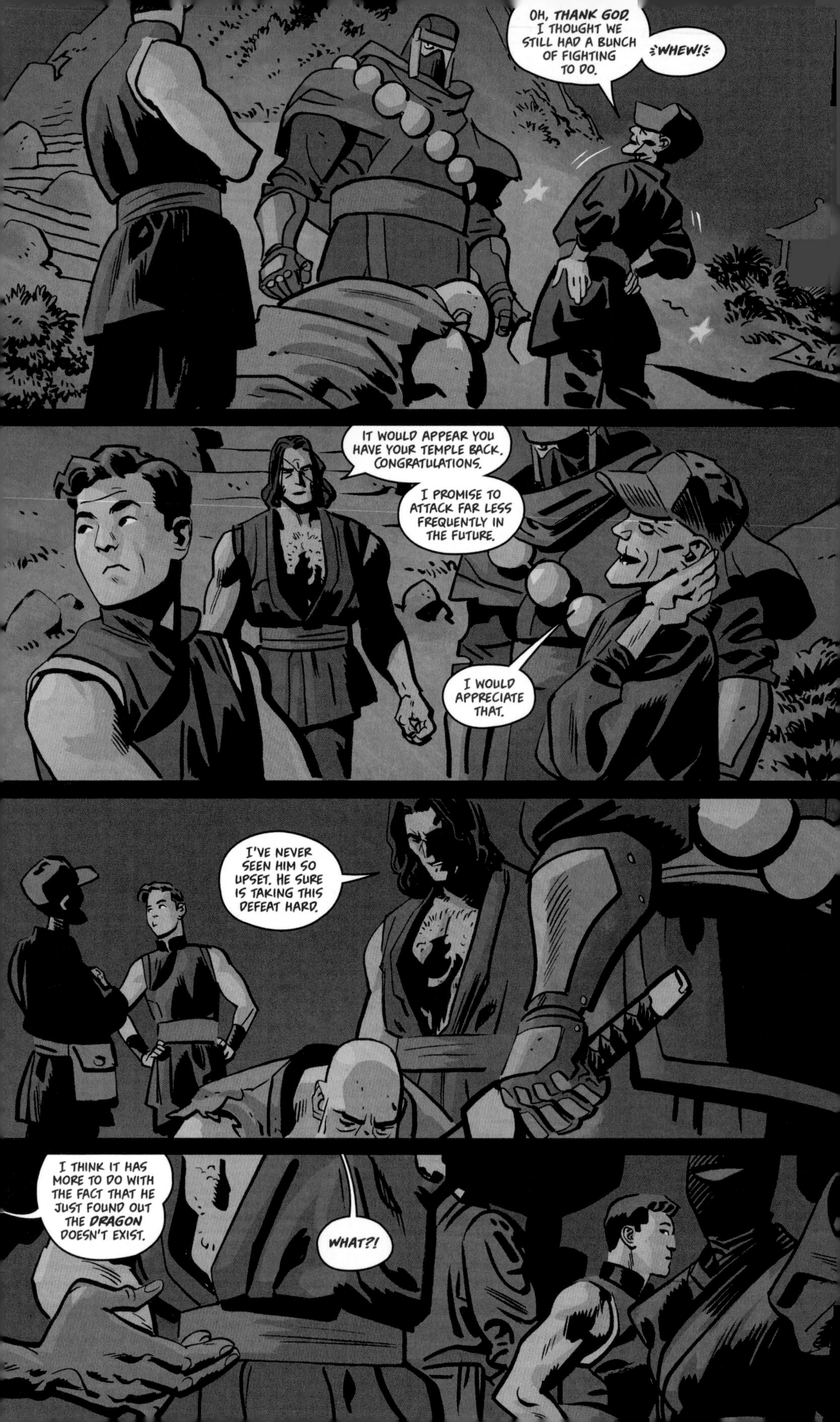
OH, THANK GOD. I THOUGHT WE STILL HAD A BUNCH OF FIGHTING TO DO.
WHEW!
IT WOULD APPEAR YOU HAVE YOUR TEMPLE BACK. CONGRATULATIONS.
I PROMISE TO ATTACK FAR LESS FREQUENTLY IN THE FUTURE.
I WOULD APPRECIATE THAT.
I'VE NEVER SEEN HIM SO UPSET. HE SURE IS TAKING THIS DEFEAT HARD.
I THINK IT HAS MORE TO DO WITH THE FACT THAT HE JUST FOUND OUT THE DRAGON DOESN'T EXIST.
WHAT?!

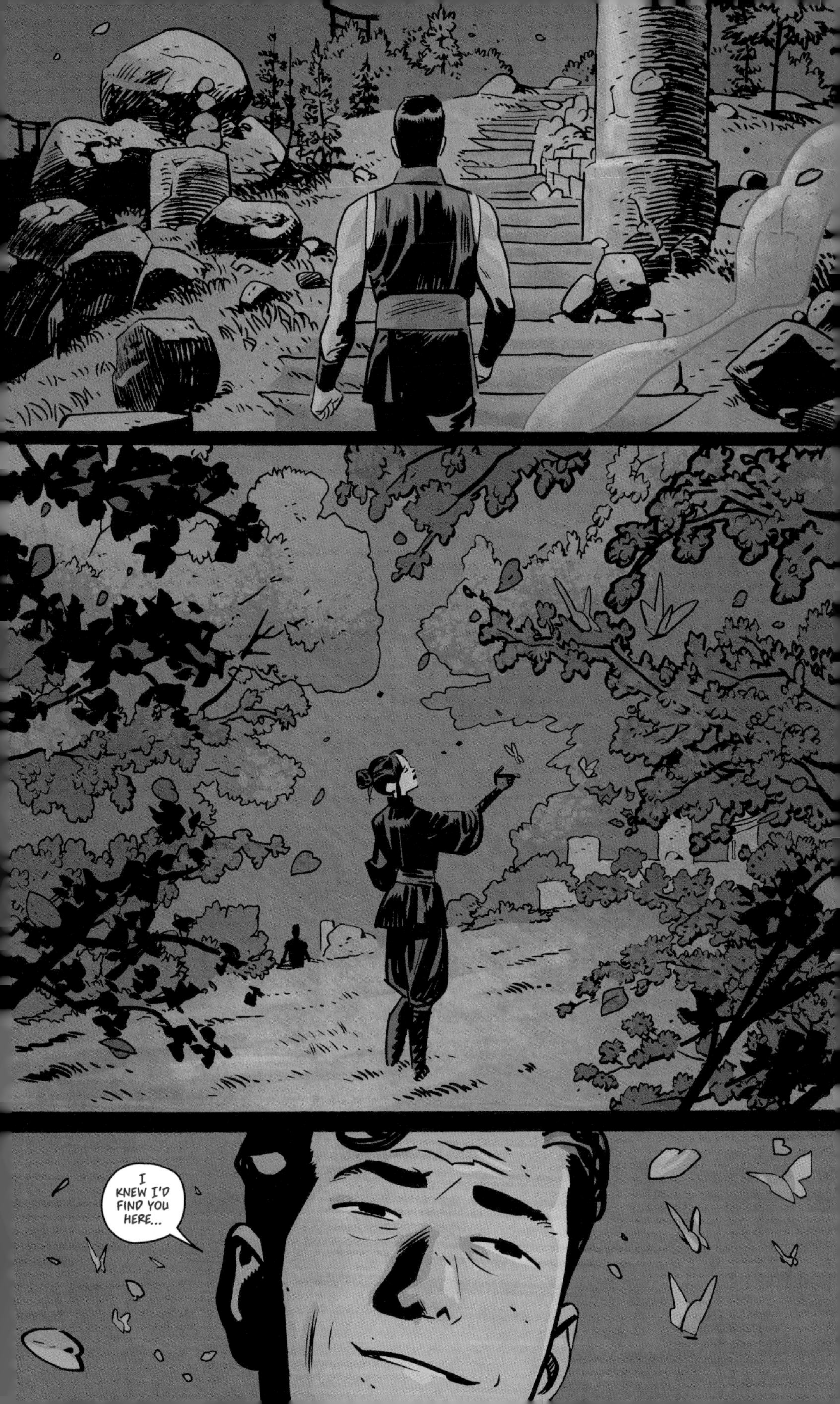
I KNEW I'D FIND YOU HERE...

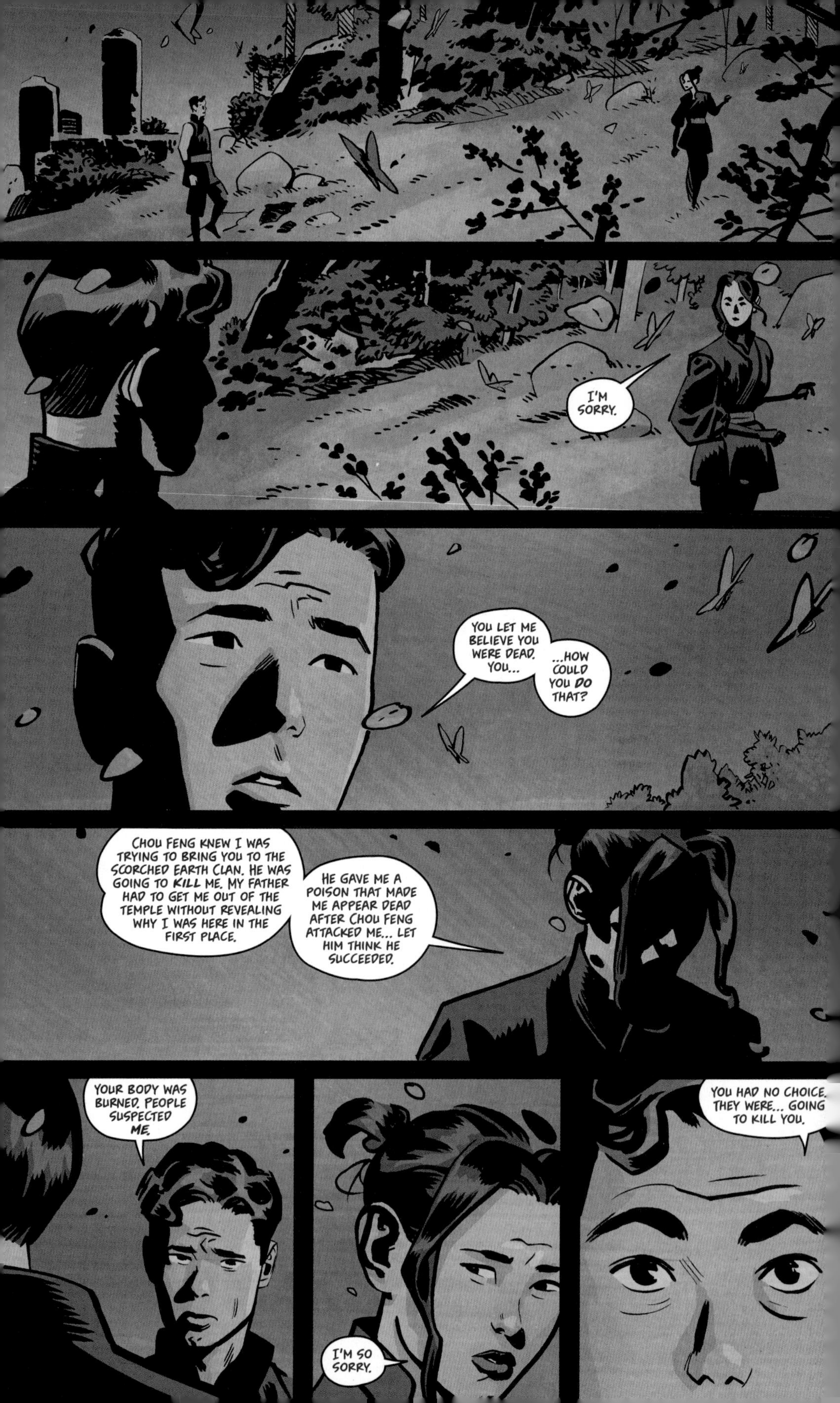
I'M SORRY.
YOU LET ME BELIEVE YOU WERE DEAD. YOU...
...HOW COULD YOU DO THAT?
CHOU FENG KNEW I WAS TRYING TO BRING YOU TO THE SCORCHED EARTH CLAN. HE WAS GOING TO KILL ME. MY FATHER HAD TO GET ME OUT OF THE TEMPLE WITHOUT REVEALING WHY I WAS HERE IN THE FIRST PLACE.
HE GAVE ME A POISON THAT MADE ME APPEAR DEAD AFTER CHOU FENG ATTACKED ME... LET HIM THINK HE SUCCEEDED.
YOUR BODY WAS BURNED. PEOPLE SUSPECTED ME.
I'M SO SORRY.
YOU HAD NO CHOICE. THEY WERE... GOING TO KILL YOU.

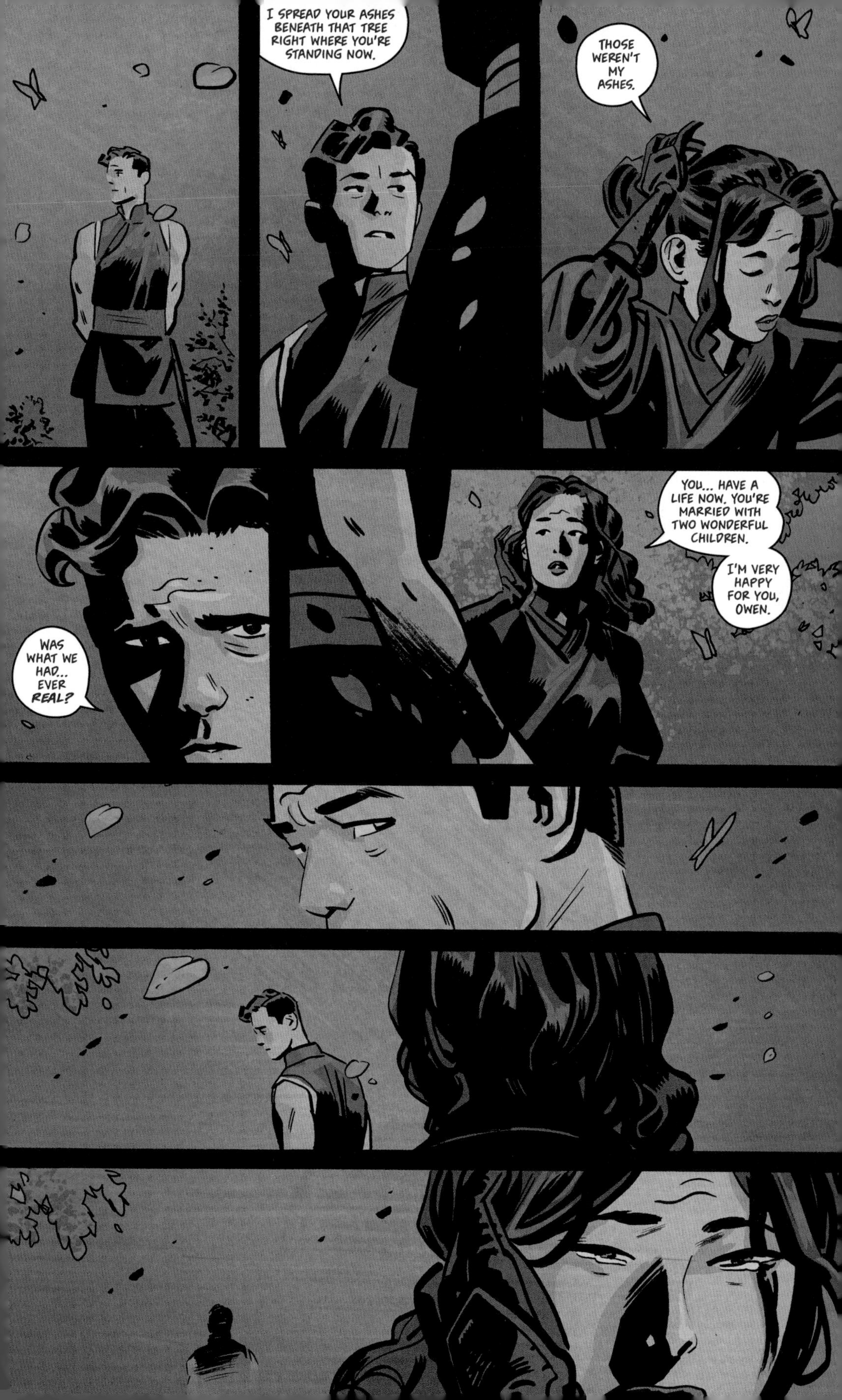
I SPREAD YOUR ASHES BENEATH THAT TREE RIGHT WHERE YOU'RE STANDING NOW.
THOSE WEREN'T MY ASHES.
WAS WHAT WE HAD... EVER REAL?
YOU... HAVE A LIFE NOW. YOU'RE MARRIED WITH TWO WONDERFUL CHILDREN.
I'M VERY HAPPY FOR YOU, OWEN.

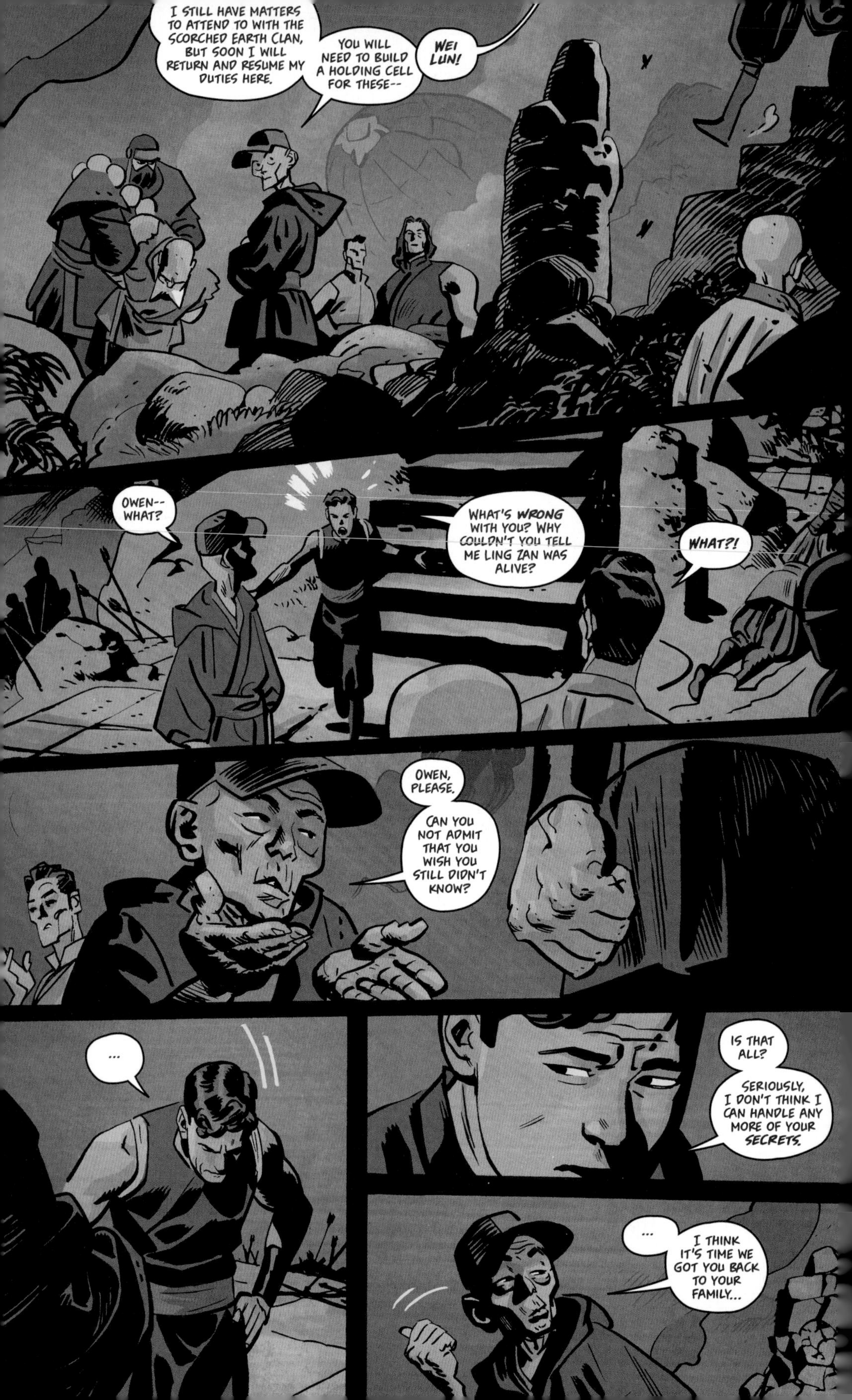
I STILL HAVE MATTERS TO ATTEND TO WITH THE SCORCHED EARTH CLAN, BUT SOON I WILL RETURN AND RESUME MY DUTIES HERE.
YOU WILL NEED TO BUILD A HOLDING CELL FOR THESE--
WEI LUN!
OWEN-- WHAT?
WHAT'S WRONG WITH YOU? WHY COULDN'T YOU TELL ME LING ZAN WAS ALIVE?
WHAT?!
OWEN, PLEASE.
CAN YOU NOT ADMIT THAT YOU WISH YOU STILL DIDN'T KNOW?
...
IS THAT ALL?
SERIOUSLY, I DON'T THINK I CAN HANDLE ANY MORE OF YOUR SECRETS.
...
I THINK IT'S TIME WE GOT YOU BACK TO YOUR FAMILY...

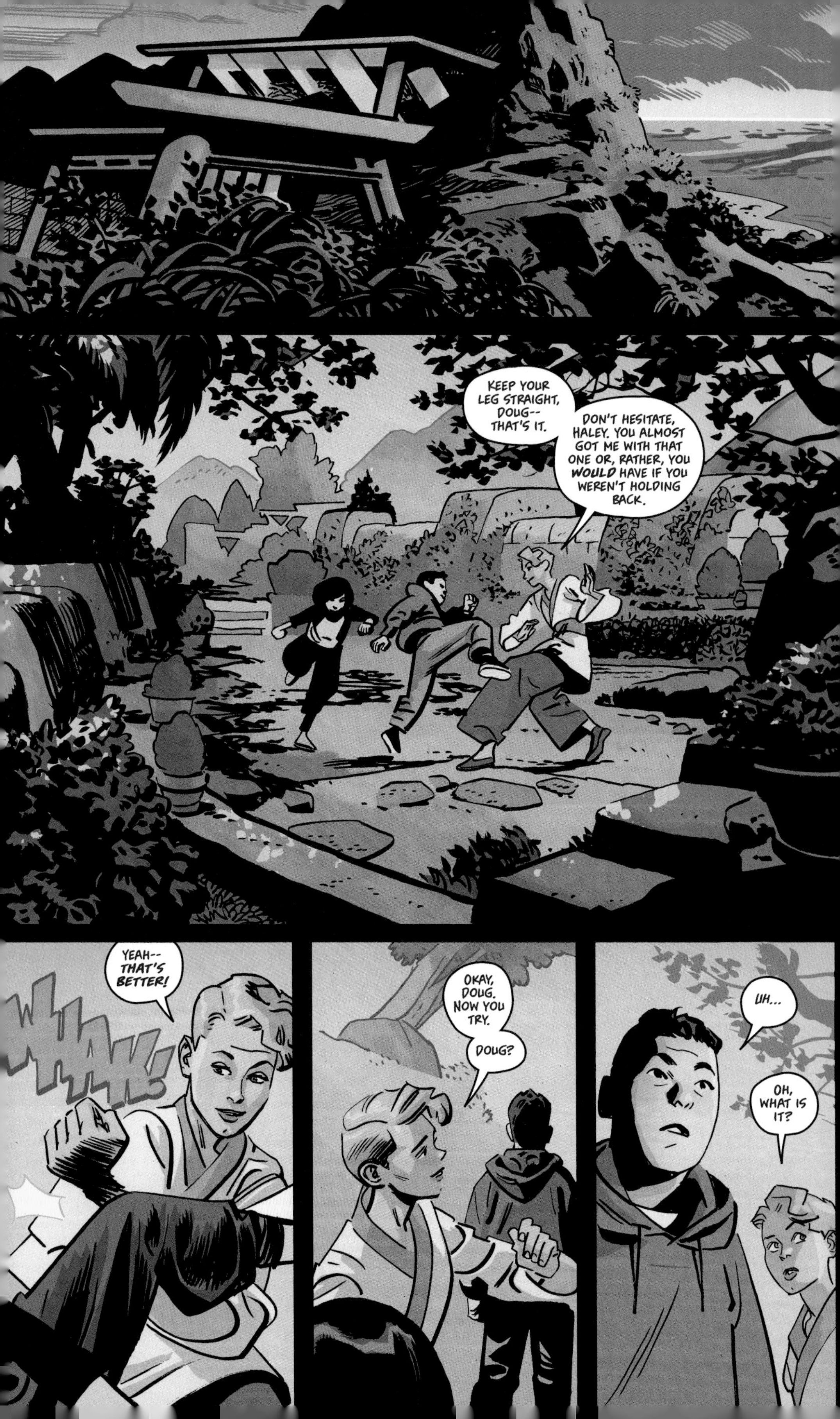
KEEP YOUR LEG STRAIGHT, DOUG-- THAT'S IT.
DON'T HESITATE, HALEY. YOU ALMOST GOT ME WITH THAT ONE OR, RATHER, YOU *WOULD* HAVE IF YOU WEREN'T HOLDING BACK.
YEAH-- THAT'S BETTER!
WHAK!
OKAY, DOUG. NOW YOU TRY.
DOUG?
UH...
OH, WHAT IS IT?

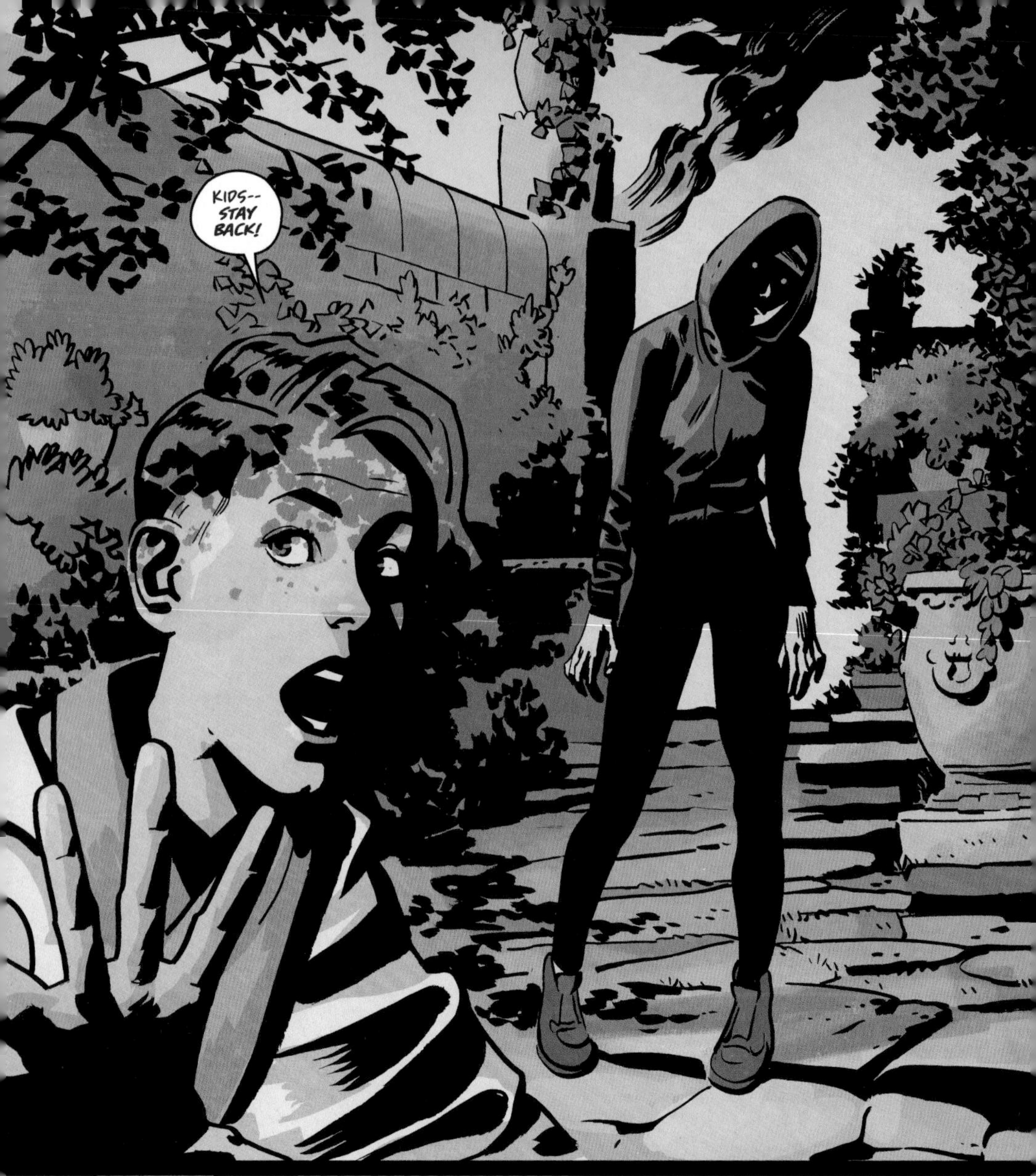
KIDS--
STAY
BACK!

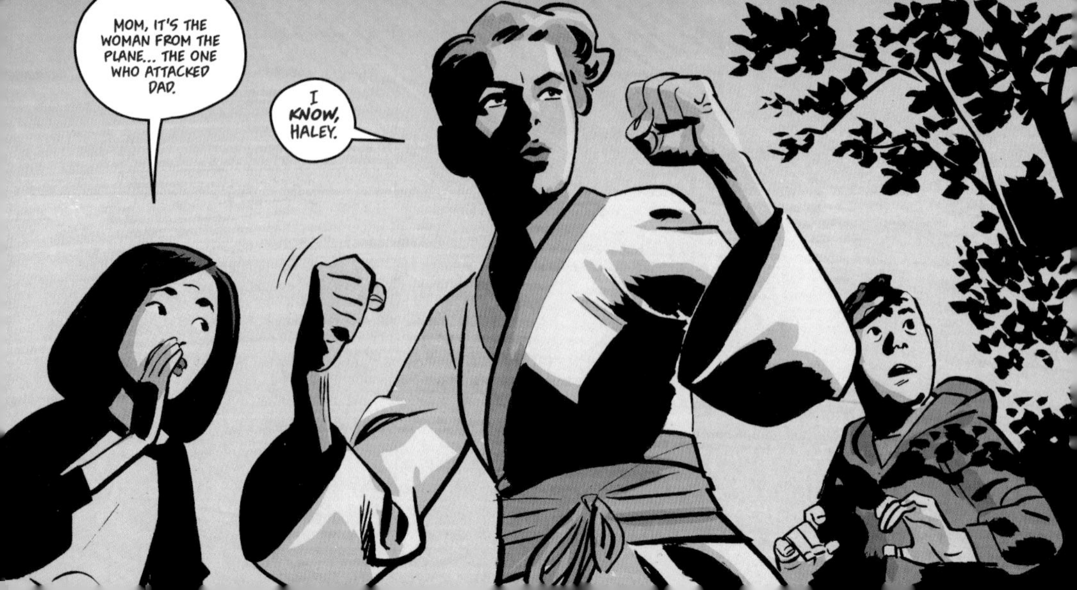
MOM, IT'S THE WOMAN FROM THE PLANE... THE ONE WHO ATTACKED DAD.
I KNOW, HALEY.

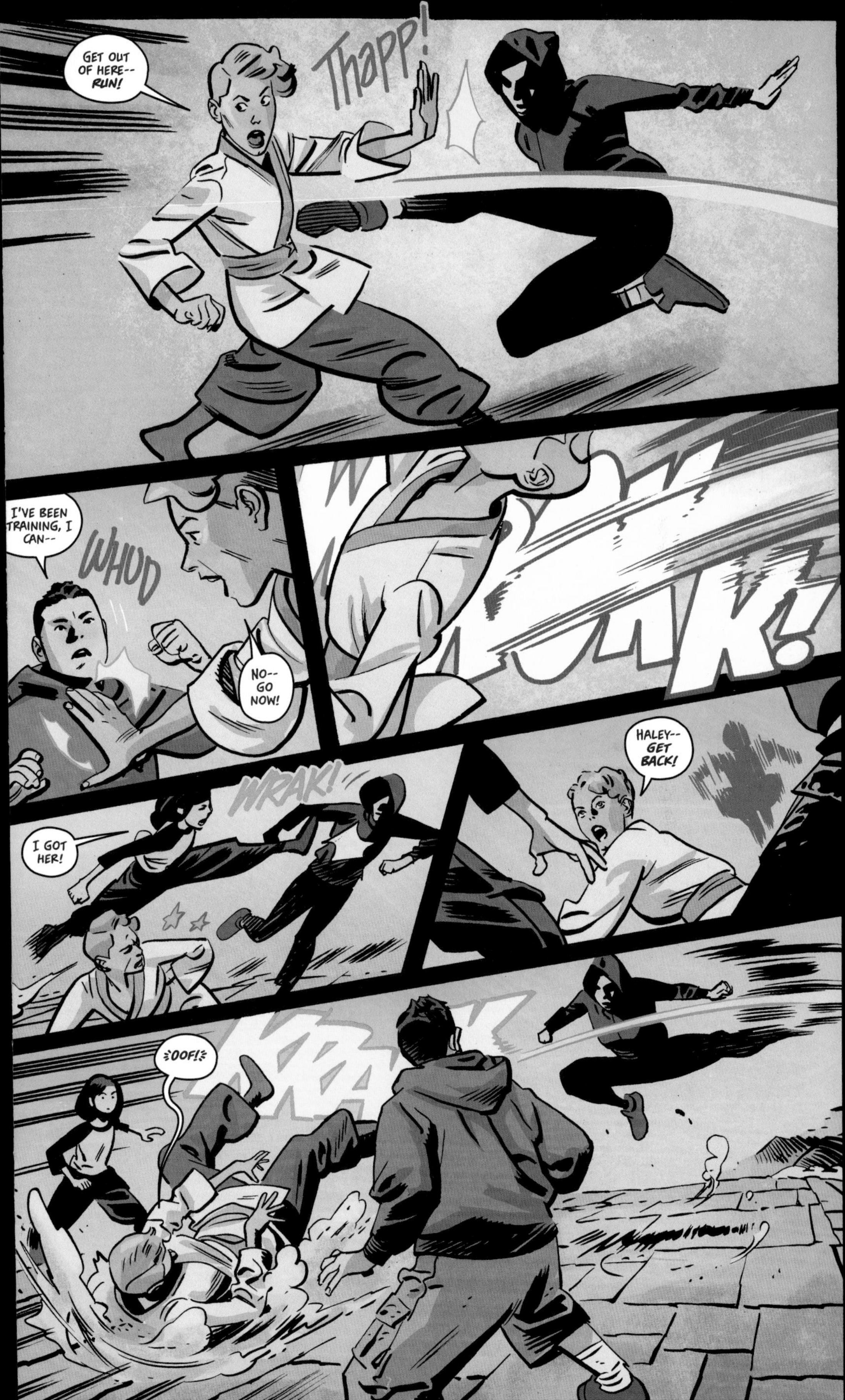
GET OUT OF HERE-- RUN!
THAPP!
I'VE BEEN TRAINING, I CAN--
WHUD
NO-- GO NOW!
I GOT HER!
WRAK!
HALEY-- GET BACK!
OOF!

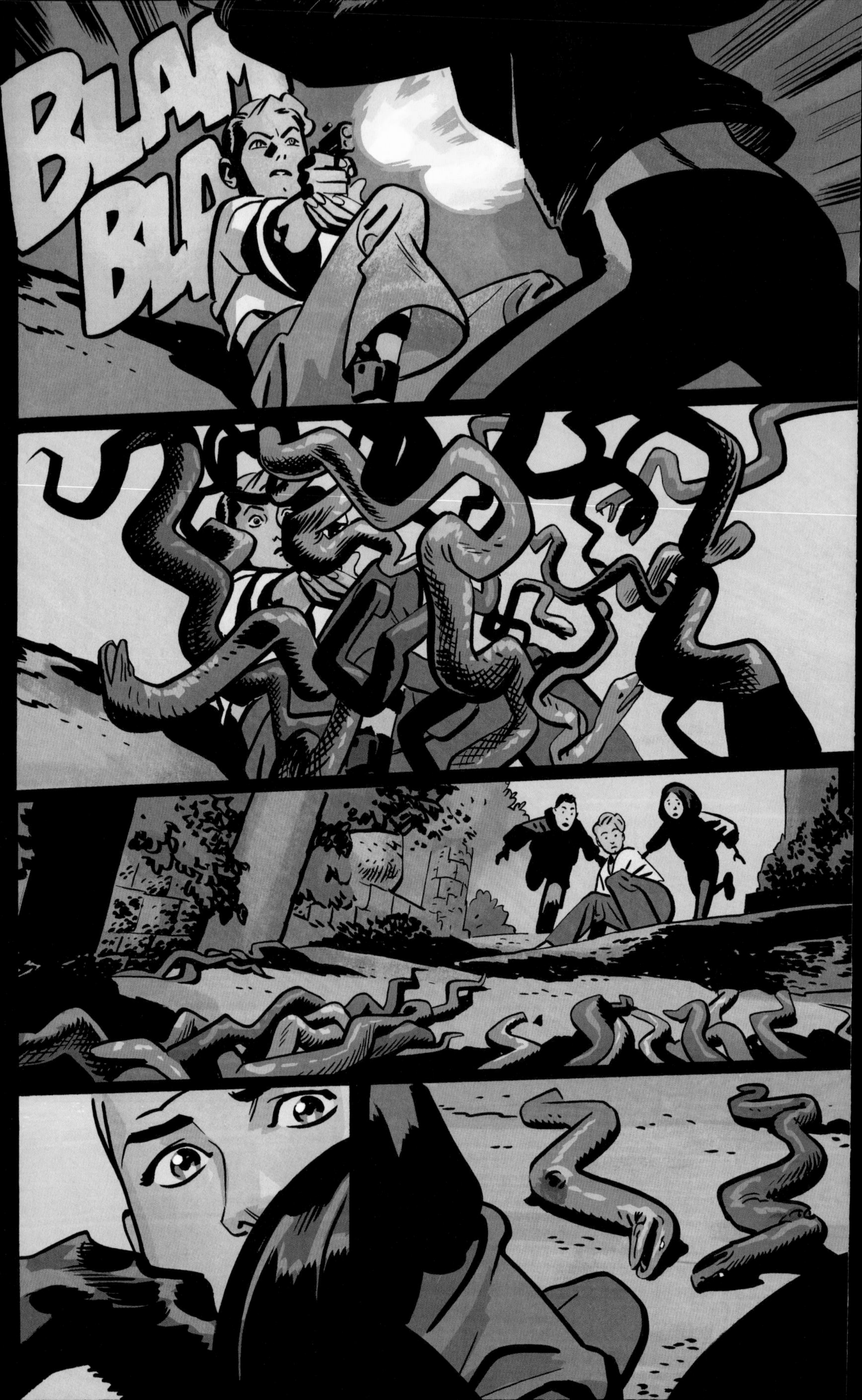
BLAM
BLA

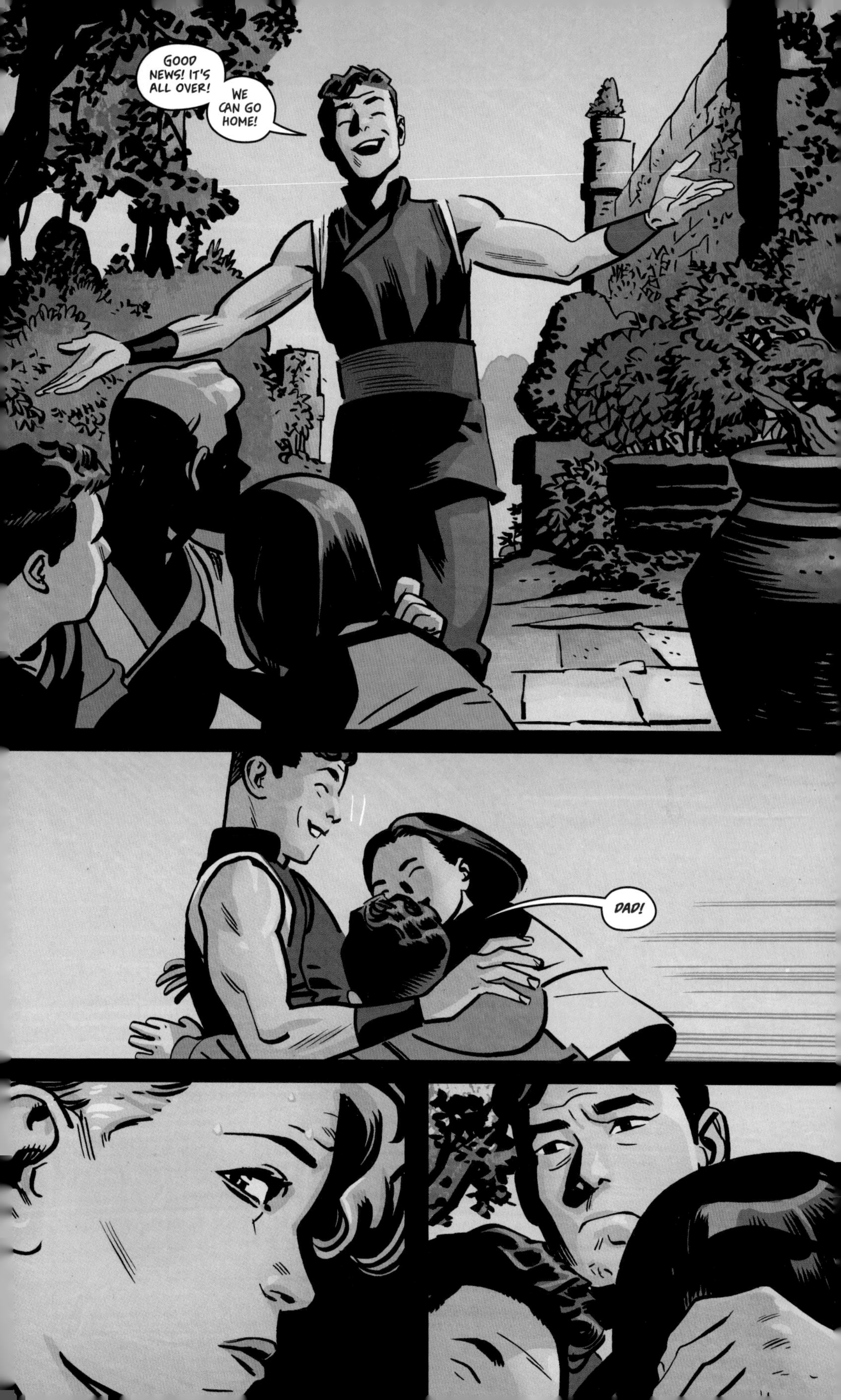
GOOD NEWS! IT'S ALL OVER!
WE CAN GO HOME!
DAD!

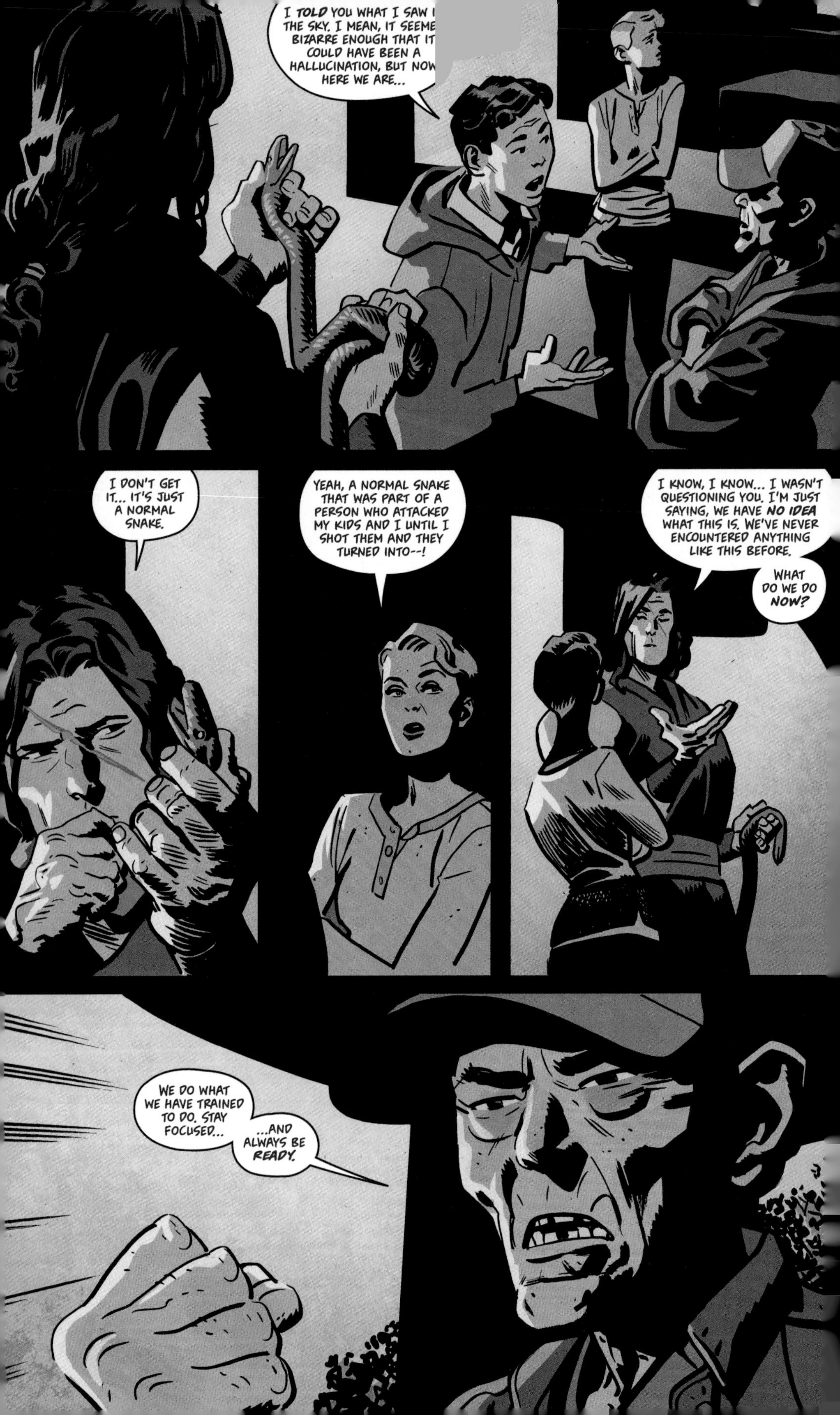
I TOLD YOU WHAT I SAW I
THE SKY. I MEAN, IT SEEME
BIZARRE ENOUGH THAT IT
COULD HAVE BEEN A
HALLUCINATION, BUT NOW
HERE WE ARE...
I DON'T GET IT... IT'S JUST A NORMAL SNAKE.
YEAH, A NORMAL SNAKE THAT WAS PART OF A PERSON WHO ATTACKED MY KIDS AND I UNTIL I SHOT THEM AND THEY TURNED INTO--!
I KNOW, I KNOW... I WASN'T QUESTIONING YOU. I'M JUST SAYING, WE HAVE NO IDEA WHAT THIS IS. WE'VE NEVER ENCOUNTERED ANYTHING LIKE THIS BEFORE.
WHAT DO WE DO NOW?
WE DO WHAT WE HAVE TRAINED TO DO. STAY FOCUSED...
...AND ALWAYS BE READY.

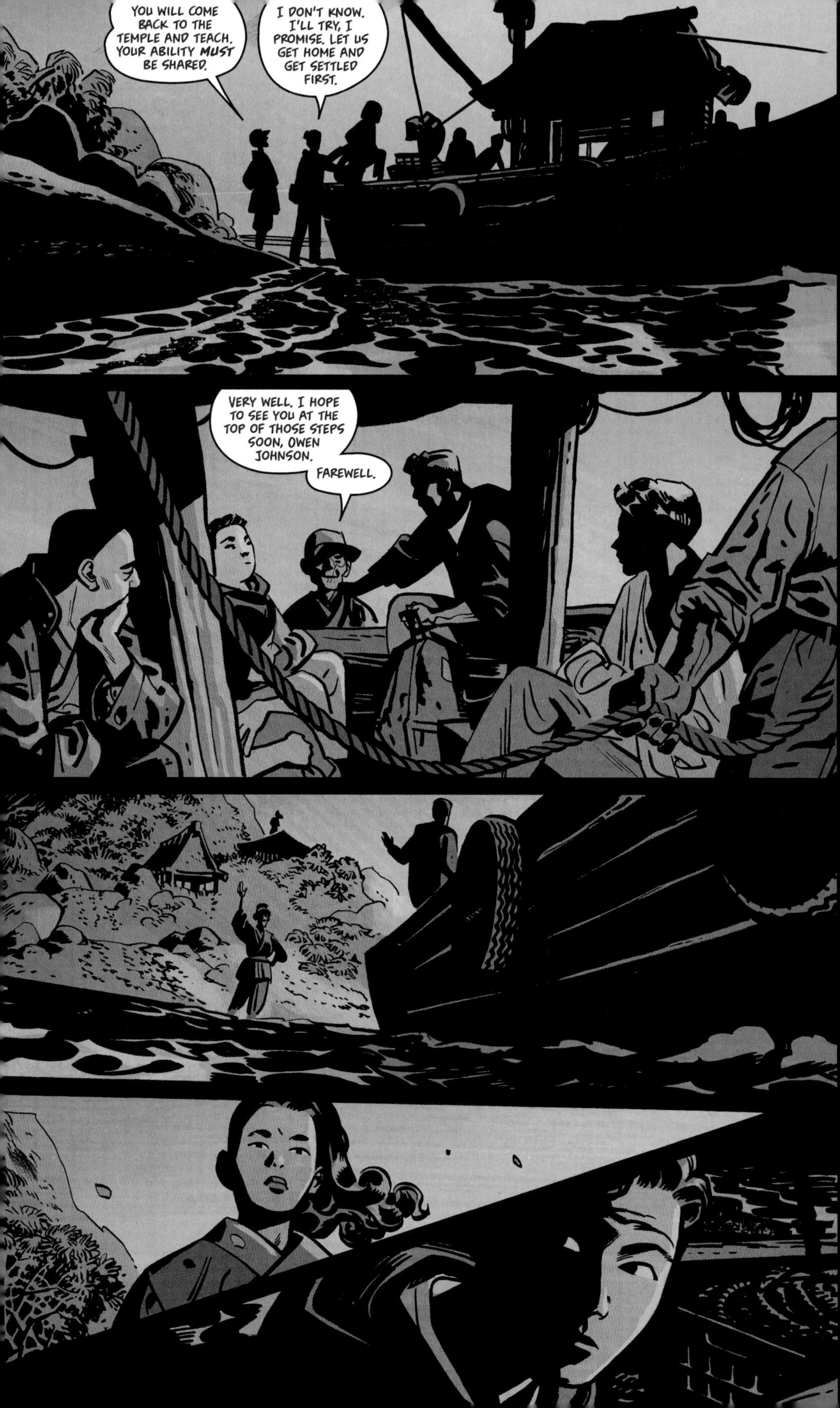
YOU WILL COME BACK TO THE TEMPLE AND TEACH. YOUR ABILITY MUST BE SHARED.
I DON'T KNOW. I'LL TRY, I PROMISE. LET US GET HOME AND GET SETTLED FIRST.
VERY WELL. I HOPE TO SEE YOU AT THE TOP OF THOSE STEPS SOON, OWEN JOHNSON.
FAREWELL.

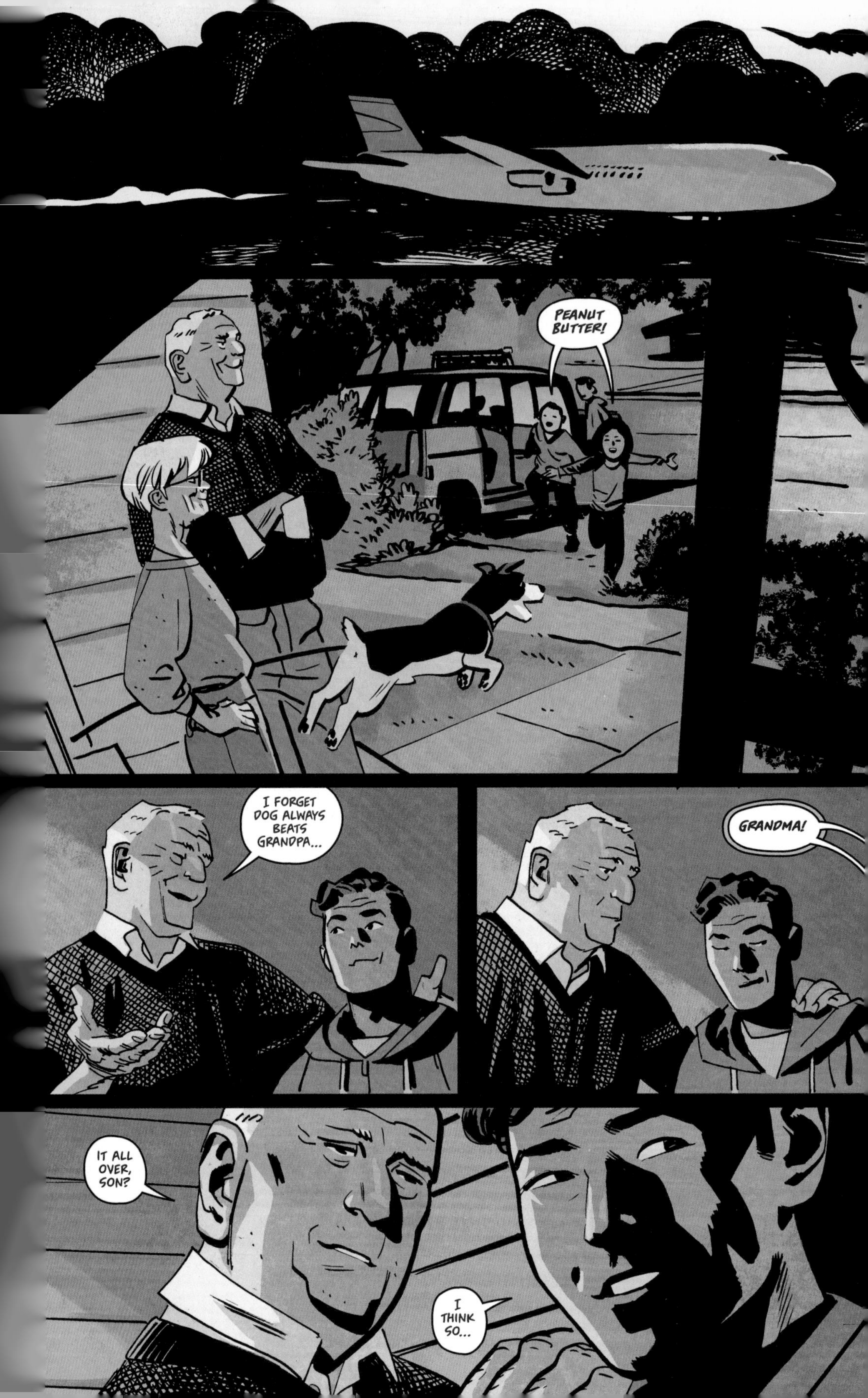
PEANUT BUTTER!
I FORGET DOG ALWAYS BEATS GRANDPA...
GRANDMA!
IT ALL OVER, SON?
I THINK SO...

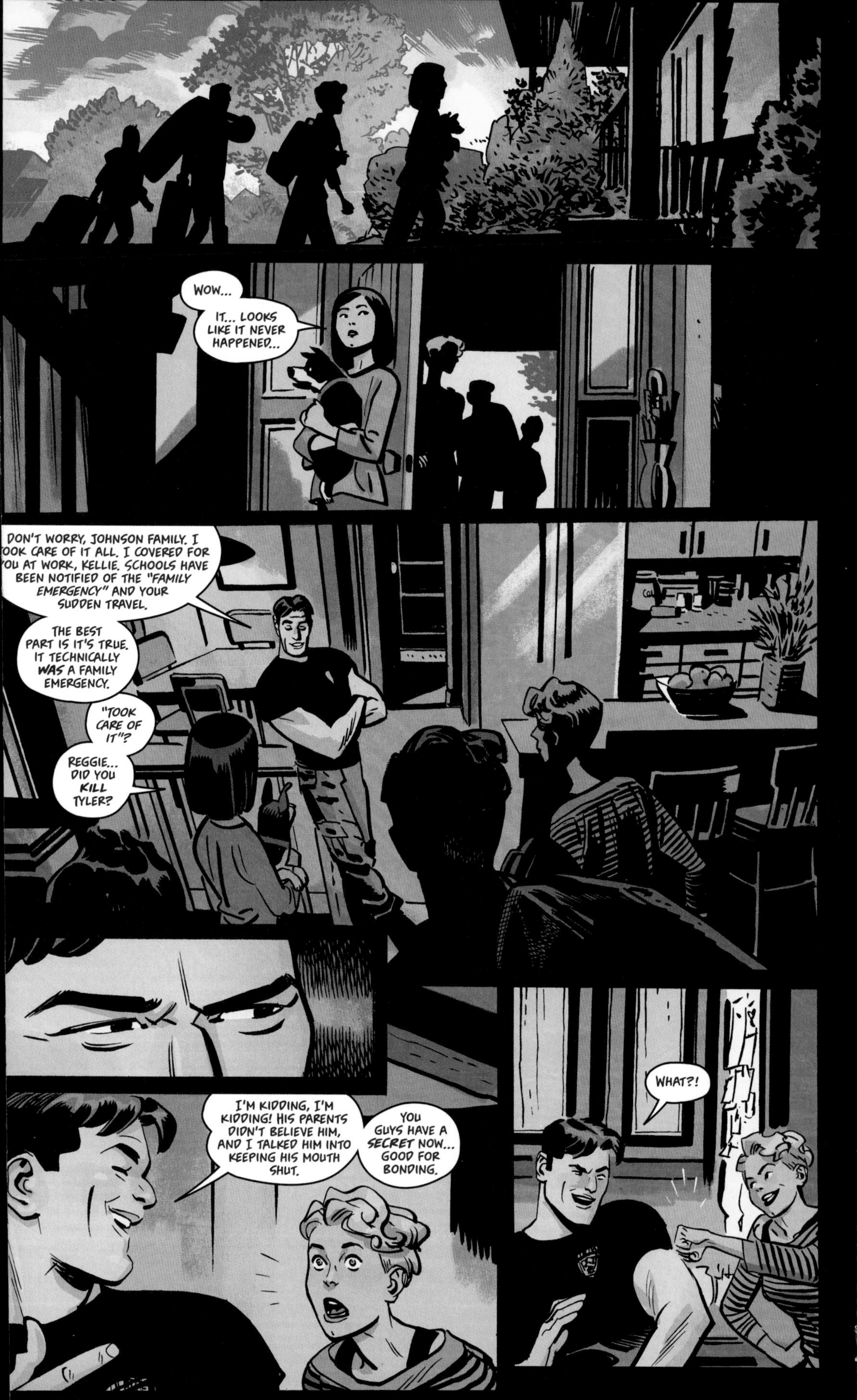
WOW...
IT... LOOKS LIKE IT NEVER HAPPENED...
DON'T WORRY, JOHNSON FAMILY. I TOOK CARE OF IT ALL. I COVERED FOR YOU AT WORK, KELLIE. SCHOOLS HAVE BEEN NOTIFIED OF THE "FAMILY EMERGENCY" AND YOUR SUDDEN TRAVEL.
THE BEST PART IS IT'S TRUE. IT TECHNICALLY WAS A FAMILY EMERGENCY.
"TOOK CARE OF IT"?
REGGIE... DID YOU KILL TYLER?
I'M KIDDING, I'M KIDDING! HIS PARENTS DIDN'T BELIEVE HIM, AND I TALKED HIM INTO KEEPING HIS MOUTH SHUT.
YOU GUYS HAVE A SECRET NOW... GOOD FOR BONDING.
WHAT?!

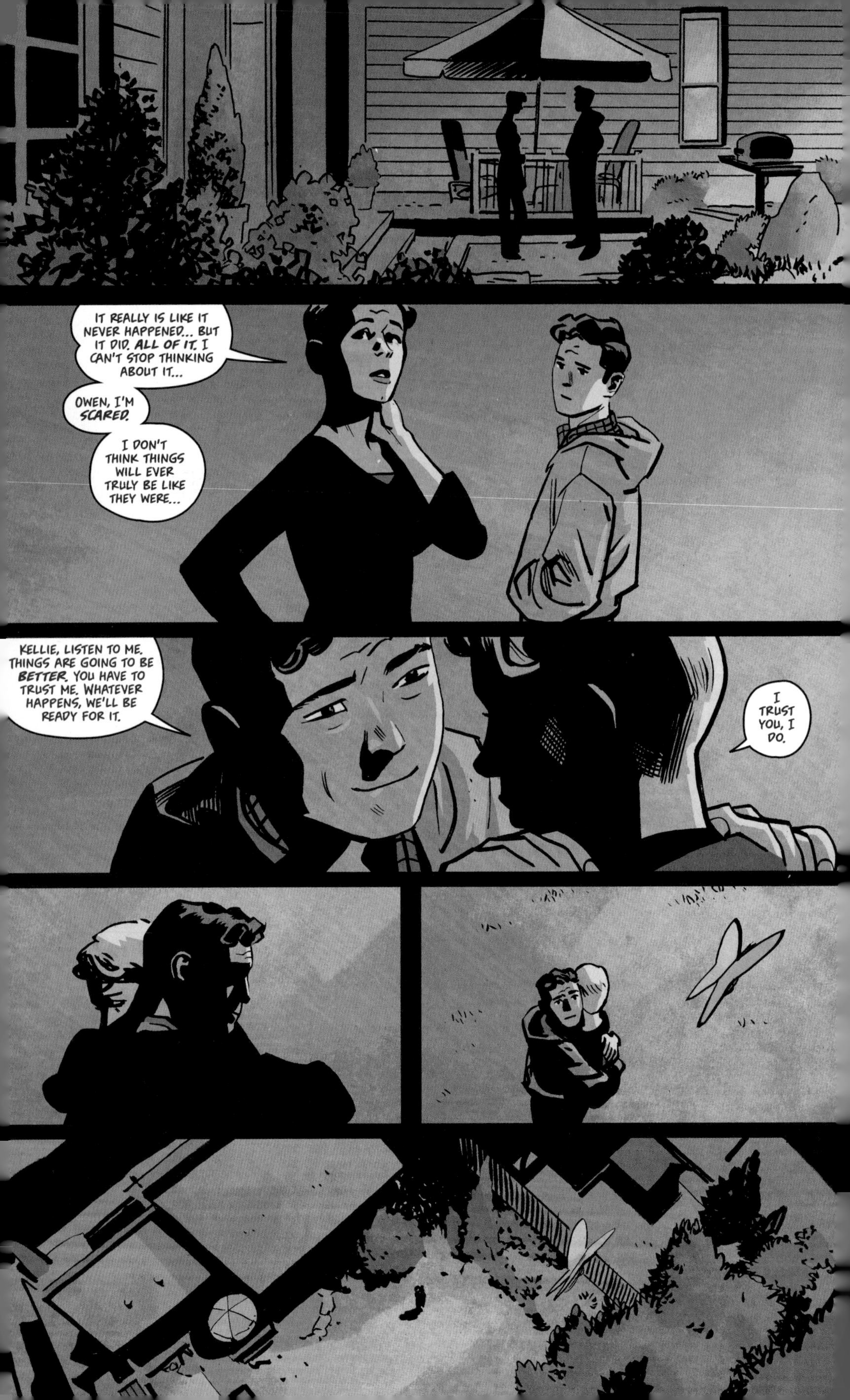
IT REALLY IS LIKE IT NEVER HAPPENED... BUT IT DID. ALL OF IT. I CAN'T STOP THINKING ABOUT IT...
OWEN, I'M SCARED.
I DON'T THINK THINGS WILL EVER TRULY BE LIKE THEY WERE...
KELLIE, LISTEN TO ME. THINGS ARE GOING TO BE BETTER. YOU HAVE TO TRUST ME. WHATEVER HAPPENS, WE'LL BE READY FOR IT.
I TRUST YOU, I DO.

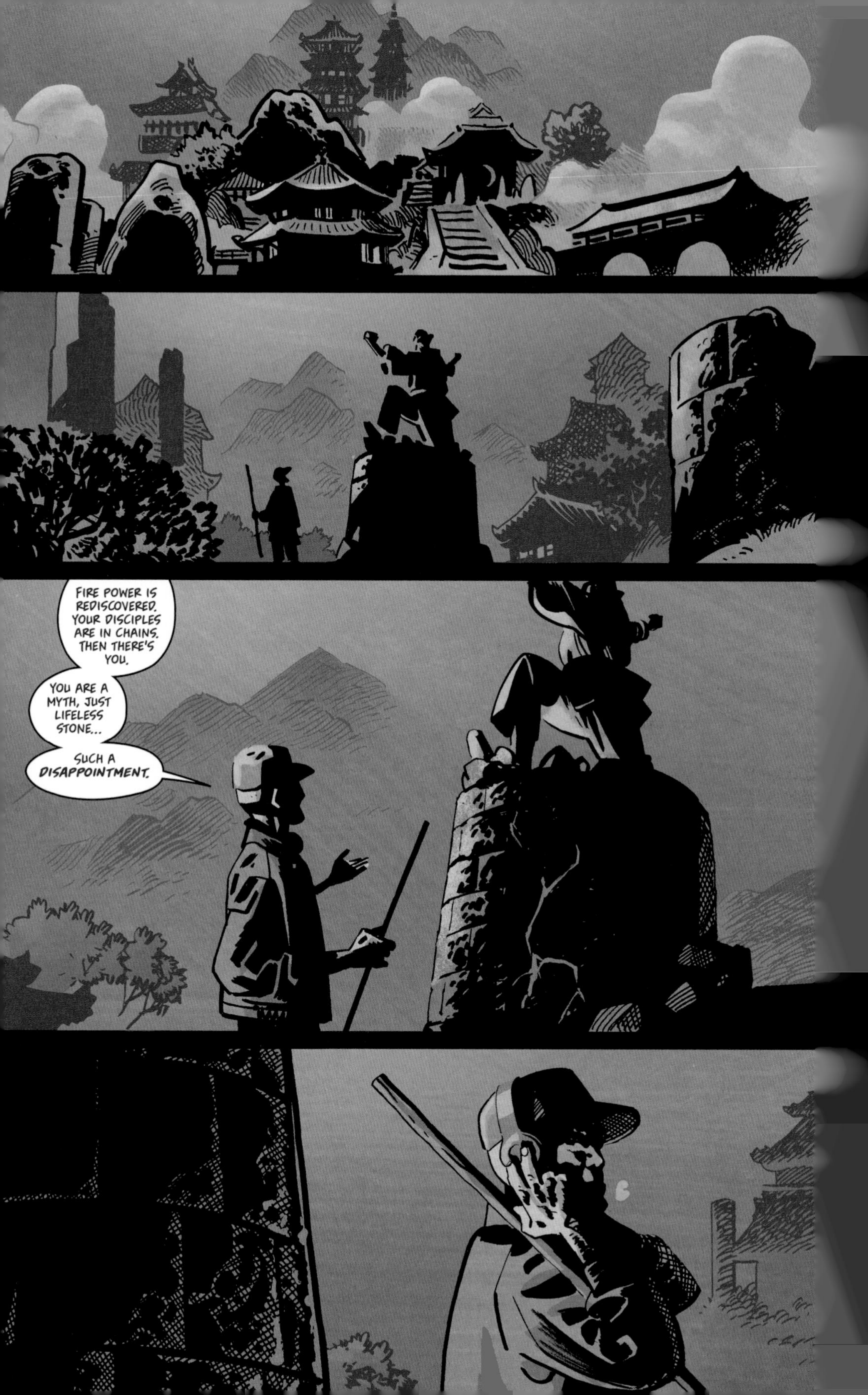
FIRE POWER IS REDISCOVERED. YOUR DISCIPLES ARE IN CHAINS. THEN THERE'S YOU.
YOU ARE A MYTH, JUST LIFELESS STONE...
SUCH A DISAPPOINTMENT.

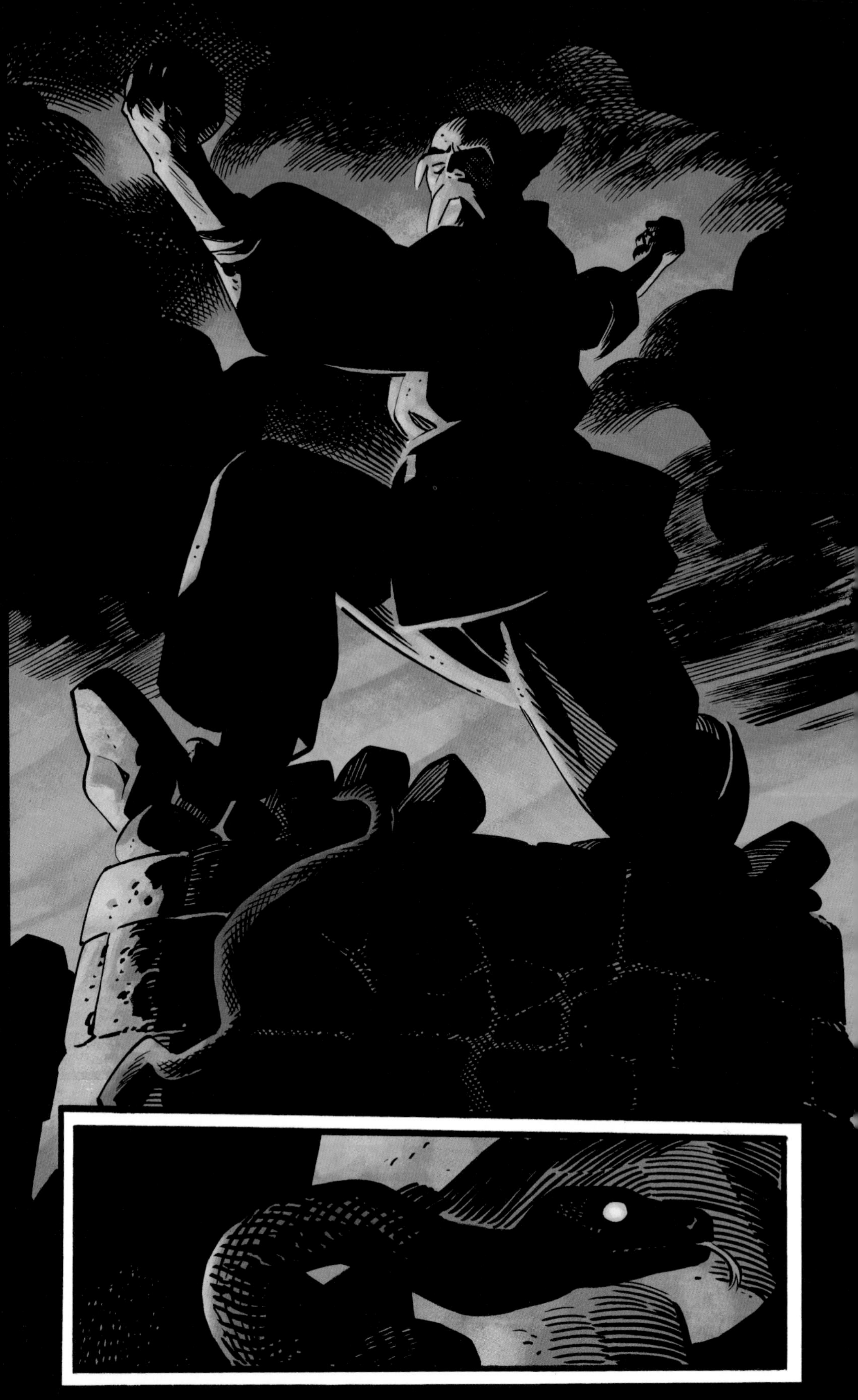

TO BE CONTINUED

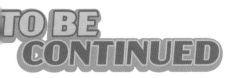

SKETCHBOOK GALLERY

CHRIS SAMNEE: Owen's "costume" look. I tried out a few options – but this is a colored-up version of my first attempt. Every time I leaned more into a "ninja" look it just felt off... just didn't work for our guy.

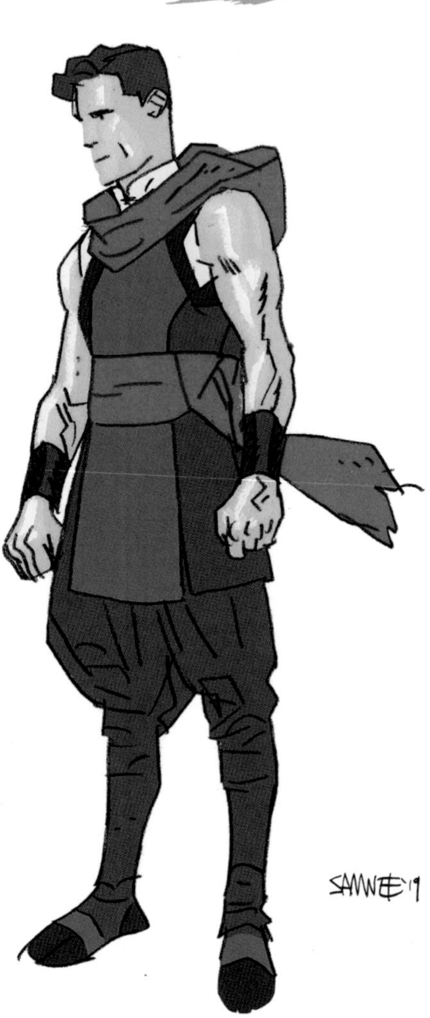
SAMNEE '19

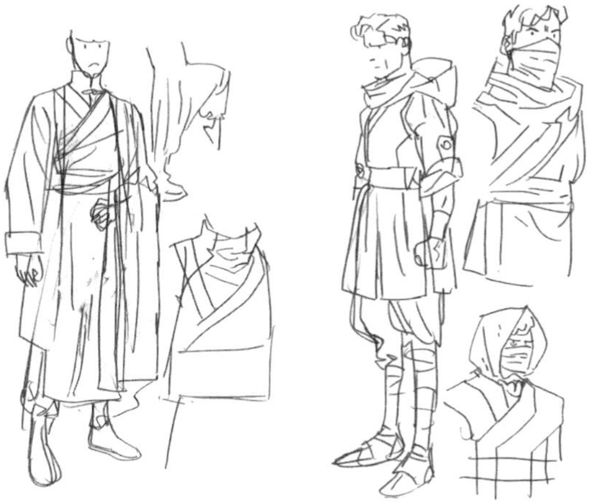

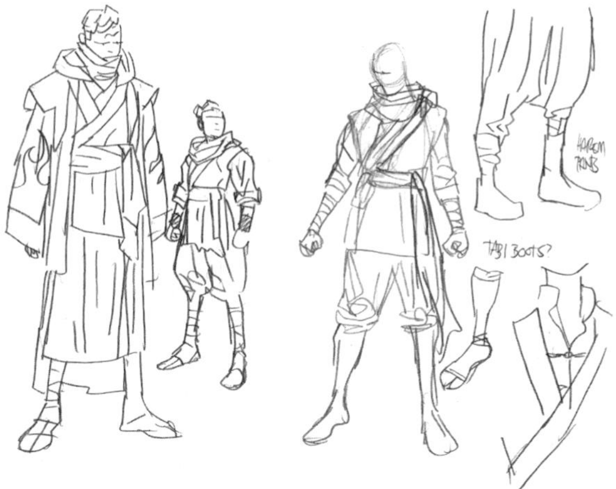
TABI BOOTS?

ROBERT KIRKMAN: This is NOT a superhero book, but I thought it would be cool if Owen had a more recognizable, iconic costume--er... outfit that he could wear into battle. Something kind of inspired by the new alliance between the Scorched Earth Clan and the Temple of the Flaming Fist (which is where we end up by the end of this volume, you did read it first... right?!)

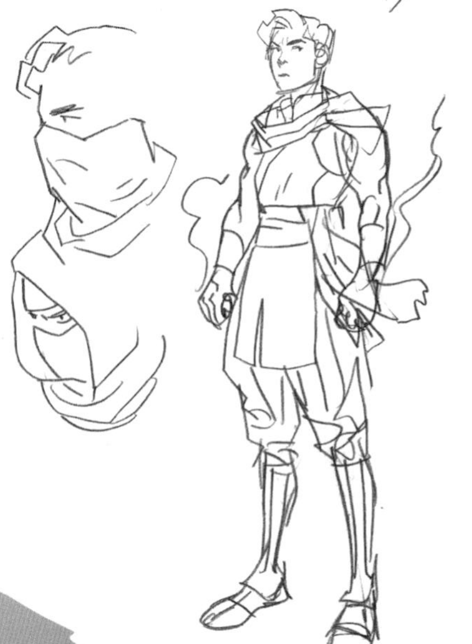

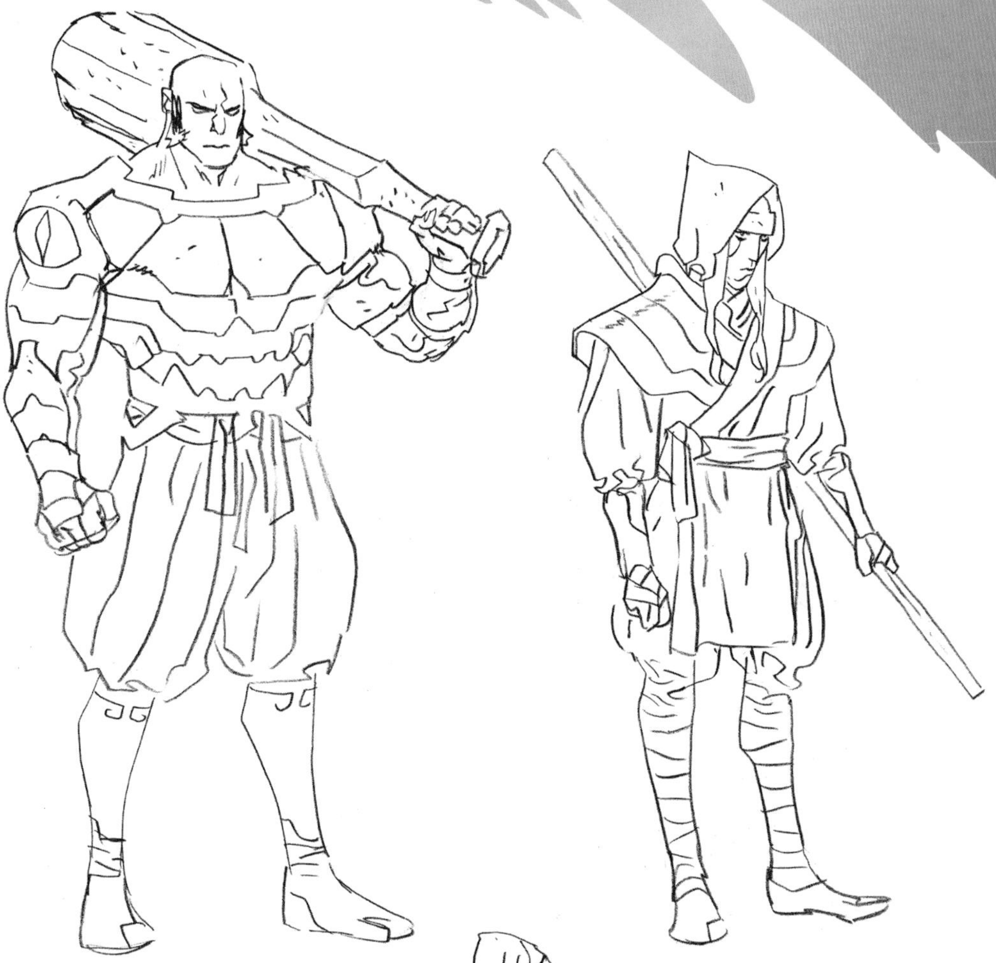

CHRIS: These were the first designs for our gang of villains. Initially, they were just throwaway baddies – but Robert dug their look and gave them all larger roles. In the scripts they were just Club, Chain, Staff, and Sword – and that's still what I call them :P

ROBERT: That's really the magic of comics, folks. "Hey, put some people in this scene – oh, they look awesome, they'll come back!" Thus Kanabo, Jin, Taiji, and Dow are born! And I had no clue Taiji would end up being the Serpent's Omen when we introduced her. That kind of stuff just comes organically as you move from issue to issue. It's what I call... the fun stuff.

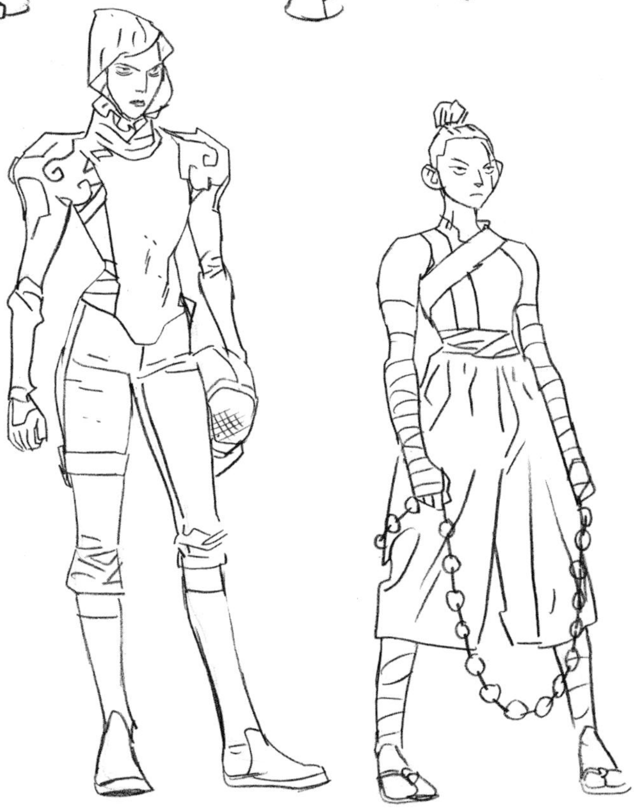

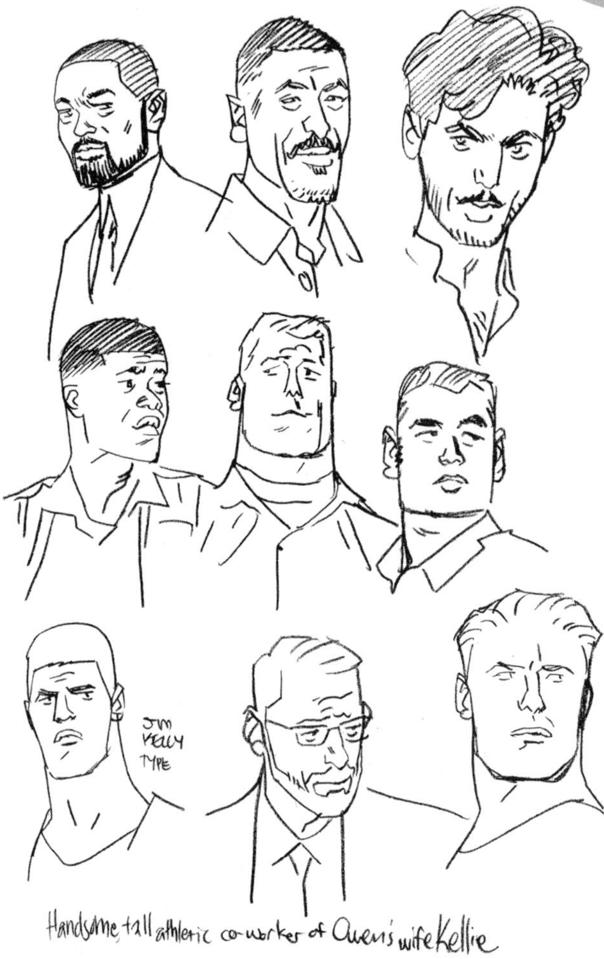
JIM KELLY TYPE
Handsome, tall athletic co-worker of Owen's wife Kellie

CHRIS: Reggie explorations...

ROBERT: My main thought with Reggie was that I wanted him to be this tall, strong, handsome guy who you'd think we were going to put in a love triangle with Owen and Kellie, but we never would. In my head, he's more or less based on my pal Patrick Fugit who is a super tall and strong looking dude who is kind of unassuming and friendly... but is a Muay Thai master and could probably kick anyone's butt.

CHRIS: Trying to find Larry.

ROBERT: Oh, man... for Larry I was picturing another father figure, but a slick, cool, crafty guy. Like the coolest wheeler and dealer at your local antique furniture place. Was I thinking of Brent Spiner as a basis for this guy? Maybe. Maybe I just really want to work with *Outcast* actors again. Watch Wrenn Schmidt in *For All Mankind*. She's great!

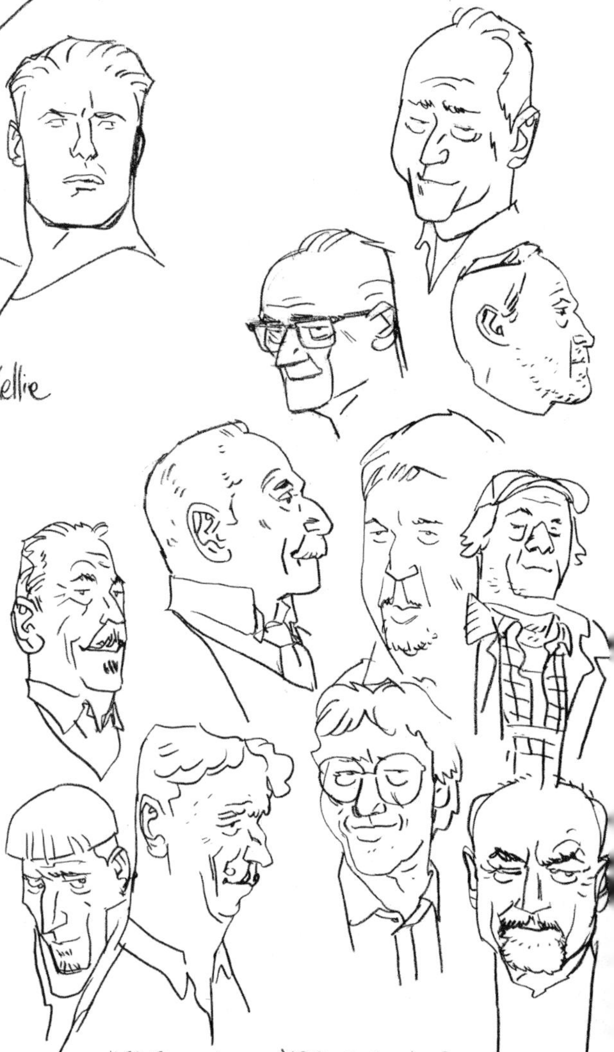
11-24-18 SHADY ANTIQUE SHOP MANAGER

CHRIS: *Thumbnails of multiple layout options for the cover to #7. I usually stick to one or two options for a cover – but found multiple moments in this issue that I thought might be cover-worthy images.*

ROBERT: Ah... the cover thumbnails in the sketchbook section. The game I like to call "Robert chose the wrong cover".

CHRIS: *Ninjas! Sad sunset!*

ROBERT: That Chen Zul cover would have been cool... the visors turning into birds probably would have won you another Eisner Award. People really flip out over stuff like that.

CHRIS: *NINJAS! NINJAS!! NINJAS!!!*

ROBERT: Yeah... maybe the profile version of this cover had a cool look to it... damn. Logo would have fit better, too...

ROBERT: For the issue #8 cover, I chose the winner. Big shot of the Serpent's Omen, rad as heck!

CHRIS: *#9A was deemed too much of a spoiler...*

ROBERT: Was it? Yeah, I guess it spoiled they fell out of the plane in the previous issue. Pretty striking, though. The cover we went with is great, but that one of the little figures in the distance? Pretty great!

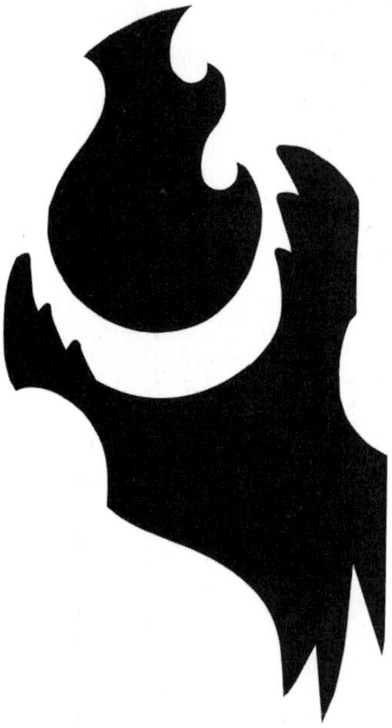

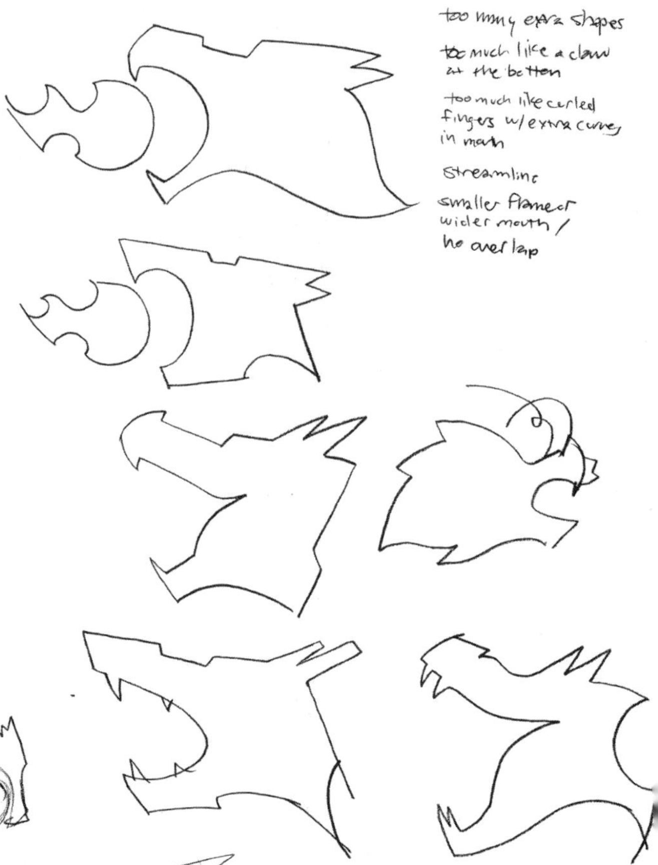
too many extra shapes
too much like a claw at the bottom
too much like curled fingers w/ extra curves in mouth
streamline
smaller flame or wider mouth /
no overlap

CHRIS: I filled a sketchbook with this tattoo... didn't think I'd ever get it. This is just a small sampling of what I sent to Robert. I'll know it works if we ever see a FIRE POWER reader with this actual tattoo.

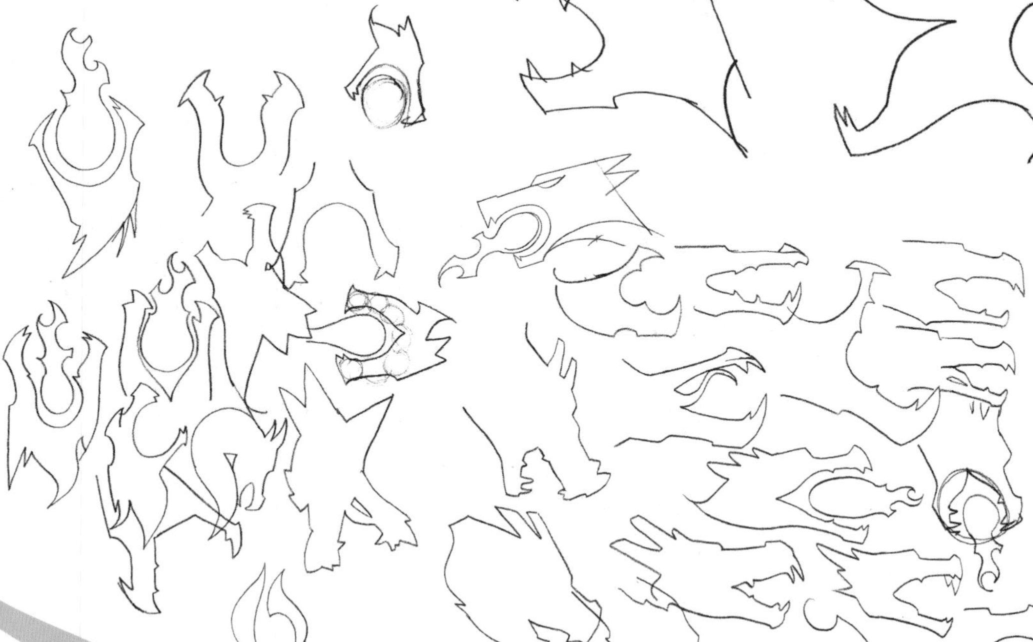

ROBERT: Yeah, this was a fun few weeks! SO MANY tattoo designs. The final one is great. I actually have it tattooed really big on my chest, just like Chen Zul, so I guess it works!!